Farmer Education

and

Farm Efficiency

A WORLD BANK RESEARCH PUBLICATION

Farmer Education

and

Farm Efficiency

Dean T. Jamison and Lawrence J. Lau

PUBLISHED FOR THE WORLD BANK

The Johns Hopkins University Press

BALTIMORE AND LONDON

The Johns Hopkins University Press
Baltimore, Maryland 21218, U.S.A.

Library of Congress Cataloging in Publication Data

Jamison, Dean.
    Farmer education and farm efficiency.

    (A World Bank research publication)
    Bibliography: p.
    Includes index.
    1. Farmers—Education. 2. Agricultural education.
3. Agricultural productivity. I. Lau, Lawrence J.,
1944– . II. World Bank. III. Title. IV. Series.
S531.J29   630'.7'15   81-47612
ISBN 0-8018-2575-X   AACR2

Contents

Map, Figures, and Tables

Map

Figures

Tables

Foreword

MARKET PERFORMANCE can provide the basis for evaluating the profitability for many potential investments, and the economic returns to investments are appropriately analyzed within enterprises in terms of profits to the investor. The World Bank, however, frequently helps to finance investments for which private profits provide only an incomplete or indirect indication of economic return, such as investments to improve an economy's infrastructure—its roads, ports, public health, public education, public security, telecommunications facilities. These improvements, in turn, encourage the development of private economic activity. Infrastructure sectors often require large resources compared with the scale of the national economy. Investments in some sectors, such as education, health, and security, not only promote private growth but help to meet the ultimate goals of development.

Because these sectors are important, then, and because market mechanisms to guide the level and composition of such investment in them are not reliable, careful economic analyses are required to provide information on economic viability. An important part of World Bank work is to undertake such analyses—both to improve the quality of the Bank's own project portfolio and to assist member governments in planning investment programs for infrastructure. The World Bank's research program plays an important role both in developing the methods for assessment and in providing a broad base of empirical information on investment costs and returns that can be used to assess any particular project.

In this book, Dean T. Jamison and Lawrence J. Lau report the results of research on the economic returns to investment in education in rural areas. Their careful and innovative treatment of extensive data sets (from Korea, Malaysia, and Thailand) and their systematic integration of previous findings with their own provide an excellent example of applied microeconomic research. Their book provides, then, not only convincing evidence for high economic returns to educational investment in rural areas; it also exemplifies how microeconomic research can illuminate important investment choices.

HOLLIS B. CHENERY
Vice President
Economics and Research

Preface

DEVELOPMENT STRATEGIES INCREASINGLY EMPHASIZE agricultural development, employment, and equity. It is therefore important to examine the role of education in light of these new emphases. The educational requirements of a capital-intensive, industrially focused growth strategy can be expected to differ in important ways from the requirements of a strategy placing greater emphasis on employment and agriculture. Nonetheless, much of the research on the economic benefits of education is limited to examination of data from the urban wage sector. One conclusion recently emerging from this research has typically been that there is overinvestment in education, particularly at the higher levels. There is strong feeling, however, that this conclusion, which is based on the structure of earnings and employment in the formal urban labor market, is inapplicable to the new growth strategies. For example, John Mellor (1976) has argued:

> All aspects of agricultural growth through technological change are based on expanding the number of rural supporting institutions to benefit the small farmer, who is a crucial part of the overall high-growth strategy. Because of the agricultural sector's massive size, the intensity of use of trained manpower, and stress on broad participation in growth, an emphasis on rural development requires a huge expansion of education at all levels. Also, the broader the participation in rural development, the more intensive the requirements for trained manpower (p. 74).

Mellor thus views investment in education in rural areas as a central ingredient in a strategy to improve agricultural productivity, principally through its complementarity with new inputs such as chemical fertilizers and pesticides, irrigation, high-yielding varieties, and effective research and extension services. Therefore, as

Schultz (1964, 1975) has emphasized, education can be expected to have a stronger effect under conditions of a changing or modernizing agricultural environment. But whereas Mellor rejects the conclusion that there is typically overinvestment in education, he offers little concrete evidence that education will play the role he expects it to. The plausibility of the arguments of Mellor and Schultz—and the importance of their conclusions for investment policy in education—suggest that the empirical validity of the arguments should be carefully tested.

In this book we examine existing and develop new empirical evidence concerning farmer education and farm efficiency. The existing literature, which is reviewed in Chapter 2, strongly suggests that more educated farmers are more productive, particularly, as Schultz hypothesized, in modernizing agricultural environments.

The robustness of previous findings is checked by examining education's effects on farm productivity using three new data sets from Korea, Malaysia, and Thailand. Still another purpose of the monograph is to bring new techniques of analysis to bear on the relation between education and efficiency. In particular, the data set from Thailand includes information on the prices at which each farmer bought his inputs and sold his outputs; this allows us to test how well education helps farmers to adjust the level and composition of output, as well as levels of farm inputs, to the prevailing prices. Finally, we introduce a new concept of efficiency—market efficiency—to examine the extent to which farmers get good prices for their inputs and outputs in imperfect product and factor markets. Again, the price data from Thailand allow us to test for education's effect on market efficiency.

The present study, however, like those that have preceded it, leaves unanswered two important questions. The first is: to what extent do the observed correlations between education and efficiency result not from the effects of education but, instead, from attributes of farmers correlated with their having education? The second question, closely related to the first, is: through which of their outcomes do schooling and extension produce their effects? A follow-on to the work reported here, involving new survey data collected in Nepal and Thailand, is now under way at the World Bank. These new surveys were designed to obtain two categories of data that were previously unavailable. The first was data on the family background of the head of the farm household and that person's spouse. The second included measures of the ability, academic achievement, agricultural knowledge, and modernity of attitudes of the adult members of the households surveyed. (In addition, the follow-on studies gathered data on the fertility, health, and nutrition of the farm households in the sample; this will allow examination of education's effects on aspects of rural development other than agricultural productivity.)

Both sets of data will help ascertain the extent to which the apparent contribution of education to productivity results not from education itself but rather from such correlates of education as ability or family background. Results from the tests will help quantify the extent to which each of education's measured outcomes increases productivity. Preliminary results of the Nepal and Thailand studies are now becoming available (Jamison and Moock 1981) and indicate an effect of education independent of family background operating (in Nepal, at least) partly through improving farmers' numerical skills.

The present work should be seen, then, as the first part of a two-part endeavor by the World Bank to understand better the linkage between providing education (and extension) opportunities, on the one hand, and expediting improvements in agricultural efficiency (and other aspects of rural development), on the other. Whereas this first part of the endeavor principally delineates the existence and size of the linkage, the second part will use new data to ascertain the mechanisms through which education produces its effects.

DEAN T. JAMISON
LAWRENCE J. LAU

Acknowledgments

WE ARE INDEBTED TO NUMEROUS INDIVIDUALS for valuable comments and assistance with various aspects of this monograph. Several of our colleagues in the World Bank—Hollis Chenery, Susan Cochrane, Risto Harma, Benjamin B. King, Timothy King, T. N. Srinivasan, and Bernard Woods—provided useful reviews of earlier drafts or comments at seminars. So, too, did Howard Barnum (University of Michigan), Pichit Lerttamrab (Food and Agricultural Organization, Bangkok), Henry M. Levin (Stanford University), Yaffa Machnes (Bar-Ilan University), Rati Ram (Illinois State University), Benjawan Tongsiri (Chiang Mai University), Pan A. Yotopoulos (Stanford University), and Kan-Hua Young (Econ, Inc.). Revision of the monograph particularly benefited from the suggestions of a review panel the Bank convened in June 1978 to comment on the manuscript; this panel comprised Mary Jean Bowman (University of Chicago), Robert Evenson (Yale University), and Peter Moock (Teachers College, Columbia University). Four referees of the manuscript also provided constructive comments.

Peter Hazell and Lyn Squire of the World Bank generously provided the data from Malaysia and helped us to use and interpret them. We very much appreciate their assistance.

Marlaine Lockheed of the Educational Testing Service is coauthor of Chapter 2 (and the article upon which it is based), and we are grateful to her both for permission to use that material and for her comments on other aspects of the manuscript. The U.S. Agency for International Development joined the World Bank in supporting her contribution.

Paul Lorton (San Francisco State University) generously ran many of the logit regressions reported in Chapter 7, and Jennie Hay (Harvard University) provided valuable assistance in preparation of Chapter 2 as well as serving as coauthor of a conference presentation dealing with our empirical findings on Malaysia. We are particularly indebted to Erwin C. Chou (Stanford University) for his expert assistance with all aspects of the data analysis.

Finally, Regina Barnes at Stanford and Carmelita Casumbal at the World Bank provided quick and efficient typing and administrative services that assisted greatly in the preparation of this manuscript. Virginia deHaven Hitchcock edited the manuscript for publication. S. A. D. Subasinghe prepared the figures. The map was compiled by Jose Z. Rodriguez and drawn by Larry A. Bowring under the supervision of the World Bank's Cartography Division. Joyce C. Eisen designed the cover.

Farmer Education

and

Farm Efficiency

CHAPTER 1

Introduction and Summary

THIS BOOK EXPLORES THE RELATION between the education farmers have received and their subsequent efficiency as farm operators. Economists assess the economic benefits of education in the wage sectors of an economy by attempting to ascertain the effect of educational level on wages or earnings; for the self-employed, however, this approach breaks down, and other methods must be used to ascertain the nature of education's effect and role.[1] Our concern here is with the self-employed in agriculture—the small farmer.

Bowman (1976b) has argued that education and information relevant to the small farmer might usefully be categorized along a continuum, the poles of which she labels "formation of competences" and "transmission of information." Basic competences— literacy, numeracy, and general cognitive skills—are best formed through schools or similar institutions. Information—on prices, new seeds or techniques, irrigation methods, and so forth—can be transmitted through a variety of institutional or noninstitutional frameworks, including extension services. Whereas the goals of information transfer services can be stated in narrowly economic terms, the development of competence can be expected to have not only economic benefits in agriculture, but also in the improvement of other aspects of household life and in the encouragement of a critical self-reliance.

---

1. See King (1978) for a thoughtful analysis of the relation between education and self-employment, and Wharton (1965) for a more specific discussion of the agricultural sector.

Important as the range of benefits of schooling (and, through it, improved intellectual competence) may be, this study is concerned solely with ascertaining empirically the effect of schooling on agricultural efficiency.[2] Likewise, when the data are available, we examine the effect of access to information, as measured by exposure to extension services. The analyses reported use data from Korea, Malaysia, and Thailand. In addition, related findings from several other countries of Africa, Asia, and Latin America are reviewed.

Methods

The data used in the empirical analyses (Chapters 5 through 7) come from surveys of individual farms in Thailand, Korea, and Malaysia. We used these data sets because they were available and contained information on education, farm inputs and outputs, and, in the case of Thailand, prices for the inputs and outputs of individual farms; thus, they provided an opportunity to test the effect of education on farm efficiency. However, it is plausible to argue that, within a community, there may be no ascertainable relation between education (or exposure to extension) and productivity, because farmers who are less educated will follow the more productive practices of their more educated neighbors. If this were the case, then the effects of education could be discovered only by examining whether communities (or other aggregates) with higher average levels of education had higher levels of productivity. This might, then, be an argument against using data on individual farms to investigate the issues we are addressing here.

2. The World Bank has recently sponsored a series of reviews, edited by Timothy King, of the effects of education on many aspects of development. In this collection Bowman (1980) surveyed the effects of education on economic growth in general; Berry (1980) reviewed the literature on education and earnings in urban areas; Fields (1980) reviewed literature on education and income distribution; and Psacharopoulos (1980) provided an update of his earlier summary of studies of the rate-of-return to education (Psacharopoulos 1973). In related efforts, Cochrane (1979) reviewed studies relating education and fertility, and Cochrane, Leslie, and O'Hara (1982) reviewed studies of the effects of parental education on child mortality, morbidity, and growth. Hicks (1980) and Wheeler (1980) have utilized newly available country-level data over time to reexamine the question of the contribution of education to aggregate growth, and have concluded that the effects of education are indeed important. The present monograph should be viewed in the context of these other related studies on the contribution of education to development.

The ideal case is when there are data on individual farms from many communities. Short of the ideal case, either data aggregated at the community level or data on individual farms within one community can be used. Both of these possibilities have shortcomings. On the one hand, there may be important problems of interpretation if production functions, as described below, are estimated from aggregated data (Chapter 4). On the other hand, as just noted, it is possible to underestimate the effect of education or extension if data on individual farms within a single community are used. A national probability sample was used to select the farms in Korea for which we have data, so we expect no problem with estimating the effect of education there. The data from Malaysia and Thailand, however, come from much more compact geographical areas, and there may be an ensuing bias.

The production function

Given a data set of this sort, the researcher can estimate the effect of education on productivity by constructing a "production function" relating the amount of farm output to the level of each of the inputs, including the farmer's education.

Take a simple example: let Y = total output (in kilograms); T = area under cultivation (in hectares); L = labor input (in person-days); E = educational level of the household head (in years of formal schooling completed); and EXT = indicator of exposure to extension services ($EXT = 1$ if the farmer was exposed, $EXT = 0$ if he was not). The studies we review use variations on the Cobb-Douglas production function to relate output, Y, to the various inputs in the following way:

$$\ln Y = \alpha_0 + \alpha_1 \ln T + \alpha_2 \ln L + \beta \ln E + \gamma\, EXT.$$

The coefficients ($\alpha_0, \alpha_1, \alpha_2, \beta, \gamma$) on the input variables are estimated from the data and indicate how strongly each input affects output. Almost all the studies we review use production functions of this general form, but include a normally distributed "error" term, the standard deviation of which is also estimated in the statistical analysis.

If there are individuals in the sample with no education ($E = 0$), then education, like exposure to extension services, can be treated as an indicator variable, or a nonhomogeneous Cobb-Douglas function can be estimated. The estimated coefficients in the production function give the elasticities of output with respect to the various inputs and, hence, in this example, β would give the elasticity of output with respect to years of education (Chapter 2). This provides a measure of the productivity of education. In the actual empirical studies that are undertaken, far more complete specifications of the production function are used than in this simplified example, including many more independent variables.

Most estimates of the effects of education on labor productivity use wage rate as a proxy for marginal productivity and examine the effect of an individual's educational level, controlling for other variables, on the wage he receives. This is reasonable, assuming competitive labor markets and an absence of screening mechanisms whereby the individual's education may simply signal productive qualities to a potential employer without actually enhancing them. Direct estimation of the marginal product of education through its coefficient in a production function provides an alternative to using wages that is superior in several respects: (a) no assumptions need to be made about the equivalence of wages and the marginal products of labor; (b) the possibility of screening does not confound interpretation of the results (though omitted variables may); and (c) only in this way is it possible to obtain estimates of the effect of education on productivity in sectors, such as agriculture, that may rely relatively little on wage employment.

Concepts of efficiency

In addition to examining the effect of education on productivity, it is also possible to examine whether it affects allocative efficiency; that is, the extent to which farmers optimally choose their input and output mix in light of their production functions and prevailing prices. In a seminal article, Welch (1970) discussed ways to assess the effect of education on allocative efficiency. Several of the studies we review have examined the issue of allocative efficiency by comparing actual with optimal allocation decisions in light of an estimated production function. The availability of farm-specific price data allowed estimation of profit and factor demand functions to test for farmers' allocative efficiency for the sample of farms in Thailand (Chapter 6). Chapter 3 provides a more thorough discussion of alternative concepts of efficiency; the first section of Chapter 6 and Appendix D explain the use of profit functions as a tool for assessing allocative efficiency.

Another concept of efficiency that we introduce, market efficiency, is defined as a farmer's ability to obtain the highest net sale price for his outputs and the lowest net purchase price for his inputs. In any market there is usually a distribution of prices for essentially the same commodity, centered around some mean price. Prices vary from the mean because of differences in access to information, in the ability to use information, and in the qualities of the commodity. If every farm household has the same information and the same ability to use the information, and there is no difference in quality, the price should be the same for all farm households, apart from transport margins.

To the extent that the market is imperfect, however, the access to and the ability to use information will make a difference. It is hypothesized that better educated farm households will on average receive higher net prices for their outputs and pay lower net prices for their variable inputs. Education enhances a farmer's ability to know his alternatives, to know when and where to buy and sell. A better educated farmer is more likely to know what prices are likely to prevail in equilibrium, and can therefore become a better bargainer. He may also have a finer discrimination of differences in quality and may be able to judge quality more accurately. In Chapter 6 we report the tests of the adequacy of the hypothesis that education improves farmers' market efficiency.

A final concept of efficiency that we explore is that of efficiency in the choice of production technique. We discuss the basic concepts in Chapter 3 and study the choice of technique empirically with the Thailand data in Chapter 7.

Findings

Before summarizing the principal findings we touch briefly on the results concerning the effect of education on the other dimensions of farmer choice. Although we are able to examine determinants of productivity for Korea, Malaysia, and Thailand, only for Thailand do we have price data for individual farms that allow the use of profit functions to examine allocative efficiency and market efficiency (Chapter 6). Again, only for Thailand can we examine the effect of education on the choice of techniques of production—in this case, the choice of whether to use chemical fertilizers (Chapter 7).

In brief, these analyses from Thailand indicate that farmers of all educational levels are maximizing profits, as assessed by comparing coefficients in the profit and factor demand functions. More educated farmers do, however, have higher levels of profits, which reflect the higher levels of productivity found in the production function analyses. We find that education (or anything else) has little effect on market efficiency. And, finally, higher levels of education and exposure to extension services do increase the probabilities of using chemical fertilizers.

Table 1–1 summarizes the findings on the effect of exposure to schooling on farmer productivity in the sample areas of Korea, Malaysia, and Thailand. The effects are positive, statistically significant, and quantitatively important. Table 1–2 summarizes the similar findings concerning the effect of (very crudely measured) exposure to extension services in Malaysia and Thailand.

The findings of seventeen other studies conducted in low-income countries concerning the extent to which the educational level of small farmers affects their production efficiency are reviewed in Chapter 2. To put the results from subsequent chapters into a comparative perspective, we summarized our own results in this chapter as well. In total, Chapter 2 discusses analyses of thirty-seven sets of farm data that allow statistical estimation of the effect of education, controlling for other variables. Although education was found to have a negative (but statistically insignificant) effect in six of these data sets, the effect was positive and usually statistically significant in the remaining thirty-one. We do realize that the results of disparate studies must be combined with caution. With that caveat, Figure 1–1 contains a histogram showing the distribution (across studies) of gain in productivity from having 4 years of education rather than none. Our overall conclusion is that farm productivity increases on average by 8.7 percent as a result of a farmer's completing 4 years of elementary education. The 8.7 percent is an average of values from those studies in which an estimate could be computed. Weighting the studies according to their relative reliability gives a slightly lower estimate of the effect of education (Figure 2–1). Several studies showed evidence that at a threshold number of years (4 to 6) the effect of education became more pronounced. The effects of education were much more likely to be positive in modernizing agricultural environments rather than in traditional ones, a fact which was ascertained both by

Figure 1–1. *Results of Thirty-one Data Sets Relating Schooling to Agricultural Productivity, Unweighted*

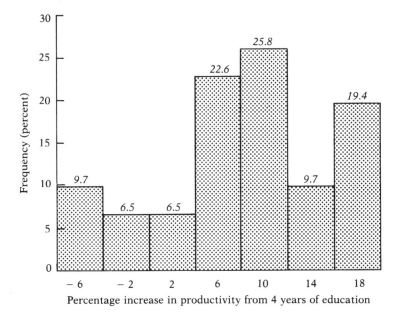

Percentage increase in productivity from 4 years of education

Note: Mean, 8.7 percent; standard deviation, 9.0 percent.

inspection and by regressing (across studies) the measured effect of education on productivity against modernization of environment and other variables. In sixteen of the samples, data were available on the farmers' exposure to agricultural extension education. Of these studies, eight provided evidence that extension was significantly positively related to efficiency.

Finally, we present the results of calculations of the internal rate of return to education based on the effects of education on the technological level of farmers (Chapter 8). This exercise is hypothetical in character, and the results are sensitive to the assumptions about the time structure of the streams of benefits and, of course, to the assumption that the benefits of education that are estimated with the production functions will continue to occur in the future. Of course, estimates of the rate of return to education in the wage

Table 1–1. *Schooling and Agricultural Productivity: Korea, Malaysia, and Thailand*

Study	Sample size, N	Coefficient of education on agricultural productivity	t statistic	R^2	Estimated percentage of increase in output for one additional year of education[a]	Comments
Korea (mechanical farms)[b]	1,363	Continuous 0.022	4.97	0.66	2.22	Analysis also undertaken with discrete variables representing different educational levels.
Korea (nonmechanical farms)[b]	541	Continuous 0.023	2.95	0.61	2.33	Analysis also undertaken with discrete variables representing different educational levels.
Malaysia	403	Indicator: literate, 0.109; 1 to 3 years, 0.071; 4 years, 0.186	1.62 1.14 2.60	0.69	5.11	None

Thailand (chemical farms)[c]	91	0.031	2.10	0.76	3.15	The coefficient for education has an increase between the dummy for primary education (4 years) and more than 4 years: Dummy (< 4 years) = 0.030 Dummy (= 4 years) = 0.124 Dummy (> 4 years) = 0.280
Thailand (nonchemical farms)[c]	184	0.024	2.27	0.81	2.43	The coefficient for education has an increase between the dummy for primary education (4 years) and more than 4 years: Dummy (< 4 years) = .066 Dummy (= 4 years) = .108 Dummy (> 4 years) = .132

a. These figures were computed from the formulas in Chapter 2.
b. Farms using no mechanical power are referred to as "nonmechanical;" others are referred to as "mechanical."
c. Farms using no chemical fertilizer or other chemical inputs are referred to as "nonchemical;" others are referred to as "chemical."

Table 1–2. *Exposure to Extension Services and Agricultural Productivity: Malaysia and Thailand*

Study	Sample size, N	Nonformal education variable	Coefficient of extension on agricultural productivity	t statistic	R^2	Evidence of interaction with formal education	Comments
Malaysia	403	Exposure to adult agricultural extension classes	0.237	1.73	0.69	Not applicable	None
Thailand (chemical farms)[a]	91	Number of extension visits to village	−0.123	−1.53	0.78	$A_5Ex_1 = 1$ if extension available $B = 0.015$ $t = 0.718$ $A_5Ex_0 = 1$ if extension not available $B = 0.036$ $t = 2.316$	Extension had negative coefficient, and education had positive coefficient on farm profits for farms using chemical fertilizer.
Thailand (nonchemical farms)[a]	184	Number of extension visits to village	0.085	2.22	0.81	$A_5Ex_1 = 1$ if extension available $B = -0.032$ $t = 2.695$ $A_5Ex_0 = 1$ if extension not available $B = -0.016$ $t = 1.291$	Education and extension had positive coefficients on farm profits for farms not using chemical fertilizer.

a. Farms using no chemical fertilizer or other chemical inputs are referred to as "nonchemical;" others are referred to as

sector are subject to these caveats and the additional, important one that wage differences may fail to reflect marginal productivity differences for reasons discussed above.

Table 8–2 shows our estimates of the internal rate of return as a function of various assumptions concerning output (rice) prices and the age of onset of the benefits of education. The estimated rates of return are quite respectable. They are highest for Malaysia (25 to 40 percent), lowest for Korea (7 to 11 percent), and intermediate for Thailand (14 to 25 percent).

PART ONE

Background and Data

CHAPTER 2

Previous Empirical Results

IN THIS REVIEW CHAPTER we synthesize the conclusions of several studies—many of them quite recent—on the effect of a farmer's educational level and exposure to extension services on his productivity.[1] The focus is on studies using data from individual farms in low-income regions.[2] These studies are examined for information concerning the correctness of three hypotheses:

Note: This chapter and Appendix A are drawn from Lockheed, Jamison, and Lau (1980).

1. Several studies have examined the effect of education on the willingness of farmers to adopt innovations. An early and important study in this area is that of Roy, Waisanen, and Rogers (1969). Villaume (1977, Chapter 2) provides a valuable review of this literature as well as an assessment of the direct and indirect effects of literacy on the adoption of innovations in Brazil and India.

2. In Chapter 4 advantages and disadvantages of using data from individual farms rather than aggregated data are discussed. Other authors (such as Griliches 1963, 1964; Fane 1975; Khaldi 1975; and Huffman 1974, 1977; and Evenson, Waggoner, and Ruttan 1979, table 3) have studied the effect of education on agricultural productivity using aggregated data (at the county or state level) in the United States, and have found educational levels positively associated with increased efficiency. Gisser (1965), also using aggregated U.S. data, found education associated with increased propensity to migrate from rural areas. Using similar methods, Hayami (1969) and Hayami and Ruttan (1970) found that educational level is an important determinant of agricultural productivity differences among nations. Herdt (1971), using much the same methodology with Indian data aggregated at the state level, found no positive effects of education, although Ram (1976) found that education contributed strongly to the productivity of Indian agriculture with data disaggregated from the state to the district level. Also using data on Indian districts, Harker (n.d.) found that average literacy levels increased productivity and, more strongly, increased the utilization of fertilizer. In other related studies Beal (1963) found that use of both education and extension services contributed to a subjective measure of

a. Higher levels of formal education increase the efficiency of farmers;

b. Education has a higher payoff for farmers in a changing, modernizing environment than in a static, traditional one (as suggested by Schultz (1979));[3] and

c. Exposure to extension services improves the productivity of farmers.

Following the suggestion of Glass (1976) we drew quantitative data from each study on the magnitude of the effects of education in a format that allows comparison across studies. As the studies differ from one another along many dimensions (including, in particular, the quality of data and data analysis), any conclusions from comparisons must be drawn with care. Nonetheless, subject to several caveats, general conclusions from the existing literature are possible. Our own results from Korea, Malaysia, and Thailand are also discussed. Appendix A contains supplemental information on the studies reviewed.

---

farmer performance in England, and Page (1978, 1979) found that exposure to technical education increased the efficiency of foresters in Ghana, but that experience rather than formal education was related to productivity of entrepreneurs in the Indian soap industry. Gerhart (1975) found that more educated Kenyan farmers were more likely to adopt hybrid maizes, and Rosenzweig (1978) found that more educated Punjabi farmers were more likely to adopt high-yielding varieties. On the other hand, Morss and others (1976) concluded that the average literacy level of farmers reached by agricultural development projects was not a determinant of project success. Although economists only began to pay systematic attention to these issues in the 1960s (beginning with the seminal work of T. Schultz), the educational research literature of the 1920s had already begun to consider the role of education in improving agricultural productivity. Folks (1920), for example, reported studies showing a strong influence of education on agricultural productivity in Indiana, Missouri, and New York.

3. When agricultural conditions are static, proper practices can be formalized and passed from generation to generation by example and adage. Buck (1937) provided interesting examples from China, such as, from Shantung: "Plant millet after millet and you will end by weeping." Evenson (1974), Bowman (1976a), Ram (1976), and Sachs (1979) provided thoughtful interpretations of how research, extension, and education, on the one hand, and market conditions, on the other, are related in transforming traditional environments into modernizing ones. Harma (1978) discussed specific ways in which education and information would help improve productivity in a range of agricultural activities. Hopper (1979) and Schultz (1979) discussed how governmental price and regulatory policies can facilitate or impede the incentive of farmers to modernize their practices and, thereby, indirectly influence the returns to education.

Methods of Analysis

Yotopoulos (1967) used a production function for agricultural output as his basic tool to analyze the effect of education on productivity. Subsequent studies used much the same methodology. We begin this section with a discussion of how a farmer's productivity and efficiency can be assessed from production functions and, if available, from price data.

The studies we review typically used data from a survey of several hundred farm households in a particular locale. These surveys contain data for each farm on some or all of the following variables: total output of the farm (say, kilograms of rice), land area under cultivation, person-days of family labor used, quantity and kind of equipment used, educational levels of the members of the household, and exposure of the farmer to extension services. Given a data set of this sort, the researcher can assess the effect of education on productivity by estimating a production function relating the quantity of farm output to the level of each of the inputs, including the farmer's education.

To take a simple example: let Y = total output (in kilograms); T = area under cultivation (in hectares); L = labor input (in person-days); E = educational level of the household head (in years of formal schooling completed); and EXT = indicator of exposure of the farmer to extension ($EXT = 1$ if exposed, $EXT = 0$ if not exposed). The studies reviewed use variations of either the Cobb-Douglas (or ln − ln) production function or the linear production function to relate output, Y, to the various inputs in one of the following ways:

(2.1) $$\ln Y = \alpha_0 + \alpha_1 \ln L + \alpha_2 \ln T + \beta \ln E + \gamma\, EXT$$

or

(2.2) $$\ln Y = \alpha_0 + \alpha_1 \ln L + \alpha_2 \ln T + \beta\, E + \gamma\, EXT$$

or

(2.3) $$\ln Y = \alpha_0 + \alpha_1 \ln L + \alpha_2 \ln T + \beta\, D + \gamma\, EXT$$

where D is an indicator variable that takes the value 1 if E takes a value in a specified range, and 0 otherwise; or

(2.4) $Y = \alpha_0 + \alpha_1 L + \alpha_2 T + \beta E$

or

(2.5) $Y = \alpha_0 + \alpha_1 L + \alpha_2 T + \beta D$.

In equations (2.1) through (2.3), the α_i's are the elasticities of output with respect to the various inputs.[4] In equations (2.4) and (2.5), the α_i's give the marginal product of the various inputs. In equation (2.1), β gives the elasticity of output with respect to years of education. In equation (2.2), β gives the percentage increase in output in response to a unit change in education. In equation (2.3), β gives the percentage increase in output of a farm with the farmer's educational level specified as D, compared with the base case, which is usually no education. (For example, if D signified "completed primary school," β would give the percentage increase in output of a farmer who graduated from primary school over that of one who had received no schooling.) In equation (2.4), β gives the marginal increase in output in response to a unit change in education. In equation (2.5), β gives the increase in output of a farm with the farmer's specified number of years of education, compared with the base case.

All of the studies use production functions of one of these general forms, in which β provides a measure of the productivity of education. Similarly γ provides a measure of the productivity of agricultural extension. In the better empirical studies, far more complete specifications of the production function, including many more independent variables, are used than in this simplified example.

In addition to examining the effect of education on productivity, it is also possible to examine whether it affects allocative efficiency; that is, the extent to which farmers optimally choose their mix of input and output in light of their production functions and prevailing prices. In a seminal article, Welch (1970) discusses ways to assess the effect of education on allocative efficiency. Several of the studies have examined the issue of allocative efficiency by compar-

---

4. The elasticity of variable Y with respect to variable X is the percentage change in variable Y induced by a 1 percent change in variable X. An elasticity of 0.2, for example, would imply that a 1 percent increase in variable X would result in a 0.2 percent increase in variable Y. The coefficients of an indicator variable, like D in equation (2.3) in the text, is approximately the percentage increase in output that would result if the indicator variable had the value 1 rather than 0.

ing actual with optimal allocation decisions in light of an estimated production function, and, in Chapter 6, farm-specific price data are used to estimate profit and factor demand functions to test allocative efficiency. This was done for a sample of farms in Thailand. Chapter 3 provides a thorough discussion of alternative types of efficiency, and Chapter 6 and Appendix D explain the use of profit functions as a tool for assessing allocative efficiency. Studies by Müller (1974) and by Shapiro and Müller (1977) analyzed the relation between information and technical efficiency and provided empirical support that familiarity with information sources improves productivity in dairy farming in the United States and cotton farming in Tanzania.

Selection of the Studies

Eighteen studies on education and small farm production in thirteen countries of Africa, Asia, Europe, and Latin America have produced thirty-seven data sets. In seventeen of the data sets the effects of education on technical efficiency in the production of a cereal crop (rice, wheat, or maize) were examined; in the remaining data sets, the effect of education on the production of a mixed crop, typically including a cereal, was examined. Only a study of dairy farms by Sadan, Nachmias, and Bar-Lev (1976) did not examine efficiency in terms of field crop production. Table 2–1 summarizes salient features of the data bases, and Table A–1 in Appendix A provides more detail on the variables used in each analysis. There are some sources of inconsistency among the studies, so criteria were developed to restrict the sample of studies for further analysis.

Although the widely differing studies had many similarities, several factors limit the scope of generalizations. The most important of these are differences in the sample characteristics, in the methods of analysis, and in the specification or measurement of both dependent and independent variables (particularly the education variables). Furthermore, as previously noted, there is substantial variation among the studies in the quality of data, data analysis, and reporting, which limits the validity of the comparisons.

Sample characteristics

Of the thirty-seven data sets, only sixteen were collected with the use of an explicit sampling design. The data sets also varied in the

Table 2–1. *Data Base Used in Each Study*

Reference to study	Area and date of data collection, sample characteristics, and crops
Calkins (1976)	Nepal, 1973–74. Sample of small farms in five panchayats of Nuwakot district of central Nepal. Rice and wheat.
Chaudhri (1974)	India, 1961–64. Reanalysis of a sample population of twenty-one villages in the wheat belt of Punjab, Haryana, and Utter Pradesh. Wheat.
Halim (1976)	Philippines, 1963, 1968, 1973. Subsample of an earlier random sample of households in twenty-eight representative rice-producing barrios of Laguna district.
Haller (1972)	Colombia, 1969. Stratified random sample of farms in Chinchiná, Espinal, Malaga, and Moniquira regions. Tobacco, coffee, corn, cassava, guayaba, cotton, sesame, rice, and livestock.
Harker (1973)	Japan, 1966. Representative sample of 971 middle-aged rice farmers in central and southern Honshu, Shikoku, and in the Fukuoka areas of Kyushu. Rice.
Hong (1975)	Korea, 1961. Subsample of random census sample of 1,200 farm households in nine provinces. Rice and other crops.
Hopcraft (1974)	Kenya, 1969–70. Subsample of a stratified random sample of 1,700 small farms collected for the Small Farm Enterprise Cost Survey. Maize, livestock, and tea.
Jamison and Lau (this volume)	Malaysia, 1973. Subsample of FAO/World Bank survey of 800 rural farming households in monoculture paddy area of Muda Irrigation Project, Kedah and Perlis States, West Malaysia. Rice.
Jamison and Lau (this volume)	Korea, 1973. Subsamples of a national survey of 2,254 farms in nine regions of South Korea. Rice and other crops.
Jamison and Lau (this volume)	Thailand, 1972–73. Reanalysis of a stratified random sample of farm households from twenty-two villages in the Chiang Mai Valley. Rice.

Table 2–1 (*continued*)

Reference to study	Area and date of data collection, sample characteristics, and crops
Moock (1973)	Kenya, 1971–72. Farms in Vihiga Division that received loans for the purchase of hybrid maize seeds and fertilizer and comparison farms that were not loan recipients. Maize.
Pachico and Ashby (1976)	Brazil, 1970. Sample of farm households in four communities of southern Brazil collected by University of Rio Grande de Sul. Mixed field crop and livestock.
Patrick and Kehrberg (1973)	Brazil, 1969. Survey of 620 farms in five regions of eastern Brazil. Maize, beans, coffee, beef cattle, and dairy cattle.
Pudasaini (1976)	Nepal, 1975. Random sample of 102 traditional and mechanized farms in Bara District. Rice, wheat, and sugarcane.
Sadan, Nachmias, and Bar-Lev (1976)	Israel, 1969–70. Population of 1,841 dairy farms under the supervision of the Settlement Agency in Israel.
Sharma (1974)	Nepal, 1968–69. Subsample of a stratified random sample of households in fifteen village panchayats in Rupandehi. Rice and wheat.
Sidhu (1976, 1978)	India, 1968–71. Sample of 150 farms in the Ferozepur district of Punjab, 1968–69; farms in four districts of Punjab, 1970–71. Wheat.
Wu (1971)	Taiwan, 1964–66. Records of bookkeeping farms: 249 farms in twenty-five hsiangs collected in 1964; 246 farms in twenty-six hsiangs collected in 1965; 154 farms in thirteen hsiangs collected in 1966. Rice, banana, pineapple, sweet potatoes, sugarcane, and poultry.
Wu (1977)	Taiwan, 1964–66. Reanalysis of a sample of 310 bookkeeping farms in three mixed farming regions; presumably same data set as Wu (1971).
Yotopoulos (1967)	Greece, 1963. Subsample of a random sample of 650 households in 110 villages and three cities of Epirus. Wheat and cotton.

number of farms that were surveyed, the size distribution of the farms, the kind of crop grown, and regional characteristics. Moreover, information on education was frequently not the primary goal of the original data collection efforts.

Data analysis

The primary method of analysis used in the studies was multiple regression with both dependent and independent variables in logarithmic form, resulting in a production function commonly referred to in economic literature as the Cobb-Douglas type, equation (2.1). In several of the studies, however, the description of the specification of the production equation was so inadequate that we were unable to determine whether the variables were actually expressed in logarithmic form. Appendix Table A–1 indicates the specifications of the equations where they could be determined.

The dependent variable

Although most of these studies were described as studies of production, the analysis of twenty-three of the thirty-seven data sets used the value of crop production as the dependent variable. Since the value of a crop depends on price structures (which may vary widely both within and among regions), studies which examine the quantity of output and those which examine the value of output should be compared with some caution. The studies also included a variety of different field crops; the dependent variables included both single field crops (typically rice, wheat, or maize) and mixed field crops (including bananas, cotton, vegetables, sugar cane, and so forth), both separately or in combination with cereal crops.

The education variable

There are three sources of variations throughout the studies regarding the education variable used: whose education is measured; what the education measure is; and how the measure is expressed. The educational level of the production unit was measured in these studies by either the education of the head of the household, the aggregate education of the family members, or the aggregate education of farm workers. Education aggregates typically excluded the education of nonworkers—the very young or the very old. The quantity of education was measured by either the number of years attended or completed, the number of grades or levels attended or completed, or simply a measure of literacy. Educational level was expressed as either an indicator or a continuous variable; continuous variables were sometimes entered in the production functions in logarithmic form and sometimes in natural form.

Whenever possible, we have reported results of equations in which the number of years or grades completed by the head of the household was used. Where more than one education variable was analyzed, however, any differences in the estimated effects have been noted.

Other factor inputs

The widest discrepancies among these studies are the extent to which other input variables are included in the specification of the production function. Land, labor, and capital are generally included, but in different ways. Land may be entered into the function as a quantity or as a value. Labor is often differentiated into family or hired, and the variable may be in terms of time or value. Capital may be entered as a single variable or differentiated into several factors. Other factor input variables may include the quantity or use of fertilizer, use of irrigation, types of seed, and regional indicator variables.

Because of the differences in samples, outputs, and factor inputs among these studies, the summary histograms and regressions include only:

   a. Agricultural production function studies (this eliminated Harker 1973)

   b. Studies in which the dependent variable was a field crop or an aggregate of several field crops (this eliminated Sadan, Nachmias, and Bar-Lev 1976)

   c. Studies in which a percentage gain per year of education could be computed (this eliminated Calkins 1976, Chaudhri 1974, and Hong 1975).[5]

Hopcraft's maize production function, reported in Table 2–2, was not included because of its finding of a negative effect of labor on output.[6] These restrictions reduced the number of data sets used to thirty-one.

   5. Chaudhri's work on India was extended and published after the present manuscript was completed; see Chaudhri (1979).

   6. See Hopcraft (1974). Although Hopcraft's maize production function did have a surprising negative coefficient for labor, labor had a positive coefficient on output in his production function for aggregate crop output.

Table 2-2. *Formal Education and Agricultural Productivity*

Area and study	Sample size, N	Coefficient of education on agricultural productivity	t statistic	R^2	Estimated percentage of increase in output for one additional year of education[a]	Comments
Brazil, Candelaria (Pachico and Ashby 1976)	117	0.126	0.89	0.71	2.69	Education was positively related to output among highly commercialized farms.
Brazil, Garibaldi (Pachico and Ashby 1976)	101	0.207	1.92	0.69	4.60	Education was positively related to output among highly commercialized farms.
Brazil, Guarani (Pachico and Ashby 1976)	63	0.072	0.55	0.67	1.49	Preliminary analysis of data indicated that less than 5 years of schooling had no significant effect on output.
Brazil, Taquari (Pachico and Ashby 1976)	101	0.244	1.66	0.68	5.53	Education was positively related to output among highly commercialized farms.
Brazil, Alto São Francisco (Patrick and Kehrberg 1973)	82	−0.013	−0.65	0.44	−1.29	Returns of schooling were negative in the traditional agricultural regions, but became positive and increased as the regions became more modern among the five samples.

Brazil, Conceicao de Castelo (Patrick and Kehrberg 1973)	54	−0.009	−0.75	0.82	−0.90	None
Brazil, Paracatu (Patrick and Kehrberg 1973)	86	−0.017	−1.41	0.59	−1.69	None
Brazil, Resende (Patrick and Kehrberg 1973)	62	0.010	1.11	0.55	1.01	None
Brazil, Vicosa (Patrick and Kehrberg 1973)	337	0.023	2.86	0.62	2.33	None
Colombia, Chinchiná (Haller 1972)	77	−0.008	−0.13	0.75	−0.29	None
Colombia, Espinal (Haller 1972)	74	0.140	1.80	0.71	6.10	None
Colombia, Málaga (Haller 1972)	74	0.047	0.94	0.53	3.09	None
Colombia, Moniquirá (Haller 1972)	75	−0.049	−1.02	0.79	−3.12	None
Greece (Yotopoulos 1967)	430	0.138	2.06	0.79	6.47	The marginal product for one year of education was 606.40 drachmas.

(Table continues on the following page)

Table 2-2 (continued)

Area and study	Sample size, N	Coefficient of education on agricultural productivity	t statistic	R^2	Estimated percentage of increase in output for one additional year of education[a]	Comments
India, Punjab, Haryana, and Utter Pradesh (Chaudhri 1974)	1,038	Family average 0.116	5.04	0.59	Insufficient information to calculate	Marginal product of family education was calculated as 107.04 rupees a year. Marginal product of education of household head was calculated as 153.12 rupees a year. No base was given. Chaudhri (1979) provides further analysis based on this same data set and calculates rates of return to education that are high indeed.
		Household head 0.114	3.65	0.59	—	
India, Punjab (Sidhu 1976) (traditional and Mexican wheat varieties)	236	0.038	1.90	0.92	1.49	Education was related to production efficiency but more strongly to allocative efficiency.

Location	Sample					Notes
India, Punjab (Sidhu 1976) (Mexican wheat)	369	0.036	2.25	0.92	1.41	In an analysis using gross farm sales as dependent variable, Sidhu finds a positive effect of education, not quite statistically significant, resulting in a 1.1 percent increase in value of sales for 1 year of education. Sidhu and Baanante (1978) use profit and factor demand functions with the same data and find a positive (but statistically insignificant) effect of education.
Israel (Sadan, Nachmias, and Bar-Lev 1976)	1,841	21.100	4.20	Not given	Marginal value added was US$21 per year of wife's schooling (1.08 percent of gross value added of production).	None
Japan, Honshu, Shikoku, and Kyushu (Harker 1973)	971	Correlation: with gross farm sales, 0.02; with communication behavior and agricultural adoption variables added, 0.31. ($p < 0.001$)	Not significant	0.38	Not applicable	None

(Table continues on the following page)

Table 2-2 (continued)

Area and study	Sample size, N	Coefficient of education on agricultural productivity	t statistic	R^2	Estimated percentage of increase in output for one additional year of education[a]	Comments
Kenya, Vihiga (Moock 1973)	152	Indicator: 4 or more years, 0.067	1.60	0.64	1.73	An indicator variable for 1 to 3 years of education had a negative coefficient.
Kenya (Hopcraft 1974)	674	Indicator: 2 to 3 years, −0.023; 4 to 6 years, −0.163; primary school, −0.148	−0.30 −2.19 −1.50	0.56	−3.26	Results are for maize production, for which the coefficient of labor on output was negative. The production functions for aggregate output, which had a positive labor coefficient, had education coefficients that were essentially zero.
Korea (Hong 1975)	895	Log-linear 0.712 Cobb-Douglas 0.927	3.05 1.46	0.85 0.85		Units of equation were hard to interpret, so figure could not be computed. Some empirical conclusions of this study are difficult to interpret.
Korea (this volume) (mechanical farms)[b]	1,363	Continuous 0.022	4.97	0.66	2.22	Analysis was also undertaken with discrete variables representing different educational levels.

Korea (this volume) (nonmechanical farms)[b]	541	Continuous 0.023	2.95	0.61	2.33	The coefficient of labor on output was negative in this study.
Malaysia, Kedah and Perlis (this volume)	403	Indicator: literate, 0.109; 1 to 3 years, 0.071; 4 or more years, 0.186	1.61 1.14 2.60	0.69	5.11	None
Nepal, Bara (Pudasaini 1976)	102	0.014	1.71	0.90	1.3	Positive effect of schooling on farm revenue. Tractor-hiring and pumpset-owning farms (the modernizing variable) were more efficient than traditional, whereas farms with tractors and farms with both tractors and pumpsets were not significantly different from traditional farms in terms of efficiency.

(Table continues on the following page)

31

Table 2-2 (continued)

Area and study	Sample size, N	Coefficient of education on agricultural productivity	t statistic	R^2	Estimated percentage of increase in output for one additional year of education[a]	Comments
Nepal, Nuwakot (Calkins 1976)	540	Indicator: 7 or more years, 0.53	3.53	0.77	Could not be computed because means of other independent variables not given.	The coefficient for 0 years of education was not significantly different from the one for 1 to 6 years of education. For 7 or more years, however, the coefficient was significant. The evidence thus suggests a minimum threshold of 6 to 7 years before education affects productivity.
Nepal, Rupandehi (Sharma 1974) (wheat farms)	87	Indicator: literate, 0.142	1.80	0.84	5.09 (Computed using literate as equal to 3 years of education.)	None
Nepal, Rupandehi (Sharma 1974) (rice farms)	138	Indicator: literate, 0.082	1.78	0.95	2.85 (Computed using literate as equal to 3 years of education.)	None

Philippines, Laguna, 1963 (Halim 1976)	274	0.020	1.53	0.77	2.0	None
Philippines, Laguna, 1968 (Halim 1976)	273	0.019	1.26	0.70	1.92	None
Philippines, Laguna, 1973 (Halim 1976)	220	0.027	2.25	0.80	2.74	None
Taiwan (Wu 1971) (rice farms)	333	0.007	0.53	0.60	0.7	Simple rate of returns for 1 year of additional schooling computed from 1 to 12 years decreased at a steady rate. Thus, there was no evidence of a threshold effect.
Taiwan (Wu 1971) (banana and pineapple farms)	316	0.038	2.83	0.65	3.87	None
Taiwan (Wu 1977)	310	0.009 quadratic form(s) −0.066 0.005	0.95 1.82 2.12	0.87	0.9	Marginal productivity of education in crop production changes from negative to positive at 6.6 years of schooling of the farm operator. The quadratic formula shows this clearly: Where $a_1S + a_2S^2$ was entered in equation $a_1 = -0.066$, $a_2 = 0.005$.

(Table continues on the following page)

Table 2-2 (continued)

Area and study	Sample size, N	Coefficient of education on agricultural productivity	t statistic	R^2	Estimated percentage of increase in output for one additional year of education[a]	Comments
Thailand, Chiang Mai (this volume) (chemical farms)[c]	91	0.031	2.10	0.76	3.15	The coefficient for education has an increase between the indicator for primary education (4 years) and more than 4 years. Indicator: < 4 years = 0.030; = 4 years = 0.124; and > 4 years = 0.280 for all equations.
Thailand, Chiang Mai (this volume) (nonchemical farms)[c]	184	0.024	2.27	0.81	2.43	The coefficient for education has an increase between the indicator for primary education (4 years) and more than 4 years. Indicator: < 4 years = 0.066; = 4 years = 0.108; and > 4 years = 0.132 for all equations.

a. These figures were computed from the formulas in the text.
b. Farms using no mechanical equipment are labeled "nonmechanical;" others are labeled "mechanical."
c. Farms using no chemical fertilizer or other chemical inputs are referred to as "nonchemical;" others are referred to as "chemical."

Results of the Studies

The results of the previous studies are summarized below. They show the effects of formal schooling in different environments as well as the effects of exposure to extension services or other nonformal agricultural education experience.

Effects of schooling

We have hypothesized that education (years of schooling) will have a positive effect on farmer efficiency; overall, our hypothesis is confirmed. For each of the thirty-seven data sets Table 2–2 reports the coefficient of education on agricultural productivity, the statistical significance of the estimate, and (for the thirty-one data sets where it was possible) the estimated percentage increase in output for each additional year of education. There was a broad range of findings among the diverse studies. In six of these data sets education had a negative (but statistically insignificant) effect, but, in the remaining thirty-one, the effect was positive and usually significant. Table A–2 in Appendix A contains additional information—in particular, about the environment from which the farm samples were drawn.

The percentage increase in output for one additional year of education at the mean educational level of the sample can be computed for most of the studies. The appropriate formula depends on the particular equation of the production function that is used in the study. Let $\bar{E}$ be the average educational level of the sample and β be the estimated coefficient of education. Then the percentage increase in output for one additional year of education may be calculated by computing the ratio of the value of output when the level of education is half a year greater than $\bar{E}$, Y_1, to the value when it is half a year less, Y_0, subtracting one, and multiplying by 100. If the production function is specified as in equation (2.1),

$$\text{Percentage increase} = [Y_1/Y_0 - 1] \times 100$$
$$= [(\bar{E} + 0.5)^\beta/(\bar{E} - 0.5)^\beta - 1] \times 100$$
$$= [(\bar{E} + 0.5/\bar{E} - 0.5)^\beta - 1] \times 100 .$$

For equation (2.2),

Percentage increase $= [e^{\beta(\bar{E} + 0.5)}/e^{\beta(\bar{E} - 0.5)} - 1] \times 100$

$$= [e^\beta - 1] \times 100.$$

For equation (2.3), if there are N years of education in the level specified by D,

Percentage increase $= [(e^\beta - 1)/N] \times 100.$

(In the calculation for equation (2.3), it is assumed that the percentage increase owing to education can be proportionally attributed to the years of education.)

For equation (2.4),

Percentage increase $=$

$$\left[\frac{\alpha_0 + \alpha_1 L + \alpha_2 T + \beta(\bar{E} + 0.5) + \gamma EXT}{\alpha_0 + \alpha_1 L + \alpha_2 T + \beta(\bar{E} - 0.5) + \gamma EXT} - 1 \right] \times 100$$

$$= \left[\frac{\beta}{\alpha_0 + \alpha_1 L + \alpha_2 T + \beta(\bar{E} - 0.5) + \gamma EXT} \right] \times 100.$$

For equation (2.5), if there are N years of education in the level specified by D,

Percentage increase $= [\beta/(\alpha_0 + \alpha_1 L + \alpha_2 T + \gamma EXT)] \times 100/N.$

In order to summarize our findings we generated histograms (based on the thirty-one studies that were not omitted for technical or comparability reasons) of the number of studies by percentage decrease or increase in output attributable to a farmer's having 4 years of education rather than none. Our estimate of the effect of 4 years is, however, simply four times the effect of 1 year as computed from the formulas just given. (This averages out threshold effects of the sort found in some of the studies.) The period of 4 years was chosen because it is often stated as the minimum for the basic education cycle.[7] Change was rounded to nearest 0.5 percent to group the studies, which were aggregated in 4 percent intervals. The histogram in Figure 1–1 showed that the mean gain in produc-

---

7. Four years is the Unesco standard for minimum primary education. Rogers (1969) provides empirical support for this as a threshold in a study of Colombian farmers, and the World Bank has a research project underway (RPO 671–55, "International Study of the Retention of Literacy and Numeracy") to assess where the threshold is.

tion for 4 years of education was about 8.7 percent, with a standard deviation of 9.0 percent.

In order to assess the reliability of our estimates of percentage gain in production for 4 years of education, we also estimated the standard errors of these estimates, based on the estimated standard errors of the coefficients in the respective studies. Table A–2 in Appendix A shows these estimated standard errors, which varied greatly among the studies. To compensate for these differences in reliability, the percentage gains were weighted by the reciprocals of the corresponding estimated standard errors and were used to generate a bar graph, shown in Figure 2–1. Thus, the more reliable an estimate is, the heavier the weight. The results are slightly lower

Figure 2–1. *Results of Thirty-one Data Sets Relating Schooling to Agricultural Productivity, Weighted by the Reciprocal of the Standard Error*

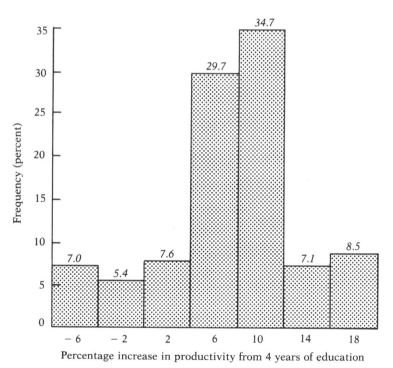

Note: Mean, 7.4 percent; standard deviation, 6.8 percent.

than those estimated from the unweighted sample in Figure 1–1, with a mean gain from 4 years of education estimated as 7.4 percent and a standard deviation of 6.8 percent.

Effects of schooling in different environments

As noted before, aspects of the environment may be important determinants of the effects of education on production. In particular, Schultz (1975) has argued that education is likely to be effective principally under modernizing conditions.[8] To test this hypothesis, the studies were divided according to whether they reflected modernizing or traditional environments.

An environment was identified as traditional if it included primitive technology, traditional farming practices and crops, and little reported innovation or exposure to new methods. Conversely, an environment was identified as modern if it included the availability of new crop varieties, innovative planting methods, erosion control, and the availability of modern inputs such as insecticides, fertilizers, and tractors or machines. Other indicators of this kind of environment were market-oriented production and exposure to extension services. In some cases, authors of the studies were explicitly testing Schultz's hypothesis, and for those we simply accepted the author's classification of whether the sample's environment was modernizing. In other cases, where information was available, we made our own subjective assessment. Twenty-three of the thirty-one data sets could be classified as modern or traditional.

The effect of a modernizing environment was assessed in two separate ways. First the bar graph of Figure 2–1 was divided into modern and traditional subsamples, as shown in Figure 2–2. Under modernizing conditions, the effects of education are substantially greater than under traditional conditions. In all the studies the mean increase in output from 4 years of education under traditional conditions was 1.3 percent compared with 9.5 percent under modern or modernizing conditions.

A second way to assess the effect of a modernizing environment on the productivity of education was to conduct a regression analysis of our estimates of the percentage of increase in farm output from 4 years of education as a function of environmental characteristics such as the adult literacy rate in the country, modernizing

---

8. See footnote 3 above.

Figure 2–2.   *Results of Twenty-three Data Sets Relating Schooling
to Agricultural Productivity, Grouped by Modern and Traditional
Samples and Weighted by the Reciprocal of the Standard Error*

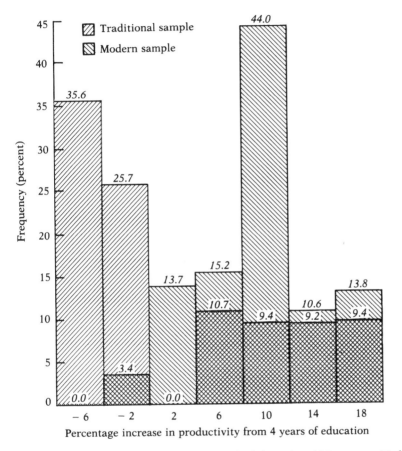

Note: Traditional: mean, 1.3 percent; standard deviation, 11.0 percent. Modern:
mean, 9.5 percent; standard deviation, 5.7 percent.

environment, regional availability of extension services, type of
crop (rice versus other crops), and real GNP per capita. Since our
estimates of the percentage gains were themselves random variables with different variances, the ordinary least-squares estimator
was inefficient, although it remained unbiased under standard
assumptions. To correct for the heteroscedasticity the generalized
least-squares estimator was used, with an estimated diagonal

Table 2–3. *Variables Used in Regression Analysis*

Independent variable	Definition
MOD1	Indicates modernizing environment (1 = modernizing; 0 = either traditional or no information available).
MOD-1	Indicates traditional environment (1 = traditional; 0 = either modernizing or no information available).
EXT1	Indicates availability of extension services (1 = services available; 0 = either no services available or no information available).
EXT-1 ·	Indicates lack of extension services (1 = services not available; 0 = either services available or no information available).
CROP	Indicates crop type (1 = rice; 0 = other).
GNP	Per capita gross national product in 1975 U.S. dollars.
LIT	Adult literacy rate expressed as percent.
MOD	Indicates modernizing environment (1 = modernizing; 0 = traditional).
M1C1	Indicates sample partition (1 = modernizing rice environment; 0 = other).
M1C0	Indicates sample partition (1 = modernizing nonrice environment; 0 = other).
M0C1	Indicates sample partition (1 = traditional rice environment; 0 = other).
M0C0	Indicates sample partition (1 = traditional, nonrice environment; 0 = other).

Note: Results of the regression analysis are given in Tables 2–4 and 2–5.

variance-covariance matrix constructed from our estimates of the variances of the percentage gains.[9] The independent variables used are defined in Table 2–3. For several studies it was not possible to determine whether the environment was modernizing or whether agricultural extension was available. Therefore two indicator variables were used, each representing the effects of modernizing environment and agricultural extension.

A number of regressions with different combinations of the independent variables were run. Table 2–4 reports only those regressions with at least one statistically significant estimated coefficient (defined as a coefficient with a t statistic exceeding 1.96 in absolute value). We found that, on the one hand, agricultural extension, type

9. When the error does not vary constantly for all the observations, it is said to be heteroscedastic.

of crop, real GNP, and literacy rate have uniformly statistically insignificant effects on the percentage gain. On the other hand, a traditional environment appears to have a decidedly negative effect on the percentage gain. The difference in the percentage increase in productivity between a modern and a traditional environment was consistently estimated to be around 10 percent. The equation with the highest $\bar{R}^2$, the coefficient of multiple correlation adjusted for degrees of freedom, indicated that in a traditional, nonrice-growing environment, the mean percentage increase may even be negative.

To identify further the nature of the environmental influence on the effectiveness of education, we dropped from the regression analysis those studies for which the modernizing/traditional classification was unavailable, and ran further regressions with the reduced sample. Table 2–5 reports that the modernizing environment variable was strongly significant. On average, the percentage gain as a result of 4 years of education was 10 percent higher in a modernizing environment than in a traditional environment. The coefficient of the crop-type variable remained statistically insignificant. Even when the independent variables were split into four indicator variables, as defined in Table 2–3, there was no evidence of interaction between environment and type of crop. We could not reject the hypothesis that the effect of a modernizing environment was independent of the type of crop (rice or nonrice) because the t-statistic for the null hypothesis was 0.34.

Effects of extension

We have further hypothesized that exposure to extension services or other nonformal agricultural education experience should have a positive effect on output. Table 2–6 summarizes the analyses of sixteen of the data sets for which information on nonformal education was provided.[10] Of these studies, eight provided evidence that

10. We should explicitly stress that this survey of the literature is not intended to cover all studies of the effectiveness of agricultural extension or other nonformal education provided for farmers; see Orivel (1981) for such a review. We merely report here any results available concerning effectiveness of extension services in the eighteen studies listed in Table 2–1; those studies included an assessment of the contribution of formal education to agricultural productivity. Benor and Harrison (1977) reported on extension services which were considerably more effective than those reviewed here, and they provide an extensive discussion of the possibilities for reforming extension systems to improve productivity.

Table 2-4. Regression Analysis of the Determinants of Productivity Gain as a Result of 4 Years of Education
(sample = 31)

Independent variable	Alternative specifications							
	1	2	3	4	5	6	7	8
Constant	6.33 (4.52)	6.00 (3.45)	5.48 (3.28)	6.77 (4.32)	5.04 (2.16)	6.33 (4.45)	3.19 (0.97)	6.05 (3.41)
MOD1	2.25 (1.31)	2.46 (1.27)	2.85 (1.55)	3.27 (1.39)	0.96 (0.38)	2.10 (1.17)	0.65 (0.25)	2.32 (1.15)
MOD-1	-8.05 (-2.55)	-8.01 (-2.29)	-7.20 (-2.18)	-6.24 (-1.47)	-9.03 (-2.59)	-8.05 (-2.51)	-9.39 (-2.50)	-7.92 (-2.22)
EXT1	—	0.34 (0.18)	—	—	—	—	0.61 (0.33)	0.18 (0.09)
EXT-1	—	1.07 (0.32)	—	—	—	—	3.19 (0.80)	1.03 (0.30)
CROP	—	—	1.93 (0.95)	—	—	—	—	—
GNP	—	—	—	-0.00 (-0.65)	—	—	—	—
LIT	—	—	—	—	0.03 (0.70)	—	0.06 (1.00)	—
MODICROP	—	—	—	—	—	1.09 (0.37)	—	1.02 (0.32)
$\bar{R}^2$	0.46	0.42	0.46	0.45	0.45	0.45	0.42	0.40

Note: The data on which the regressions are based are presented in Table A–2. This table shows the estimated coefficients with their t statistics in parentheses below them.

To take into account the differences in the variances of the estimates of the percentage productivity gains, generalized least squares with an estimated variance-covariance matrix were used. The dependent variable is the percentage increase in output from 4 years of education. Let $Y_1, \ldots, Y_T$ be the percentage gains and the row vectors and, $X_1, \ldots, X_T$ be the independent variables. The regression model is

$$Y_i = X_i \delta + \xi_i, \, i = 1, \ldots, T$$

where

$$V(Y) = V(\xi) = \begin{bmatrix} V(Y_1) & & & 0 \\ & V(Y_2) & & \\ & & \ddots & \\ 0 & & & V(Y_T) \end{bmatrix}.$$

By transforming both the dependent and the independent variables, we obtain:

$$\frac{Y_i}{\sqrt{V(Y_i)}} = \frac{X_i \delta}{\sqrt{V(Y_i)}} + \frac{\xi_i}{\sqrt{V(Y_i)}}. \qquad (i = 1, \ldots, T)$$

This, by a redefinition of variables, becomes

$$Y_i^* = X_i^* \delta + \xi_i^* \qquad (i = 1, \ldots, T)$$

with

$$V(\xi^*) = I$$

so that ordinary least squares can be applied. But $V(Y)$ is unknown. $V(Y)$ is substituted for by a consistent estimator of $V(Y)$ calculated from the estimated variance-covariance matrixes of the coefficients of each of the underlying studies (see footnote b, Table A–2).
— Not applicable.

Table 2–5. *Regression Analysis of the Determinants of Productivity Gain as a Result of 4 Years of Education* (sample = 23)

Independent variable	Alternative specifications			
	1	2	3	4
Constant	− 1.72 (− 0.56)	− 1.72 (− 0.57)	7.14 (5.47)	—
MOD	10.16 (3.07)	10.31 (3.22)	—	—
CROP	1.09 (0.34)	—	2.39 (0.64)	—
M1C1	—	—	—	9.53 (3.20)
M1C0	—	—	—	8.44 (7.15)
M0C1	—	—	—	—
M0C0	—	—	—	− 1.72 (− 0.56)
$\bar{R}^2$	0.47	0.50	0.26	0.47

Note: This table shows the estimated coefficients with their *t* statistics in parentheses below them. See note to Table 2–4 for information on data sources and regression methods.
— Not applicable.

extension was significantly positively related to productivity, one provided evidence that extension was significantly negatively related to productivity, and the remaining seven showed no significant effect.

These results can be compared across studies only to a limited extent because of the differences in the actual measures of exposure to nonformal education, which may be indicated by the number of contacts a farmer has with the extension agent, the monetary investment in extension in that region, or the years of exposure to nonformal education. In addition, extreme variability in the program content and method of communication may also reduce comparability.

We also explored whether formal education and nonformal education acted as substitutes or complements. A few studies incorporated interaction terms between formal and nonformal education in their production function regressions. Most of the coefficients of interaction were positive, suggesting a possible complementary relation between the two forms of education, even though few of the coefficients were statistically significant.

Conclusions

This chapter has surveyed the findings of eighteen studies conducted in low-income countries concerning the extent to which the educational level of small farmers affects their production efficiency.[11] The eighteen studies contain analyses of thirty-seven sets of farm data that allow, with other variables controlled, a statistical estimation of the effect of education. In six of these data sets, education had a negative (but statistically insignificant) effect, but in the remaining thirty-one, the effect was positive and usually statistically significant. Although the results of disparate studies must be combined with caution, our overall conclusion is that farm productivity increases, on the average, by 7.4 percent as a result of a farmer's completing 4 additional years of elementary education rather than none. This figure is a weighted average of values from those studies for which an estimate could be computed. Several studies showed evidence of a threshold number of years (from 4 to 6) at which the effect of education became more pronounced. None of the studies addressed the issue of which of education's outcomes

11. Several studies were published or came to our attention after this chapter was completed. Among these is a paper by Welch (1979) including a review with (qualitative) conclusions similar to ours. In other specific studies, Bhalla (1979) found that education enhanced productivity in an Indian sample of more than 2,000 farmers; Bhati (1973) found that the technical knowledge of Malaysian farmers was related to their productivity; Freire (1981) found that education is significantly associated with the productivity of Guatemalan farmers and with their propensity to use innovative methods; Halim and Husain (1979) found the education of farm operators in Bangladesh enhanced output, although not quite statistically significantly, whereas the highest education level of anyone in the farm household bore a negative but insignificant relation to productivity; Pachico (1979) found education increased productivity of farmers in Nepal; Singh (1974) found that education (particularly secondary education) enhanced farmers' productivity in the Haryana State of India; and Valdes (1971) found that the education of agricultural laborers in Chile was significantly associated with their daily wages. These results, though not incorporated in the analyses we report, are consistent with our findings. (Bhalla's findings are not yet reported, but a description of his sample and a report of other analyses based upon it appear in Bhalla (1979).)

Table 2–6. *Nonformal Education and Agricultural Productivity*

Area and study	Sample size, N	Nonformal education variable	Coefficient of extension on productivity	t statistic	R^2	Evidence of interaction with formal education	Comments
Brazil (Pachico and Ashby 1976)	382 (total sample)	Number of direct contacts between the farm operator and government extension agent	−0.010	−2.50	0.65	The interaction term between schooling and extension indicates these factors to be complements, but the relation was statistically insignificant.	None
Brazil, Alto São Francisco (Patrick and Kehrberg 1973)	82	Number of direct contacts between farmer and extension agent	0.004	0.98	0.44	Not applicable	Mean social benefit-cost ratio for extension contacts was reported as 1.35.
Brazil, Conceicao de Castelo (Patrick and Kehrberg 1973)	54	Number of direct contacts between farmer and extension agent	0.009	2.65	0.82	Not applicable	Mean social benefit-cost ratio for extension contacts was reported as 3.02.
Brazil, Paracatu (Patrick and Kehrberg 1973)	86	Number of direct contacts between farmer and extension agent	0.001	0.20	0.59	Not applicable	Mean social benefit-cost ratio for extension contacts was reported as 0.42.

Study	N	Variable					Comments
Brazil, Resende (Patrick and Kehrberg 1973)	62	Number of direct contacts between farmer and extension agent	0.001	1.11	0.55	Not applicable	Mean social benefit-cost ratio for extension contacts was reported as 0.165.
Brazil, Vicosa (Patrick and Kehrberg 1973)	337	Number of direct contacts between farmer and extension agent	0.003	1.03	0.62	Not applicable	Mean social benefit-cost ratio for extension contacts was reported as 0.68.
Japan, Honshu, Shikoku, and Kyushu (Harker 1973)	971	Use of agricultural magazines, extension agents, and agricultural broadcasts	$r = 0.14$	$(p < 0.001)$	0.38	Not applicable	A path analysis was used; coefficient is standardized partial correlation coefficient.
Kenya (Hopcraft 1974)	674	Extension visits— Indicator:				Not applicable	The interaction between schooling and extension was significant and negative.
		(1 – 3)	0.153	1.67	0.56		
		(4 –)	0.272	2.72			
		(> 7)	0.035	0.47			
		Farmers training center course— Indicator:					
		(1 course)	− 0.014	0.12			
		(≥ 2 courses)	0.135	1.23			
		Demonstrations— Indicator:					
		(1 or 2)	0.393	4.68			
		(≥3)	0.197	1.83			

(Table continues on the following page)

Table 2-6 (continued)

Area and study	Sample size, N	Nonformal education variable	Coefficient of extension on productivity	t statistic	R²	Evidence of interaction with formal education	Comments
Kenya (Moock 1973)	152	Extension index computed by multiplying rotated factor scores of different extension measures by standardized observations and summing the products	0.003	0.77	0.64	Moock (1981) in a reanalysis of his original data finds a negative interaction between education and extension.	None
Korea (Hong 1975)	895	Log-linear investment in extension	0.832	3.55	0.85	Log-linear Ext × Ed B = 0.6039 t = −3.871	Investment in extension had a significant effect on both technical and allocative efficiency. One won investment in extension per farm a year increased rice production by 4.49 wons a year. Extension efforts for older farmers with more schooling contributed more than extension efforts
		Log-log investment in extension	3.240	6.00	0.85	Cobb-Douglas Ext × Ed B = 0.605 t = 121.0	

Study	N	Extension variable	Coefficient	t	R^2	Interaction	Comments
Malaysia, Kedah and Perlis (this volume)	403	Exposure to adult agricultural extension classes	0.237	1.73	0.69	Not applicable	None
Philippines, Laguna, 1963 (Halim 1976)	274	Number of weighted extension contacts	0.00663	3.44	0.77	Formal schooling × extension $B = -0.00028$ $t = 0.205$ Formal schooling × extension × barrio, development index, $B = 0.00008$ $t = 0.727$	Overall rate of return to extension was P8.12 for each P5.69 invested or 70 percent (combined samples). Schooling and extension effects were negatively related in all periods, but when a development index (constructed by Guttman scaling) was added, the relation was positive. Schooling and extension effects could substitute for each other in less developed barrios, but the effects could be complementary in the dynamic conditions of more developed barrios.

(Table continues on the following page)

Table 2–6 (continued)

Area and study	Sample size, N	Nonformal education variable	Coefficient of extension on productivity	t statistic	R^2	Evidence of interaction with formal education	Comments
Philippines Laguna, 1968 (Halim 1976)	273	Number of weighted extension contacts	0.004	2.40	0.70	Formal schooling × extension $B = -0.00038$ $t = -0.118$ Formal schooling × extension × barrio, development index, $B = 0.00001$ $t = 0.333$	See comments for 1963 sample.
Philippines, Laguna, 1973 (Halim 1976)	220	Number of weighted extension contacts, 1963–68	-0.000	-0.77	0.80	Formal schooling × extension $B = -0.0006$ $t = -0.352$ Formal schooling × extension × barrio, development index, $B = 0.0001$ $t = 1.00$	See comments for 1963 sample.

Thailand, Chiang Mai (chemical farms)[a] (this volume)	91	Number of extension visits to village	−0.123	−1.53	0.78	$A_5Ex_1 = 1$ if extension available $B = 0.015$ $t = 0.718$ $A_5Ex_0 = 1$ if extension not available $B = 0.036$ $t = 2.316$	Extension had negative coefficient, and education had positive coefficient on farm profits for farms using chemical fertilizer.
Thailand, Chiang Mai (nonchemical farms)[a] (this volume)	184	Whether extension was available in village	0.085	2.22	0.81	$A_5Ex_1 = 1$ if extension available $B = -0.032$ $t = 2.695$ $A_5Ex_0 = 1$ if extension not available $B = -0.016$ $t = 1.291$	Education and extension had positive coefficients on farm profits for farms not using chemical fertilizer.

a. Farms using no chemical fertilizer or other chemical inputs are referred to as "nonchemical;" others are referred to as "chemical."

(such as literacy, numeracy, modernity, and so forth) is producing the effects; research now under way in Nepal and Thailand is addressing this question.[12]

The effects of education were much more likely to be positive in modernizing agricultural environments than in traditional ones. This likelihood was ascertained both by inspection and by regressing (across studies) the measured effects of education on productivity against the degree of modernization of the environment and other variables. Our results lend support to T. W. Schultz's hypothesis that the effectiveness of education is enhanced in a modernizing environment.

12. Cole, Sharp, and Lave (n.d.) provide an insightful discussion of the role of the cognitive consequences of education, and Jamison and Moock (1981) report results from Nepal that suggest that numeracy is probably an important consequence of education for improving farmer efficiency.

CHAPTER 3

Concepts of Efficiency

THE PURPOSE OF OUR EMPIRICAL ANALYSIS in Part Two is to ascertain the extent to which farmers' educational levels affect their efficiency. We therefore begin by defining the concepts of efficiency that the empirical analysis will address. A nontechnical overview of the efficiency concepts is followed by discussions of efficiency in production and extensions of the efficiency concept.

There is no discussion of empirical methods, only a conceptual delineation of the various notions of farmer efficiency that are subsequently examined. Each of the empirical chapters begins with a discussion of the methods used in it to test for efficiency.

General Concepts

Efficiency in production is defined in terms of the production function that relates the level of output to the levels of the various inputs. In Chapter 2 a range of agricultural production functions of the sort we and others use were defined. These functions all had one output (quantity of rice produced, say) and multiple inputs (land, labor, and so forth). The basic efficiency concepts we use, however, can be intuitively described with a one-input, one-output production function that is denoted here as

$$Y = F(X).$$

This explicitly denotes the dependence of the level of output, Y, on the level of input, X, through the function F. In general Y will increase as X increases, but the diminishing returns to a single input factor might cause the incremental gain in Y for a fixed increase in X

to decrease as X increases. Figure 3–1 shows a production function with these characteristics.

It is possible, however, for a manager not to get the most out of the quantity of input available to him. The shaded area underneath the production function in Figure 3–1 consists of combinations of input and output that are possible for the manager to choose. The set of these possible choices is called the production possibility set. Points above the production function are impossible for him to choose, given the nature of his farm and his own characteristics, including educational level. Points k_1, k_2, and k_3 depict technically efficient choices; they are technically efficient in the sense that they are in the production possibility set, and there is no way to obtain more output than depicted by these points without using more of the input. Point k_4 is technically inefficient, in that more output could be obtained with no more input. Technical inefficiency results from combining available inputs poorly; for example, by plowing the insecticide into the ground or spraying fertilizer on the plant leaves.

Given that a farmer produces technically efficiently, there remains the question of just which technically efficient point should

Figure 3–1. *Technically Efficient and Inefficient Points*

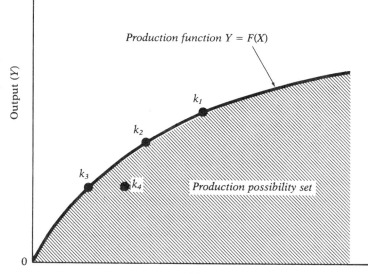

be chosen. Prices determine this. If the input price, q, is very high and the output price, p, is very low, the farmer will probably want to use little input to produce relatively little output. With high output and low input prices, however, there will be an incentive to produce quite a lot. A farmer is said to be allocatively efficient if he chooses his combination of input and output so as to maximize profit, Π, where profit is defined as the difference between the value of the output and the value of the input:

$$\Pi = pY - qX.$$

For any given level of profit and prices, the input-output pairs that will generate that level of profit can be determined, given those prices. This is simply the solution of the above equation for Y in terms of X:

$$Y = (\Pi/p) + [(q/p)X].$$

This is a straight line that will be steeper the greater the ratio of q to p. Figure 3–2 shows such an iso-profit line. At a given q–p ratio, the

Figure 3–2. *Allocatively Efficient and Inefficient Points*

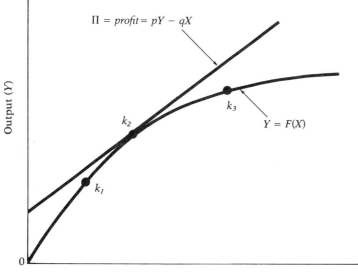

iso-profit lines are parallel, but shifted up or down depending on the level of profit. Maximizing profit at given prices amounts to choosing the highest iso-profit line that includes a point in the production possibility set; point k_2 in Figure 3–2 is the allocatively efficient level of operation for the farm at the indicated prices. Shifting the iso-profit line up would leave it with no points in common with the production possibility set; shifting it down would obviously lower profit. If the output price increases relative to the input price, the optimal (allocatively efficient) level of output will shift upward toward k_3; if output price decreases relative to input price, the optimal choice will move toward k_1.

The technical and allocative efficiency of a farm have been defined in terms of the range of options open to it. Some farms will, however, be better able to produce than other farms because they have better endowments (or better-educated managers). In other words, they have better production possibility sets or, as we shall phrase it, a higher technological level, as shown in Figure 3–3. Farm 1, with production function F_1, has an unambiguously higher tech-

Figure 3–3. *Different Technological Levels*

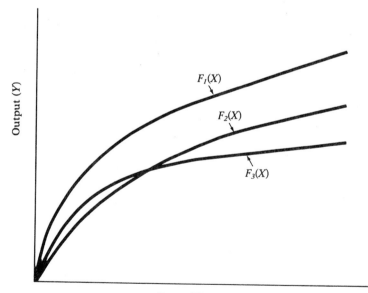

nological level than either farm 2 or farm 3. The relation between farms 2 and 3 is less clear. Farm 3 can get more output from low input levels than farm 2, but less from high input levels. Thus, at relatively high input prices farm 3 will have a higher technological level than farm 2; at relatively high output prices, farm 2 has a higher level than farm 3.

The analysis of production efficiency in Chapter 5 tests the hypothesis that the education of members of the farm household increases the technological level of the farm.[1] The analysis of the effect of education on profitability in Chapter 6 examines the extent to which education affects both technological level and allocative efficiency.

Efficiency in Production

In this section we provide a more technical treatment of the concepts discussed above.

Production possibilities

Our discussion of production possibilities follows the conventions used in economic analysis.[2] For this discussion, production is carried out by farms, each of which chooses an activity vector for each time period from within its production possibility set. If there are n commodities in the economy, an activity vector consists of a point in the n-dimensional commodity space. Negative components of the activity vector signify commodities used as inputs to the farm and positive components signify outputs.

The previous discussion followed a different and more intuitively natural convention of measuring inputs positively. For reasons that will shortly become clear, it is notationally simpler to treat inputs as negative components of the activity vector when considering

---

1. In the absence of information on the shape of the production function, such as might be available from agronomic research, it is difficult to disentangle differences in technical efficiency from differences in technological level. Welch's (1970) concept of the worker effect of education on productivity combines both concepts; his concept of the allocative effect of education corresponds to our notion of the effect of education on allocative efficiency. Levin (1976) provides a clear discussion of different concepts of efficiency, with further references to the (extensive) literature.

2. Our terminology closely follows that of Arrow and Hahn (1971, chapter 3).

multiple inputs and outputs without specifying, for any particular firm, which commodities are inputs and which are outputs.

It would be ideal, of course, if a farm could choose an activity vector that had all, or almost all, positive components. But the impossibility of creating a product from nothing or even producing a great quantity from very little implies that each farm has constraints on the activity vector it can choose. These constraints are delimited by its production possibility set. The production possibility set for farm f, denoted Y_f, is the subset of the commodity space from which the farm operator may choose. Different farms may have different (short-term) production possibility sets because of commodities (such as soil quality or access to water) particular to the farm. In this discussion certain standard assumptions are made about the production possibility sets for farms. For all f: (a) Y_f includes the zero vector and is closed, (b) Y_f contains no vector except the zero vector without at least one strictly negative component, and (c) Y_f is convex, that is, there are no economies of scale.[3] Of these assumptions, only convexity might possibly be considered an inappropriate abstraction of the real world.

The relation between the production possibility set discussed here and the production function concepts used in Chapters 2 and 5 is straightforward. Suppose, for example, that farm f can produce commodity 3 from commodities 1 and 2 by the production function $y_3 = g_f(y_1, y_2)$. Then

$$Y_f = \{(-y_1, -y_2, y_3) | y_1 \geq 0, y_2 \geq 0, \text{ and } y_3 \leq g_f(y_1, y_2)\}.$$

Naturally, the restrictions on Y_f that were stated above imply restrictions on the possible functions g_f. Jorgenson and Lau (1974) discuss in detail the relation between production functions and production possibility sets.

If there are prices for the commodities, these prices can be represented by a vector $p = (p_1, \ldots, p_n)$ in the unit simplex P_n in n-space ($P_n = \{p | \Sigma_{i=1}^{n} p_i = 1 \text{ and } p_i \geq 0\}$).[4] For any given set of prices, then, if farm f chooses an activity vector $y_f (y_f \varepsilon Y_f)$, the value of y_f will equal

---

3. The zero activity vector corresponds to the firm's doing nothing; it uses zero inputs to produce zero outputs. Other restrictions on production possibility sets, in addition to those listed here, are frequently added.

4. Assuming that prices can be represented in P_n is equivalent to assuming that only relative prices matter. It does not matter whether these relative prices are expressed, for example, in dollars or baht.

$p \cdot y_f = \Sigma_{i=1}^{n} p_i y_{fi}$, where y_{fi} is the ith component of y_f. Since inputs are negative components and outputs are positive components of the activity vector, the value of y_f is the difference between the value of the outputs and the value (cost) of the inputs. It represents the profit to the farm of choosing y_f if the prices are p.[5] A central behavioral assumption of standard economic theory is that all firms, including farms, will choose y_f to maximize profit at the existing prices.

Economic efficiency

The first concept of efficiency to be defined, that of economic efficiency (or simply efficiency), deals with the extent to which a farm maximizes profit. Let $\pi_p(Y_f) = \max_{y \in Y_f}\{p \cdot y\}$. $\pi_p(Y_f)$ is defined as the maximum profit possible for farm f when the prices are p. Convexity and closure of Y_f help assure that $\pi_p(Y_f)$ will have a well-defined maximum, and the inclusion of zero in Y_f assures that $\pi_p(Y_f) \geq 0$. A production decision (activity vector) for farm f, y_f, is economically efficient at prices p if and only if $p \cdot y_f = \pi_p(Y_f)$. If it is assumed that no farm will choose to operate at negative profit, an economic efficiency index can be assigned to choice y_f by taking the ratio of $p \cdot y_f$ to $\pi_p(Y_f)$. If this index is 1 (assuming $\pi_p(Y_f) \neq 0$), the farm is economically efficient; if it is less than 1, it indicates the extent to which the farm is economically inefficient.

Two conceptually distinct sources of economic inefficiency exist. The first of these is usually labeled technical inefficiency, for example, by Timmer, and that terminology is followed here.[6] A production decision $y \in Y_f$ is technically inefficient if and only if there exists a $y' \in Y_f$ such that $y_i' \geq y_i$ for all i and, for some j, $y_j' > y_j$. This says that the firm is technically inefficient if it could have chosen, but failed to choose, an activity vector with more of some output or less of some input, everything else being equal. Although Timmer and others have devised ways of empirically measuring technical inefficiency, this is difficult to do unless there exists a method of ascertaining Y_f without using observable choice data concerning the inputs and outputs of individual farms. Agronomic research

---

5. In many small farms much of the output is consumed by the farm household rather than marketed. Self-consumed output is, of course, included as part of gross output in measuring profit.
6. See Timmer (1970) and the discussions in Müller (1974) and Shapiro and Müller (1977).

does, in principle, provide a mechanism for ascertaining Y_f, although this study had no access to such data. Estimation of "frontier" production functions provides another alternative.[7]

The second source of economic inefficiency is frequently labeled allocative inefficiency. Let Y'_f be the set of all technically efficient points in y_f. Under reasonably general assumptions there will exist a production function, that is, a function g_f such that $g_f(y) = 0$ if and only if $y \, \varepsilon \, Y'_f$. Assuming that g_f can be differentiated, the marginal rate of substitution of any two commodities for one another can be computed by implicit differentiation, that is, values can be obtained for $\partial y_i / \partial y_j$. A technically efficient activity vector is said to be allocatively efficient at prices p if and only if, for all i, j ($i, j = 1, \ldots, n$), $\partial y_i / \partial y_j = - p_j / p_i$. If, for example, commodities 1 and 2 were outputs and $\partial y_1 / \partial y_2 > - p_2 / p_1$, the total value of output could be increased by increasing the output of commodity 1 at the expense of having less of commodity 2. Thus a reallocation of output would increase the total value of output, and the original situation would have been allocatively inefficient.

At this point three concepts of efficiency have been introduced. A farm is economically efficient at the prevailing prices if it maximizes the profit resulting from the activity vector it chooses from its production possibility set. If it is economically inefficient this may be due either to technical or allocative inefficiency. Thus, the economic efficiency of a farm is defined in terms of the range of options open to it. If that range is narrow for farm f, then f can be economically efficient even though it might use up substantially more resources than farm g to produce the same level of output. If so, then in some sense g has access to a better technology than does f. We refer to "access to a better technology" as being at a higher technological level, and define the concept more precisely below.

---

7. The analysis of farm efficiency reported in Chapter 6 categorizes farms into several broad groups (in terms of farmers' educational levels) and then compares the efficiency of those groups by using properties of the parameters of the profit functions estimated for each group. Use of frontier production or profit functions represents a qualitatively different approach, in which observed input-output data are used to estimate the production possibility set (or its frontier). This allows assessment of the extent to which each individual farm is off the frontier and hence inefficient; that inefficiency could then, in principle, be related to characteristics of the farmer such as his educational level. Førsund, Lovell, and Schmidt (1980) provide an exceptionally clear exposition of the literature on frontier production functions and relate frontier methods to nonfrontier ones such as those used here.

Technological level

Whereas economic efficiency is defined for a single farm in terms of its actual choice in relation to its range of possible choices, technological level is a relation between different farms (or the same farm at different points in time). Farm f is at a higher technological level than farm g if Y_g is a proper subset of Y_f, that is, farm f has open to it all the production possibilities available to farm g and then some. To return to Figure 3–3, farm 1, represented by production function F_1, is at a higher technological level than farms 2 and 3, as previously discussed. When production functions cross, as with farms 2 and 3, neither production possibility set is a subset of the other, but one can, by introducing prices, indicate that farm f is at a higher technological level at prices p if and only if $\pi_p(Y_f) > \pi_p(Y_g)$. That is, farm f is more technically efficient if its potential profit (assuming economic efficiency) exceeds that of g.

The concept of relative economic efficiency combines aspects of both technological level and economic efficiency and is used in Chapter 6. Let farm f choose $y_f \,\varepsilon\, Y_f$, and farm g choose $y_g \,\varepsilon\, Y_g$ when prices are p. In making this choice, farm f is said to have greater relative economic efficiency than farm g if its profit is higher, that is, if $p \cdot y_f > p \cdot y_g$. Notice that higher profits could result either from better choice within the production possibility set (greater economic efficiency) or from having access to a better production possibility set (higher technological level).

There is an extensive empirical literature concerning measurement of technological level, but most of it is at a highly aggregated level, treating an entire economy as a firm. (In this literature there is some tendency to use the term "technical efficiency" both for the concept we have defined as technological level and for what we, too, define as technical efficiency.) The analyses generally examine the extent to which technological level has improved over time. Most authors conclude that a substantial fraction of the growth in output per capita over time in the advanced economies can be attributed to improvements in technological level.[8] Chapter 5 examines the extent to which the educational level of farmers in Korea, Malaysia,

---

8. Nadiri (1970) and Kennedy and Thirlwall (1972) provide surveys of this literature. The paper by Kennedy and Thirlwall reviews, in addition, studies concerning the sources of increased technological level.

and Thailand affects their technological level. The analysis assumes that the educational level of the farm is (in the short run) an attribute of the farm and affects the range of production options open to it.

Productivity

Productivity, loosely speaking, is the ratio of output to input, or the amount of output per unit of input. It is a frequently used summary index of how well an economy, industry, or firm is doing, and we occasionally use the term in this study in discussing the relative performance of different farms.[9] Productivity is related to efficiency, as discussed below.

To take an example, Robinson Crusoe might well measure his productivity by the number of coconuts he picks per hour. Generally, however, it will be impossible to have the units of productivity measurement be actual output per unit of actual input (for example, coconuts per hour); multiple outputs from and inputs to the production process preclude this. If a set of weights exists to allow aggregation of outputs into a single aggregate output and inputs into a single aggregate input, a productivity ratio can again be constructed. The weights most typically used are prices, and the resulting ratio is the dimensionless number giving value of output divided by value of input. Economists term this number total factor productivity.

This can be phrased in terms of the notation already developed for a farm's activity vector y_f. Two new n-dimensional vectors y_f^I and y_f^O are defined in terms of y_f. The symbol y_f^I is equal to y_f in all negative components and zero elsewhere; y_f^O is equal to y_f in all positive components and zero elsewhere. Thus, $y_f = y_f^I + y_f^O$. Obviously, y_f^I is the vector of inputs to farm f, and y_f^O is the vector of outputs from f. The productivity of an activity vector y_f at prices p is $p \cdot y_f^O / (-p \cdot y_f^I)$. The problem with using prices as weights is that if one wishes to compare the productivity of the same firm at different points in time (or different firms at the same time in different countries), there may be different price vectors from which to choose. This is the much-discussed index number problem.

There are several points to be made concerning the relation be-

---

9. An industry is defined as a group of firms producing approximately the same set of outputs.

tween productivity and the various notions of efficiency. First, improvements in technological level lead to increases in potential productivity. Second, moving from a technically inefficient activity vector to one that is technically superior to it will always increase productivity. Third, moving from an allocatively inefficient point to an allocatively efficient one may actually decrease productivity. This can occur whenever there are decreasing returns to scale.[10] For this reason maximizing productivity (or benefit-cost ratios) may be undesirable. The concern should be with the difference between benefit and cost—profit or gain—and this is reflected in the concept of economic efficiency.

Efficiency in the absence of output prices

When there are prices for all commodities, a farm's choice of an economically efficient activity vector provides answers to two sorts of questions. First, which commodities should the farm produce, and how much of each? Second, which inputs should be used in the production process, and how much of each should be used? Without prices for the commodities that are potentially outputs—and this is often true in the public sector, though, of course, seldom true for farming—it becomes impossible to provide an answer to the first question in terms of economic efficiency.

Consider a strictly positive vector y' in the n-dimensional commodity space. y' may be viewed as the target output vector, that is, the vector that the farm—for whatever reason—has decided to produce.[11] The economically efficient way for farm f to meet this demand at prices p is to choose a vector $y_f \in Y_f$ (if one exists) such that $y_f^O \geq y'$ and $-p \cdot y_f^I$ is minimized.[12] This definition of economic

---

10. To continue with the Robinson Crusoe example, if Robinson experiences decreasing returns in coconut picking (for example, he picks fewer the second hour than the first because he tires), then output per unit of input is highest when he picks few coconuts. If Robinson is hungry, however, the price of a coconut relative to the price of an hour of his time may be very high. It would be allocatively inefficient for him to pick only a few coconuts.

11. y' need not be strictly positive, although that assumption simplifies the exposition here. A completely symmetrical argument, and one perhaps more relevant for farming, holds if y' is negative in all components, that is, if all inputs are fixed.

12. Here, the sign $\geq$ between vectors means greater than or equal to in every component, and p is the n-dimensional vector whose nonzero components are the prices of the commodities for which prices exist. The symbols y_f^O and y_f^I represent, as before, the vectors yielding the outputs and inputs corresponding to activity vector y_f.

efficiency simply asserts that the efficient choice to make is the one that minimizes cost subject to the constraint that outputs attain at least the specified level y'. The definitions of technical efficiency, allocative efficiency, and technological level also extend in an obvious way to the case where prices for the outputs fail to exist.

The definition of productivity fails, however, unless there is some arbitrary weighting scheme to aggregate the outputs into a single number or unless there is only one component of output. The previous definition of productivity can easily be extended to cover either of these cases.

Extensions of the Concept of Efficiency

We now explore extensions of the concepts of production efficiency just discussed: market efficiency and efficiency in the choice of technique. This discussion does not deal with questions of efficient choice under uncertainty or of efficient intertemporal choice.[13] Although in a formal sense problems of uncertainty and intertemporal choice can be dealt with by appropriate redefinition of the objects of choice, in substance these remain areas of choice behavior not dealt with here.[14]

Market efficiency

For various reasons, individuals in roughly the same circumstances may end up paying different prices for the same good or service. The concept of the market efficiency of farms (or individuals) denotes their capacity to get a good price for their inputs and outputs. Wharton (1965) has suggested that education may

13. Krantz, Luce, Suppes, and Tversky (1971, chapter 5) review and provide references to the vast literature on choice under uncertainty; Jamison (1970, part two) similarly reviews the literature concerning intertemporal choice.

14. See Debreu (1959, chapter 6). Roumasset (1976) provides a valuable empirical study of the riskiness of alternative methods of rice production and of the extent of aversion to risk among rice farmers. Binswanger (1980) has experimentally measured aversion to risk among small farmers in India; he finds formal schooling tends to reduce risk aversion. Just (1978) discusses welfare implications of the riskiness of agricultural decisions and assesses the relative desirability of several approaches—price stabilization by buffer stocks, crop insurance, forward contracting, improving forecasts, guaranteed credit, and futures markets—for reducing the adverse consequences of risk.

improve the market efficiency of farmers. In Chapter 6 we describe an explicit empirical test of that hypothesis for farmers in Thailand.

The previous discussion of efficiency in production assumes prices to be given, that is, the price vector consists simply of a vector with positive components in a space with as many dimensions as the number of commodities. This concept can be generalized in two steps, as indicated in Figure 3–4. To simplify the pictorial representation only two prices are considered, p_1 and p_2, the prices of two inputs to the farm. The top panel of Figure 3–4 depicts the case where the price of each input is completely independent of the price of the other. The best price is the lowest price pair possible. Since the farm can pay more for either input, the shaded region above and to the right of the best price is the price possibility set.

The bottom panel of Figure 3–4 depicts a slightly more complicated situation in which the prices of different commodities might be tied to one another. Tied prices can occur naturally if the farmer is shopping for his inputs in several different markets, and the prices differ from market to market. Market A may have a better price for seeds, and market B for fertilizers, and so forth. If the farmer chooses to buy both inputs in the same market because of credit availability or shopping costs or whatever, he will face a price frontier like the one on the lower left of the shaded price possibility set.[15]

The empirical work in Chapter 6 deals only with the determinants of market efficiency under the assumption of independent prices. The appropriate empirical techniques for estimating a price frontier and an individual farm's proximity to it remain to be worked out.

The market efficiency of a farmer, as defined, clearly improves only at the expense of someone else: the buyers of his output or suppliers of his inputs. The efficiency concept is thus private rather than social. Nonetheless, higher levels of education all around might lead to a lower variance in prices, as would be expected if education increases individual market efficiency, and the resulting price stabilization could provide net welfare gains.[16]

15. The concept of a price frontier generalizes naturally to situations with multiple inputs and outputs. Jamison is now examining the nature of the conditions that will lead to an equilibrium distribution of prices when prices can vary from market to market.

16. See Figlewski (1978) and Rogerson (1978) for discussions of these issues.

Figure 3–4. *Market Efficiency: Independent and Tied Prices*

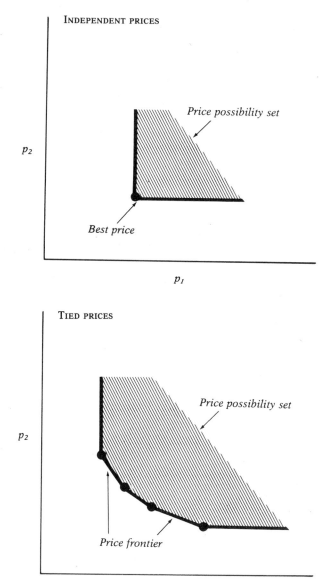

Note: p_1, price of input 1; p_2, price of input 2.

Choice of production technique

Earlier in this chapter we dealt with efficiency of production choice under the assumption that the choice of activity vector for farm f was constrained to lie in a production possibility set Y_f. Another dimension of choice that may arise, particularly in conditions of modernization and change, is that the farmer may implicitly face a choice from among several possible production possibility sets. This is the problem that farmers face when considering whether to adopt innovations in technique or new varieties of seed. The choice from within one production possibility set is considered a managerial choice; the choice from among several alternative production possibility sets is considered an entrepreneurial choice.

If switching from one production possibility set to another were costless, then, of course, the farm would have a large production possibility set that was the union of the small ones. Changing production possibility sets, however, may entail physical moves, investment of time in contemplating alternatives, and investment of time (and output forgone) while learning to be technically and allocatively efficient in a new production environment.[17] For these reasons it is useful to think both of short-term choice within production possibility sets and of longer-term, entrepreneurial choice among them.

Treatment of efficiency in entrepreneurial choice would involve in an essential way the consideration of tradeoffs between the short run and the long run and the risky character of such choice. There is indeed a substantial literature on certain aspects of such choice (for example, the "putty-clay" discussion in dealing with long- versus short-term choice), but those issues are not reviewed here. There are, however, several important points. First, this issue of choice of technique is conceptually rather different from the earlier discussion of efficiency in production, and the tools for assessing efficiency are less well developed. Second, whereas managerial choice will typically involve choice along a continuum of alternatives (for example, how much labor to use in transplanting), entrepreneurial choice will usually be from among a discrete, probably rather small

---

17. Rosenzweig (1978), for example, provides a valuable empirical treatment of the time cost of the decision of Indian farmers to switch to high-yielding varieties.

set of alternatives (for example, whether to adopt high-yielding varieties).

Thus, the treatment of choice of technique in Chapter 7 is descriptive, with only passing attention to efficiency considerations. The purpose is to understand the factors influencing Thai farmers' choice of whether to switch to production techniques using chemical fertilizers.

CHAPTER 4

The Data

THE DATA SETS USED IN THE EMPIRICAL ANALYSES in Chapters 5 through 7 came from surveys of individual farms in Thailand, Korea, and Malaysia. We used these data sets because they were readily accessible and contained comparable information on education, agricultural extension, farm inputs and outputs, and, for Thailand, prices for the inputs and outputs of individual farms. They thus provided an opportunity for testing the effects of education and agricultural extension services on individual farm efficiency.

Using these data sets, empirical analyses were performed for the individual farms without further aggregation. It has been argued, however, that within a community there may be no ascertainable relation between individual education or exposure to extension services and individual productivity, because farmers who are less well educated may benefit by simply following the more productive practices of their more educated neighbors.[1] Thus, it might appear from the individual farm data that the productive efficiency of individual farms is unrelated to the level of education or exposure to extension of the individual farmers, even though in fact education and exposure to extension might have raised the productive efficiency of the whole community. If this were the case, then the effects of education (or extension) could be discovered only by examining whether communities with higher average levels of education (extension) had higher levels of productivity. This might, then, be an argument against using data on individual farms. If, however, the effect of individual education (or exposure to exten-

1. The point was made in Sen (1971), pp. 154–55.

sion) on individual farm efficiency were measured using data on individual farms within the same community, it would represent a lower bound, since an analysis based on such data would, in general, be expected to understate the effect of education (or extension) for the reason discussed above.

In the ideal case one has data on individual farms from many different communities. (We are deliberately vague about the size of a community.) Short of the ideal case, one can either use data aggregated at the community level, or one can use data on individual farms from within a particular community. Both these possibilities have shortcomings. On the one hand, there may be important problems of interpretation of coefficients and bias of simultaneous equations if production functions are estimated from aggregate data. On the other hand, as just noted, it is possible to underestimate the effect of education if only data on individual farms from within a single community are used. Since the individual farms included in the Korean data survey were selected from a national probability sample and obviously not restricted to a single community, the estimates of the effects of education there should be free of this particular downward bias. The data from Malaysia and Thailand, however, came from much more compact geographical areas, and there may be an ensuing downward bias in the estimated effects of education.

Because of the importance of the proper choice of the level of aggregation for this analysis, the issues involved in data aggregation are discussed first.[2] The three data sets used in the subsequent analyses are then discussed in detail.

Issues in Data Aggregation

The data used in the empirical analyses consist of information on the values of variables at the level of the individual farm for a cross section of farms at a single point in time. There are advantages and disadvantages in using such individual farm data as opposed to data that have been aggregated or averaged over a group of farms or a community. Data sets of the latter kind are much more common

2. We are indebted to Mary Jean Bowman for emphasizing to us the importance of the data aggregation issue and for pointing out the useful role aggregate data can play (and indeed have played) in analyzing the effect of education on farm efficiency.

than the former. In particular, published data frequently are averages or aggregates over a group or a community.

Aggregation bias

The first issue that arises in connection with the use of average or
aggregate data concerns the assumptions that have to be maintained to justify the aggregation procedure. Suppose that there are
N farms, each with a production function, $f_i(K_i, L_i)$, $i = 1, \ldots, N$,
where K_i and L_i are the quantities of capital and labor, respectively,
employed by the ith farm. By using average or aggregate data,
average or aggregate output is being expressed as a function, say
$F(\cdot)$, of average or aggregate capital and labor, so that for all
possible K_i, L_i, the average or aggregate outputs of the individual
farms are precisely equal to the value of the average or aggregate
production function $F(\cdot)$:

(4.1) $$[\Sigma_{i=1}^{N} f_i(K_i, L_i)]/N = F[(\Sigma_{i=1}^{N} K_i/N), (\Sigma_{i=1}^{N} L_i/N)]$$

or

(4.2) $$\Sigma_{i=1}^{N} f_i(K_i, L_i) = F(\Sigma_{i=1}^{N} K_i, \Sigma_{i=1}^{N} L_i).$$

If the average or aggregate production function exists, it implies
that all the individual production functions must be identical and
linear.[3] Differentiating equation (4.1) with respect to K_j and L_j produces:

(4.3) $$\frac{1}{N} \frac{\partial f_j}{\partial K_j}(K_j, L_j) = \frac{\partial F}{\partial K}\left(\Sigma_{i=1}^{N} \frac{K_i}{N}, \Sigma_{i=1}^{N} \frac{L_i}{N}\right)$$

and

(4.4) $$\frac{1}{N} \frac{\partial f_j}{\partial L_j}(K_j, L_j) = \frac{\partial F}{\partial L}\left(\Sigma_{i=1}^{N} \frac{K_i}{N}, \Sigma_{i=1}^{N} \frac{L_i}{N}\right).$$

But the left-hand sides of equations (4.3) and (4.4) depend only on
K_j and L_j, whereas the right-hand sides depend on $\Sigma_{i=1}^{N}(K_i/N)$, and
$\Sigma_{i=1}^{N}(L_i/N)$. It is possible to vary the values of the latter variables by
changing K_i and L_i, $i \neq j$. But such variations leave the left-hand
sides unchanged and hence must also leave the right-hand sides

3. We are indebted to Benjamin King for a suggestion that simplified this proof
substantially. For a further discussion of these issues, see Bridge (1971), pp. 348–52.

unchanged. We conclude that the right-hand sides must be independent of their arguments and therefore must be constants. Thus,

(4.5)
$$(\partial f_j/\partial K_j)(K_j, L_j) = \alpha_1$$

and

(4.6)
$$(\partial f_j/\partial L_j)(K_j, L_j) = \alpha_2$$

which holds for all j, $j = 1, \ldots, N$.

From the two partial differential equations (4.5) and (4.6) one can readily integrate back to the underlying production function, which, making use of the fact that $f_j(0, 0) = 0$, that is, zero output for zero inputs, must have the form:

$$f_j(K_j, L_j) = \alpha_1 K_j + \alpha_2 L_j \qquad (j = 1, \ldots, N).$$

A similar proof applies to equation (4.2). Thus, for an average or aggregate production of the form described in equations (4.1) and (4.2) to exist, the production functions of each individual farm must be identical and linear.

Now, the assumption of identical production functions is not an especially bad assumption. Even if cross-sectional individual farm data are used, a similar assumption will have to be made before it is possible to estimate the production function. The linear production function, however, is not a particularly realistic description of the agricultural technology. It implies that all the factor inputs are perfect substitutes—that is, it is possible to produce using only capital and no labor or vice versa—an implication that is clearly contradicted by almost every piece of systematic or casual empirical evidence on agricultural production. It is no accident that almost no empirical studies of agricultural production functions at either the individual or the aggregate level are based on the assumption of linearity.

Moreover, the above line of reasoning implies directly that whenever average or aggregate data are used in the empirical analysis of production functions in the absence of the assumption of linearity there is a mis-specification. A concrete example illustrates this. The Cobb-Douglas production function is probably the most commonly used functional form in the empirical study of agricultural production. Suppose that the production functions of individual farms are identical and Cobb-Douglas, that is,

$$\ln Y_i = \ln Y_0 + \alpha_1 \ln K_i + \alpha_2 \ln L_i \quad (i = 1, \ldots, N)$$

where α_1 and α_2 are positive constants. The aggregate output is given by

$$Y = \Sigma_{i=1}^{N} Y_i = Y_0 \, \Pi_{i=1}^{N} K_i^{\alpha_1} L_i^{\alpha_2}$$

which in general depends on all of the individual K_i's and L_i's and is different from the output that can be produced from the aggregate inputs,

(4.7) $$Y = Y_0 (\Sigma_{i=1}^{N} K_i)^{\alpha_1} (\Sigma_{i=1}^{N} L_i)^{\alpha_2}$$

or from the aggregate output that can be produced with the set of inputs of each individual at the average levels,

(4.8) $$Y = N \, Y_0 \, [(I/N) \, \Sigma_{i=1}^{N} K_i]^{\alpha_1} [(1/N) \, \Sigma_{i=1}^{N} L_i]^{\alpha_2}$$
$$= N^{[1-(\alpha_1+\alpha_2)]} \, Y_0 (\Sigma_{i=1}^{N} K_i)^{\alpha_1} (\Sigma_{i=1}^{N} L_i)^{\alpha_2}.$$

In fact, for a given α_1 and α_2, if $K_i > 0, L_i > 0, i = 1, \ldots, N$, and the K_i's are not proportional to the L_i's, it is shown in Appendix B that,

(a) If $\alpha_1 + \alpha_2 < 1$,

$$Y_0 \, \Sigma_{i=1}^{N} K_i^{\alpha_1} L^{\alpha_2} < N^{[1-(\alpha_1+\alpha_2)]} Y_0 (\Sigma_{i=1}^{N} K_i)^{\alpha_1} (\Sigma_{i=1}^{N} L_i)^{\alpha_2},$$

and,

(b) If $\alpha_1 + \alpha_2 \geq 1$,

$$Y_0 \, \Sigma_{i=1}^{N} K_i^{\alpha_1} L_i^{\alpha_2} < Y_0 \, (\Sigma_{i=1}^{N} K_i)^{\alpha_1} (\Sigma_{i=1}^{N} L_i)^{\alpha_2}.$$

Thus, equation (4.7) always overstates the aggregate output if there are constant or increasing returns to scale. Equation (4.8) always overstates the aggregate output if there are constant or decreasing returns to scale. The direction of the bias cannot be determined for equation (4.7) if there are decreasing returns to scale and for equation (4.8) if there are increasing returns to scale.

These biases refer to situations in which the parameters α_1 and α_2 are given. The problem of aggregation bias is further complicated by the need to estimate these parameters in general. If aggregate data are used to estimate the production function parameters, one will be estimating the equation

(4.9) $\ln (\Sigma_{i=1}^{N} Y_i) = \ln Y_0^{*} + \alpha_1^{*} \ln (\Sigma_{i=1}^{N} K_i) + \alpha_2^{*} \ln (\Sigma_{i=1}^{N} L_i).$

If averaged data are used to estimate the production function parameters, one will be estimating the equation

$$\ln [(1/N) \, \Sigma_{i=1}^{N} Y_i] = \ln Y_0^{**} + \alpha_1^{**} \ln [(1/N) \, \Sigma_{i=1}^{N} K_i]$$
$$+ \alpha_2^{**} \ln [(1/N) \, \Sigma_{i=1}^{N} L_i]$$

or

(4.10) $\ln (\Sigma_{i=1}^N Y_i) = \{\ln Y_0^{**} + [1 - (\alpha_1^{**} + \alpha_2^{**})] \ln N\}$

$+ \alpha_1^{**} \ln (\Sigma_{i=1}^N K_i) + \alpha_2^{**} \ln (\Sigma_{i=1}^N L_i).$

Equations (4.9) and (4.10) are statistically equivalent for given N, and the estimated α_i^*'s will be identical to the estimated α_i^{**}'s. These two equations may be compared with the true aggregate relation:

(4.11) $\Sigma_{i=1}^N \ln Y_i = \Sigma_{i=1}^N \ln Y_0 + \alpha_1 \Sigma_{i=1}^N \ln K_i + \alpha_2 \Sigma_{i=1}^N \ln L_i.$

Given that Y_i, K_i, and L_i are all positive quantities, the arithmetic means of Y_i's, K_i's, and L_i's are always greater than the corresponding geometric means, that is,

$$(1/N) \Sigma_{i=1}^N Y_i \geq (\Pi_{i=1}^N Y_i)^{1/N}$$

$$(1/N) \Sigma_{i=1}^N K_i \geq (\Pi_{i=1}^N K_i)^{1/N}$$

$$(1/N) \Sigma_{i=1}^N L_i \geq (\Pi_{i=1}^N L_i)^{1/N}$$

which implies

$$\ln (\Sigma_{i=1}^N Y_i) - \ln N \geq (1/N) \Sigma_{i=1}^N \ln Y_i$$

$$\ln (\Sigma_{i=1}^N K_i) - \ln N \geq (1/N) \Sigma_{i=1}^N \ln K_i$$

$$\ln (\Sigma_{i=1}^N L_i) - \ln N \geq (1/N) \Sigma_{i=1}^N \ln L_i.$$

Thus, the variables as measured in equation (4.9), $\ln (\Sigma_{i=1}^N Y_i)$, $\ln (\Sigma_{i=1}^N K_i)$, and $\ln (\Sigma_{i=1}^N L_i)$ are all biased estimates of the corresponding variables in the true relation: $(\Sigma_{i=1}^N \ln Y_i)$, $(\Sigma_{i=1}^N \ln K_i)$, and $(\Sigma_{i=1}^N \ln L_i)$. This can be seen most clearly if equation (4.9) is rewritten as

$$\ln (\Sigma_{i=1}^N Y_i) - \ln N = [\ln Y_0^* + (\alpha_1^* + \alpha_2^* - 1) \ln N]$$

$$+ \alpha_1^* [\ln (\Sigma_{i=1}^N K_i) - \ln N]$$

$$+ \alpha_2^* [\ln (\Sigma_{i=1}^N L_i) - \ln N]$$

which can be compared directly with $1/N$ times equation (4.11). It is an open question whether in general the values of α_1^* and α_2^* estimated from equation (4.9) are close approximations of the true production function parameters α_1 and α_2, the biases depending in a complicated way on the distributions of the Y_i's, K_i's, and L_i's. If individual farm data are used, then of course such aggregation biases will disappear. In general, an equation such as (4.9) can only be regarded as an approximation of the true relation in equation (4.11).

Figure 4–1. *Data Aggregation: Regional versus Pooled Analysis*

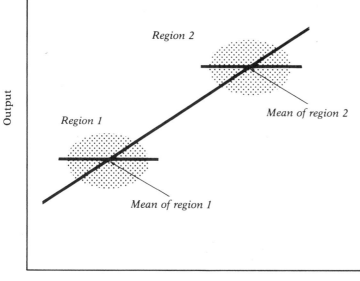

Insufficient variation and externalities

A significant problem in using individual farm data from a single region lies in the lack of sufficient variation in the independent variables, which results frequently in imprecise and possibly biased estimates of the production function. In addition, if there are positive or negative externalities because of one farm's use of a particular factor that is specific to the community, then production functions estimated from individual farm data within a single region may result in biased estimates for the coefficient of that factor.[4]

For example, in Figure 4–1, if each region's individual farm data are run separately, then the production function may appear essentially flat. If the data are pooled from several regions, however, and if the production functions are identical for all regions, a much more precise estimate of the production function can be obtained. The regional average data can also be used for this purpose. This

---

4. As discussed in the beginning of this chapter, there are reasons to believe that education might have positive externalities, resulting, therefore, in estimates of their effects that are biased downward.

will result in more or less the same estimate of the production function as the pooled individual farm data. The reasoning here then argues for pooling data across regions, whether they are individual farm data or regional average or aggregate data, rather than for using one kind of data over another.

Systematic regional differences

Although it is generally true that there is greater variation among regions than within a region, it is also more likely that the production functions may be more different among regions than within a region. The use of a single cross section of regional average or aggregate data invariably involves pooling data from different regions. The validity of the pooling operation depends crucially on the assumption that the production function is identical for all regions. Thus, to the extent that the production functions differ systematically among regions, the use of a single cross section of regional average or aggregate data runs into difficulties. The systematic differences may be in the intercepts of the production functions, in the slopes of the production functions, or both. In even the simplest case of differences in the intercepts only, the estimated production function based on regional average or aggregate data will be in general biased, as illustrated in Figure 4–2.

It is apparent from Figure 4–2 that if the intercept term is allowed to vary across regions (which cannot be done with a single cross section of regional average or aggregate data), an estimate can be obtained of the slope of the production function without bias. If differences in the intercepts are not allowed, however, then using regional average or aggregate data, or pooling the individual farm data from all the regions, will result in a biased estimate of the slope.

The hypothesis of no regional differences in the intercepts can be tested if individual farm data are available. It has to be maintained for a single cross section of regional average or aggregate data. It can, however, also be tested if a time series of cross sections of regional average or aggregate data are available.

Covariance of individual data

One consideration that makes the use of regional average or aggregate data relatively more attractive than data from individual

Figure 4–2. *Data Aggregation: Effects of Regional Intercepts*

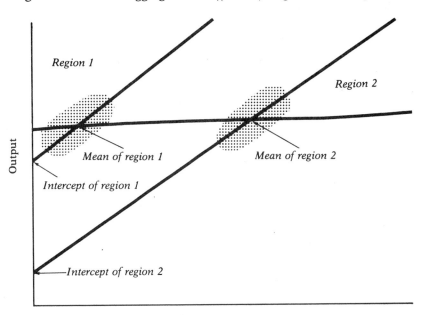

farms is the possible covariance of the stochastic disturbances which affect the individual farm data. To take an extreme case, if all the stochastic disturbances on individual farm outputs have their origins in weather, it is reasonable to assume that they will be correlated within a given region. If the correlation were perfect, then using the output data from one farm would be the same as using that from another, since they would contain the same statistical information. In this case, using the regional average or aggregate data and using the individual data will not make any difference in the precision of the resulting estimates.

Covariance is also relevant in another way. Suppose that within a given region, certain independent variables tend to move together. Then it will in general be difficult to identify the effects of the two variables separately using only data from that region. It is possible, however, that the degree of covariance may be different for different regions, so that by pooling data or by using regional average or aggregate data, the separate effects of locally multicolinear independent variables can be identified. Again, this is an argument for pooling data from different regions, and not necessarily for using regional average or aggregate data rather than individual farm data as such.

Simultaneous equations bias

An argument in favor of using individual farm data in the profit function analysis is based on the fact that in a localized market, the aggregate quantities and the prices are simultaneously determined by the equilibrium of supply and demand. Thus, if regional average or aggregate data are used, it cannot be assumed that the average or aggregate quantities demanded of the factors do not affect the equilibrium supply prices. It is reasonable to assume, however, that for the individual farm, the prices facing the farm are independent of the farm's actions. Thus, in analyzing the individual farm data, treating the prices as exogenous variables is justified, whereas in the analysis of regional average or aggregate data, it is not. However, the possible existence of simultaneous equations bias is not an insurmountable problem. There are estimators that will eliminate the bias, but this involves additional computation.

There is, however, another possible source of simultaneity resulting from the use of aggregate data that is perhaps more important for the purposes of this study. A historically and currently more productive region might also have purchased more education for its inhabitants as a consumption good, and the possible positive effect of education on productivity must be disentangled from a positive income elasticity of demand for education. This is less serious a problem with data from individual farms, since relatively much less variation in historical patterns of productivity is expected within a region than among regions.

Technical change

One drawback with the use of a single cross section of individual farm data is the inability to identify technical change. Nor can this be done with a single cross section of regional average or aggregate data. It can be done only with time-series average or aggregate data, or a time series of cross sections. Technical change, however, as well as the adoption of technical innovations, is a very important aspect of agricultural production. As mentioned earlier, there have been few studies that are based on a panel of farms observed over time. In a follow-up study to this one, we are developing some panel data that cover five consecutive years. At least some of the components of technical change and innovation adoption behavior should be identified.

The Data Sets

For the purpose of this study, cross-sectional production data from individual farm households are used. The advantages and disadvantages of individual versus average or aggregate data have been discussed above. Suffice it to say that with individual data the quantity of output of each individual farm can be related directly to the quantities of inputs used by that farm and to the characteristics of that farm household. In addition, at the microeconomic level, it is also more likely that the prices faced by the individual farms are not affected by the quantities of outputs produced and inputs used by individual farms, so that prices may be assumed to be exogenous. At the macroeconomic level, the prices and quantities will be related because they are simultaneously determined by equilibrium in the market, which implies the possible existence of simultaneous equations bias and requires more complicated methods of estimation.

For all three countries in this study—Thailand, Korea, and Malaysia—data are available on individual farm households, selected on the basis of stratified random sampling. These data sets have all been carefully collected, compiled, and verified, and are very reliable. Thus, the empirical findings will need to be confronted directly, as one can no longer take refuge in the poor quality of the data. The sizes of the usable samples differ: 275 for Thailand, 1,904 for Korea, and 403 for Malaysia.

The samples for Thailand and Malaysia are both local in geographical coverage: Chiang Mai Valley for Thailand and the Muda River area for Malaysia. The sample for Korea is a national probability sample. Thus, the results for Korea may be more representative of the country as a whole than the results for Thailand and Malaysia.

The Thailand survey was conducted by interviews. The Korean and the Malaysian surveys relied substantially on written records collected monthly. The Thailand survey period includes the rainy season (April) of 1972 and the dry season (July) of 1973. The Korean survey period is from January 1, 1974 to December 31, 1974. The

Malaysian survey period is from November 1972 to November 1973. Thus, the three survey periods are very close together.

The data sets for all three countries include the quantities of output and inputs. Price data, however, are available for the Thailand sample only and were not collected in the Korean and Malaysian samples. Thus, only the production function analysis can be applied to the Korean and Malaysian data sets. Allocative and market efficiency, which depend on prices, are analyzed only for the Thailand data set.

The main crop that is grown in all three countries is rice. Thus, the results are potentially comparable. Factor endowments differ substantially among the three countries, however, and the differences are most pronounced between Thailand and Malaysia on the one hand, and Korea on the other. Table 4–1 presents some statistics on the agricultural environment of the three countries, and Table 4–2 presents factor ratios prevailing in the different countries. It is evident that Korea is the most poorly endowed with natural agricultural resources, whereas Thailand and Malaysia are more comparable. In Korea also the applications of labor and fertilizer per hectare are more than ten times more intense than in Thailand or Malaysia. The fertilizer-labor ratios in Korea and Thailand are quite comparable.

Table 4–1. *Agricultural Environment of Korea, Malaysia, and Thailand, 1973*

Country	Arable land[a] (millions of hectares)	Population[b] (millions)	Arable land per capita[c] (hectares)	Normal annual temperature (°C)	Normal annual precipitation (inches)
Republic of Korea	2.24	33.30	0.066	5–27[d]	36–52[d]
Malaysia (Peninsular)	2.87	9.56	0.302	19–30[e]	75–110[e]
Thailand	14.00	39.41	0.353	15–35[f]	80–120[f]

a. FAO (1976), pp. 14–16.
b. Ibid., p. 30.
c. Arable land divided by population.
d. Kim (1979), pp. 30–33.
e. Vreeland (1977), p. 17.
f. Henderson (1971), pp. 12–13.

Table 4–2. *Output and Inputs per Hectare in Korea, Malaysia, and Thailand*

Country	Our sample (kilograms of output per hectare)	FAO national average[a] (kilograms of output per hectare)	Our sample	
			Labor days per hectare	Kilograms of fertilizer per hectare
Korea				
Mechanical farms	5560.74[b]	5129.00	1643.96	351.57
Nonmechanical farms	3738.07[b]		1073.49	231.22
Malaysia	4077.40[c]	2979.00	65.03	n.a.
Thailand				
Chemical farms	3022.01[c]	1831.00[d]	90.99	26.91
Nonchemical farms	3136.84[c]		109.12	—

n.a. Not available.
— Not applicable.
a. FAO (1976), p. 4.
b. The total value of output was divided by the price of output to get a quantity figure. The prices used are from Republic of Korea (1975a), p. 410.
c. Per crop hectare.
d. A figure of 2,500 to 3,000 kilograms per hectare for the Chiang Mai region is mentioned in Ishii (1978), p. 21.

Thus, although in principle it is possible to pool the data for all three countries to estimate a single production function, this has not been done. As Table 4–2 reveals, the relative factor ratios prevailing in the different countries are so different—that is, the farms in the different countries are operating in such different regions of the production function—that a simple functional form such as the Cobb-Douglas function cannot possibly model the technology for all three countries adequately. Thus the study only compares qualitatively the nature of the results obtained in different countries.

There are many factors that may lead to differences in the technology of agricultural production among these countries, despite the fact that the predominant crop in all three countries is the same—rice. The climate, terrain, soil fertility, and population pressures differ markedly, especially between Malaysia and Thailand on the one hand, and Korea on the other.[5] The differences are

5. Population pressure can affect the pattern of cropping and land use practices.

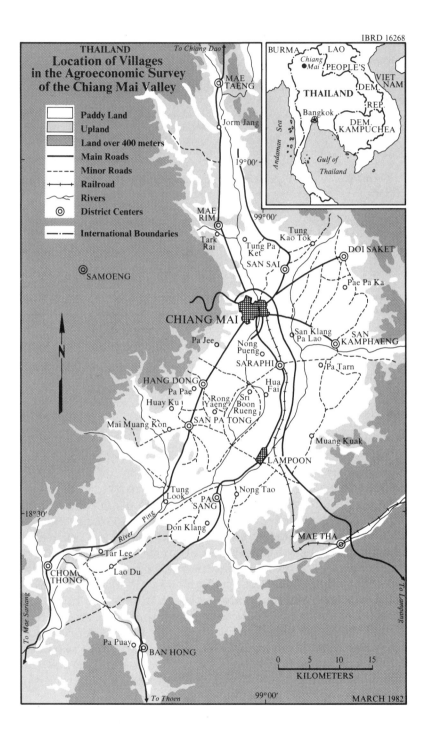

IBRD 16268

THAILAND
**Location of Villages
in the Agroeconomic Survey
of the Chiang Mai Valley**

Paddy Land
Upland
Land over 400 meters
Main Roads
Minor Roads
Railroad
Rivers
District Centers
International Boundaries

KILOMETERS

MARCH 1982

82

also borne out by the production function estimates. The different production functions for the three countries may be regarded as different local approximations of the same production function for rice, with Malaysia and Thailand operating at low levels of labor per hectare, and Korea operating at a high level.

Thailand

Most of the farm households in Thailand own and operate their farms. There are also a small number of tenant-farmers, who only work on farms. Together they constitute approximately 90 percent of all farm households in Thailand. Approximately another 5 percent of the farm households are headed by landless laborers, and another 5 percent are primarily engaged in fisheries and forestry. Members of the farm households do engage in other activities occasionally, but the primary occupation of the head of household is to work on his own farm. Agriculture is organized on the basis of individual households. There is very little cooperative or plantation-type farming.

Our study of Thai agriculture was based on a survey of 440 farm households located in the Chiang Mai area in northern Thailand. The survey was conducted from April to July 1973 by Tongsiri, Lerttamrab, and Thodey (1975). It covered the rainy season of 1972 and the immediately following dry season of 1973. Villages and farm households were initially selected in November 1972. This sample of 440 farm households spread throughout the valley in twenty-two villages was interviewed in April/May 1973. Follow-up interviews were conducted of farmers growing dry-season crops not already harvested at the time of the main survey. Every effort went into trying to acquire accurate data from farmers, including having two interviewers live in each village for a week, measuring fields with surveying equipment and sampling crop yields. The survey households were chosen through stratified random sampling. The Chiang Mai Valley was stratified into five areas, villages were selected systematically within each strata, and twenty farm households were selected systematically within each village. The actual villages selected are listed in Table 4–3. The locations of these villages are depicted the map on the opposite page. There are an estimated 82,000 farm households in the Chiang Mai Valley. Agricultural census data verified that the villages chosen constituted a representative sample of the Chiang Mai Valley.

Table 4–3. *Villages in the Thai Sample*

Name	District	Province
Jorm Jang	Mae Taeng	Chiang Mai
Tark Rai	Mae Rim	Chiang Mai
Pa Jee	Muang	Chiang Mai
Pa Pae	Hung Dong	Chiang Mai
Rong Yaeng	Hung Dong	Chiang Mai
Huay Ku	San Pa Tong	Chiang Mai
Mai Muang Kon	San Pa Tong	Chiang Mai
Tung Look	San Pa Tong	Chiang Mai
Tar Lee	Jorm Tong	Chiang Mai
Tung Pa Ket	San Sai	Chiang Mai
Tung Kao Tok	San Sai	Chiang Mai
Pae Pa Ka	Doi Sa-Ket	Chiang Mai
San Klang Pa Lao	San Kampaeng	Chiang Mai
Pa Tarn	San Pa Tong	Chiang Mai
Nong Pueng	Sarapee	Chiang Mai
Sri Boon Rueng	Sarapee	Chiang Mai
Hua Fai	Muang	Lampoon
Muang Kuak	Muang	Lampoon
Nong Tao	Muang	Lampoon
Don Klang	Pa Sang	Lampoon
Lao Du	Pa Sang	Lampoon
Pa Puay	Ban Hong	Lampoon

Table 4–4. *Variables for Thai Farms That Produce Rice*

Independent variable	Definition
Y	Output (kilograms)
Π	Profit (kilograms) (value normalized by price of output)
L	Labor days
W	Labor wage rate (kilograms per day) (money wage rate normalized by the price of output)
CH	Chemical inputs (kilograms)
PCN	Chemical inputs price (kilograms per kilogram) (money price normalized by the price of output)
K	Value of equipment (baht) (US\$1 = 20.65 bahts, 1973)

Table 4-4 (*continued*)

Independent variable	Definition
T	Land area cultivated (rai) (1 rai = 0.164 hectare)
$R1$	Region dummy, villages 1, 2, 10, 11, 12
$R2$	Region dummy, villages 3, 4, 5, 6, 7, 13, 14, 15, 16, 17
$R3$	Region dummy, villages 9, 21, 22
$R4$	Region dummy, villages 8, 19, 20
$A5$	Maximum education of either head of household (years)
$A6$	Average educational level of household members 17 to 60 years old, including head of household (years)
$A7$	Maximum age of either head of household (years)
$E1$	Education dummy, 1 if $A5 = 0$; 0 otherwise
$E2$	Education dummy, 1 if $0 < A5 < 4$; 0 otherwise
$E3$	Education dummy, 1 if $A5 = 4$; 0 otherwise
$E4$	Education dummy, 1 if $A5 > 4$; 0 otherwise
$E5$	Education dummy, 1 if $A5 > 0$; 0 otherwise
$E6$	Education dummy, 1 if $A5 = 0$; 0 otherwise
$E7$	1 if chemical inputs used, $E5 = 1$; 0 otherwise
$E8$	1 if no chemical inputs used, $E5 = 1$; 0 otherwise
$E9$	1 if chemicals used, $E5 = 0$; 0 otherwise
EXT	1 if agriculture extension services available: 0 otherwise
CR	1 if credit is taken or available; 0 otherwise
HM	1 if male head of household; 0 if female head of household
$A5^2$	$A5 \cdot A5$
$A7^2$	$A7 \cdot A7$
$A5EX1$	$A5 \cdot EX1$, where $EX1 = 1$ if extension services available; 0 otherwise
$A5EX0$	$A5 \cdot EX0$, where $EX0 = 1$ if extension services available; 0 otherwise
$A6EX1$	$A6 \cdot EX1$, where $EX1$ same as above
$A6EX0$	$A6 \cdot EX0$, where $EX0$ same as above
$A7EX1$	$A7 \cdot EX1$, where $EX1$ same as above
$A7EX0$	$A7 \cdot EX0$, where $EX0$ same as above
$A7SE1$	$A7 \cdot A7 \cdot EX1$, where $EX1$ same as above
$A7SE0$	$A7 \cdot A7 \cdot EX0$, where $EX0$ same as above
$A7A5$	$A7 \cdot A5$
$D35$	1 if head of household ≤ 35 years old; 0 otherwise
$D35A5$	$D35 \cdot A5$
$D35PA5$	$D35P \cdot A5$, where $D35P = 1$ if head of household > 35 years old; 0 otherwise

Table 4-5. Sample Means of Variables for Thai Farms: Chemical and Nonchemical Farms

Independent variable	Chemical farms, sample = 91		Nonchemical farms, sample = 184	
	Mean	Standard deviation	Mean	Standard deviation
Output (kilograms)	4,352.264	2,881.781	3,823.788	2,166.085
Normalized profit (kilograms)	3,067.998	2,416.550	2,700.149	1,814.089
Output price (baht per kilogram)	1.213	0.142	1.163	0.156
Labor days	131.451	87.865	129.380	75.513
Normalized labor wage rate (kilograms per day)	8.808	1.947	8.258	2.008
Chemical inputs (kilograms)	35.741	21.011	—	—
Normalized chemical inputs price (kilograms per kilogram)	5.037	3.328	—	—
Chemical inputs price (non-normalized) (baht per kilogram)	5.940	3.733	—	—
Value of equipment (baht)	90.406	55.341	90.266	54.743
Land area (rai) (1 rai = 0.164 hectare)	10.111	7.082	8.048	4.609
Region 1	0.209	0.406	0.261	0.439
Region 2	0.571	0.495	0.533	0.499
Region 3	0.121	0.326	0.087	0.282
Region 4	0.099	0.299	0.120	0.324
A5 (education of head of household) (years)	3.143	2.434	3.011	1.769
A6 (average education) (years)	3.523	1.605	3.535	1.265
A7 (age of head of household) (years)	50.363	12.231	47.179	12.601

E1 (education dummy, A5 = 0)	0.253	0.223	0.435	0.416
E2 (education dummy, 0 <A5 < 4)	0.088	0.098	0.283	0.297
E3 (education dummy, A5 = 4)	0.604	0.663	0.489	0.473
E4 (education dummy, A5 >4)	0.055	0.016	0.228	0.127
E5 (head of household education dummy)	0.747	0.777	0.435	0.416
EXT (1 if extension services available)	0.692	0.511	0.462	0.500
CR (1 if credit taken or available)	0.813	0.734	0.390	0.442
HM (1 if male, 0 if female)	0.978	0.995	0.147	0.074
$A5^2$ (A5 · A5)	15.802	12.196	25.149	9.974
$A7^2$ (A7 ·A7)	2,686.0	2,384.7	1,344.0	1,275.3
A5EX1 (A5 · EX1, EX1 = 1 if EXT = 1)	1.912	1.554	1.976	1.983
A5EX0 (A5 · EX0, EX0 = 1 if EXT = 0)	1.231	1.456	2.594	1.930
A6EX1 (A6 · EX1, EX1 = 1 if EXT = 1)	2.401	1.823	2.066	2.019
A6EX0 (A6 · EX0, EX0 = 1 if EX0 = 0)	1.125	1.713	1.926	1.944
A7EX1 (A7 · EX1, EX1 = 1 if EX1 = 1)	34.868	24.299	25.044	25.269
A7EX0 (A7 · EX0, EX0 = 0 if EX0 = 0)	15.495	22.880	24.555	25.143
A7SE1 (A7 · A7 EX1, EX1 = 1 if EX1 = 1)	1,843.0	1,229.0	1,589.2	1,480.5
A7SE0 (A7 · A7 EX0, EX0 = 1 if EX0 = 0)	843.01	1,155.7	1,545.3	1,508.3
A7A5 (A7 · A5)	144.25	127.17	106.13	79.798
D35 (1 if head of household ≥ 35 years old; 0 otherwise)	0.055	0.168	0.228	0.374
D35A5 (D35 · A5)	0.253	0.668	1.403	1.487
D35PA5 (D35P = 1 if head of household ≥ 35 years old; 0 otherwise)	2.890	2.342	2.327	2.013

— Not applicable.

Table 4–6. *Sample Means of Variables for Thai Farms: All and Selected Farms*

Independent variable	All farms, sample = 440		Selected farms, sample = 275	
	Mean	Standard deviation	Mean	Standard deviation
Output (kilograms)	3,597.866	2,411.819	3,998.665	2,433.830
Profit (baht)	3,075.910[a]	2,523.944	3,314.566	2,395.208
Output price (baht per kilogram)	1.357[b]	0.663	1.180	0.153
Labor days	135.487[a]	87.689	130.065	79.657
Labor wage rate (baht per day)	9.715[a]	2.517	9.880	2.352
Value of equipment (baht)	90.006	54.233	90.312	54.841
Land area (rai) (1 rai = 0.164 hectare)	8.904[a]	6.177	8.731	5.622
Region 1	0.227	0.420	0.244	0.430
Region 2	0.455	0.498	0.545	0.499
Region 3	0.136	0.344	0.098	0.298
Region 4	0.136	0.344	0.113	0.317

A5 (education of head of household) (years)	2.945[d]	2.058	3.055	2.018
A6 (average education) (years)	3.478[d]	1.346	3.531	1.390
A7 (age of head of household) (years)	47.093[c]	14.124	48.233	12.592
E1 (education dummy, A5 = 0)	0.264	0.441	0.233	0.423
E2 (education dummy, 0 < A5 < 4)	0.091	0.288	0.095	0.293
E3 (education dummy, A5 = 4)	0.611	0.488	0.644	0.480
E4 (education dummy, A5 > 4)	0.034	0.182	0.029	0.168
E5 (head of household education dummy)	0.736	0.441	0.767	0.423
EXT (1 if extension services available)	0.500	0.501	0.571	0.496
CR (1 if credit taken or available)	0.800	0.400	0.760	0.428
HM (1 if male, 0 if female)	0.966	0.182	0.989	0.104

a. Computation based on sample of 310 farms after eliminating farms with missing values.
b. Computation based on sample of 439 farms after eliminating farms with missing values.
c. Computation based on sample of 431 farms after eliminating farms with missing values.
d. Computation based on sample of 438 farms after eliminating farms with missing values.

The main survey included a questionnaire administered to each selected household; a questionnaire about the village administered to various village leaders, particularly the headman; and the measurement of all fields farmed by each household. In villages with significant dry-season cropping, a village resident was hired and trained to sample dry-season crop yields.

After eliminating households with missing or inconsistent data—for example, no entry for capital, land, or labor, or an abnormally high or low quantity of output or input—only 275 of the sample households could be used in the study. These 275 Thai farm households were further divided into two groups: the 91 farms that used chemical inputs and the 184 farms that did not use chemical inputs. They will be referred to here as chemical and nonchemical farms, respectively.

The variables used in the Thai production function analysis are defined in Table 4–4. Table 4–5 gives the means and standard deviations of these variables. The Thai production data used in this study cover only the rainy season of 1972. The rainy season is chosen because essentially only one crop is produced then—rice—whereas several crops—such as cotton—are produced in the dry season, and there would be problems in comparing farms with different crops. Glutinous rice constitutes 91.1 percent of total output; nonglutinous rice constitutes 8.4 percent of total output.

Table 4-6 shows the means and standard errors of the variables for the whole sample of 440 farms in order to evaluate whether any systematic bias was introduced by the sample selection procedure. A comparison of the two tables indicates that there was no substantial bias in the sample selection procedure with regard to farm household characteristics. The selected farms as a group appear to have higher average output and profit, and lower labor and land inputs, but the differences are well within the bounds of sampling variation.

Korea

Most of the farm households in Korea, as in Thailand, are also operated by owners or tenants. For the tenants, their tenure is secure and hereditary by tradition and custom, if not by law. Agricultural activities are carried out on the basis of individual households. There is very little cooperative or plantation-type farming, although sometimes cooperatives are formed for credit and market-ing purposes.

The study of Korean agriculture was based on the Farm House-hold Economy Survey of 1974 conducted by the Ministry of Agricul-ture and Fisheries of the Republic of Korea. The survey was based on a three-stage stratified random sample (Republic of Korea 1975a,b). The sample households maintained daily logs of their transactions. Enumerators would help to make entries in the daily log if any household was unable to do so on its own.

Originally, the sample contained 2,254 farms, which constituted approximately 0.1 percent of all farm households in the country. After eliminating farms with missing and inconsistent data, how-ever, only 1,904 farms remained in the sample. This was then divided into two groups: farms that used mechanical power and farms that did not. There were 1,363 farms using mechanical power

Table 4–7. *Variables for Korean Farms*

Independent variable	Definition
Y	Value of agricultural crop output (wons)
L	Labor hours (own, hired and exchange)
AN	Animal power, own and hired (hours)
$MECH$	Mechanical power, own and hired (hours)
CH	Chemical inputs, such as fertilizers and pesticides (wons)
K	Value of assets (won) (US\$1 = 405.97 wons, 1974)
T	Land area cultivated (pyung) (1 pyung = 0.0003 hectare)
$R1$ to $R9$	Region dummy, one for each of the nine provinces: (1) Kyeonggi, (2) Kangwon, (3) Chungbuk, (4) Chungnam, (5) Cheonbuk, (6) Cheonnam, (7) Kyeongbuk, (8) Kyeongnam, and (9) Cheju. 1 if the farm is located in the province, 0 otherwise.
$A5$	Education of head of household (years)
$A6$	Average educational level of household members 17 to 60 years old, including the head of household (years)
$A6^*$	Average educational level of household members 17 to 60 years old, excluding the head of household (years)
$A7$	Age of the head of household (years)
$E1$	Education dummy, 1 if $A5 = 0$; 0 otherwise
$E2$	Education dummy, 1 if $0 < A5 < 6$; 0 otherwise
$E3$	Education dummy, 1 if $A5 = 6$; 0 otherwise
$E4$	Education dummy, 1 if $A5 > 6$; 0 otherwise
HM	1 if male head of household; 0 if female head of household

Table 4–8. Sample Means of Variables for Korean Farms: Mechanical and Nonmechanical Farms

Independent variable	Mechanical farms, sample = 1,363		Nonmechanical farms, sample = 541	
	Mean	Standard deviation	Mean	Standard deviation
Output (wons)	363,725.125	277,465.250	259,856.00	186,334.50
Labor (hours)	2,133.219	1,257.190	1,767.962	1,066.046
Animal power (hours)	88.964	87.181	67.468	64.868
Mechanical power (hours)	22.037	40.900	—	—
Chemical inputs (wons)	21,013.578	21,362.246	14,918.93	14,068.74
Value of assets (wons)	216,480.875	229,709.500	213,885.375	207,876.938
Land area (pyungs)	1,574.309	1,506.121	1,338.796	1,249.632
A5 (education of head of household) (years)	5.246	3.069	4.826	3.116
A6 (average education) (years)	5.148	2.754	4.950	2.770
A7 (age of head of household) (years)	47.530	11.613	47.323	12.220
E1 (education dummy, A5 = 0)	0.099	0.299	0.142	0.350
E2 (education dummy, 0 < A5 < 6)	0.289	0.453	0.303	0.460
E3 (education dummy, A5 = 6)	0.459	0.498	0.427	0.495
E4 (education dummy, A5 > 6)	0.153	0.360	0.128	0.334
HM (1 if male; 0 if female)	0.902	0.297	0.876	0.330

— Not applicable.

Table 4-9. Sample Means of Variables for Korean Farms: All and Selected Farms

Independent variable	All farms, sample = 2,254		Selected farms, sample = 1,904	
	Mean	Standard deviation	Mean	Standard deviation
Output (wons)	319,994.140	250,812.865	334,212.125	259,131.500
Labor (hours)	1,953.383	1,216.561	2,029.436	1,216.896
Animal power (hours)	81.309[a]	81.086	82.856	82.024
Mechanical power (hours)	21.304[b]	41.377	22.037[e]	40.900
Chemical inputs (wons)	18,503.272	20,637.184	19,281.855	19,756.930
Value of assets (wons)	212,645.100[c]	216,905.340	215,743.000	223,670.250
Land area (pyungs) (1 pyung = 0.0003 hectare)	1,494.451[d]	1,422.111	1,507.390	1,441.501
A5 (education of head of household) (years)	5.132	3.141	5.400	2.495
A6 (average education) (years)	5.404	2.564	5.127	3.087
A7 (age of head of household) (years)	47.480	11.885	47.471	11.786
E1 (education dummy, A5 = 0)	0.116	0.321	0.111	0.315
E2 (education dummy, 0 < A5 < 6)	0.288	0.453	0.293	0.455
E3 (education dummy, A5 = 6)	0.447	0.497	0.450	0.498
E4 (education dummy, A5 > 6)	0.149	0.356	0.146	0.353
HM (1 if male; 0 if female)	0.894	0.309	0.895	0.307

a. Computation based on sample of 2,147 farms after eliminating farms with missing values.
b. Computation based on sample of 1,570 farms after eliminating farms with missing values.
c. Computation based on sample of 2,251 farms after eliminating farms with missing values.
d. Computation based on sample of 2,044 farms after eliminating farms with missing values.
e. Computation based on sample of 1,363 farms after eliminating farms with missing values.

(henceforth, mechanical farms) and 541 farms not using mechanical power (henceforth, nonmechanical farms).

The definitions of the variables used in the production function analysis are in Table 4–7. Originally, education was coded as a categorical variable. This was converted into equivalent number of years so that it could be compared directly with the other countries included in this study as follows:

Original code number and description	*Years*
1—Yet to attend school	0
2—Illiterate	0
3—Literate	3
4—Elementary school	6
5—Middle school	9
6—High school	12
7—College and above	16

Table 4–8 presents the means and standard deviations of the variables used in estimating production functions for Korean mechanical and nonmechanical farms. For comparison, Table 4–9 presents the means and standard deviations of the variables for the whole original sample. The selected farms as a group have slightly higher outputs and inputs than the sample average, but the differences are well within the bounds of sample variation.

Malaysia

In Malaysia agricultural activities are carried out in both individually organized household farms and in plantations. Our analysis covers only the individual farm households. The data were taken from a survey of farm households located in the Muda River area (Kedah and Perlis) in northwestern peninsular Malaysia conducted between November 1972 and November 1973 (FAO/World Bank 1975).

The sample was selected by first taking a random sample of all rural population census enumeration blocks within the project area, using a 25 percent sampling fraction. The result was then reduced by 32 percent to only those households primarily engaged in paddy cultivation. Households with paddy farms on qualitatively inferior acid soils (8 percent of the original) were discarded as well as those which failed to report labor usage in paddy cultivation activities or paddy output. The remaining sample was reduced to

Table 4–10. *Variables for Malaysian Farms*

Independent variable	Definition
Y	Paddy output (gantangs) (1 gantang = 2.42 kilograms)
L	Labor hours; male and female labor hours are weighted equally.
CH	Other variable inputs; includes fertilizers and insecticides (M$) (US$1 = M$2.443, 1973)
K	Capital input in weighted hours; includes tractor and bullock inputs weighted in terms of time required to bring an area of land into the same state of readiness for planting.
T	Land area cultivated (relongs) (1 relong = 0.284 hectare)
$STR4$	Dummy variable for 1 year of experience in double-cropping
$STR6$	Dummy variable for 2 years of experience in double-cropping
$STR8$	Dummy variable for 3 or more years of experience in double-cropping

Education variables

LIT	Can read and write Jawi, but had no formal education
EDS	Some education, but did not complete primary school or had from 1 to 3 years of religious education
EDL	Completed primary school or had more than 3 years of religious education
EDU	Had at least some secondary school
EDA	Attended adult classes only

Table 4–11. *Sample Means of Variables for Malaysian Farms*
(sample = 403)

Independent variable	Mean	Standard deviation
Output (gantangs) (1 gantang = 2.42 kilograms)	2,765.83	2,418.45
Labor (hours)	988.60	726.10
Chemical—other variable inputs (M$)	64.48	73.29
Capital (hours)	98.03	120.35
Land area operated (relongs) (1 relong = 0.284 hectare)	5.812	4.489
LIT (can read and write Jawi but no formal education)	0.21	0.41
EDS (some education but did not complete primary school or had from 1 to 3 years of religious education)	0.28	0.45
EDL (completed primary school or had more than 3 years of religious education)	0.19	0.39
EDU (had at least some secondary school)	0.17	0.13
EDA (attended adult classes only)	0.03	0.18

double-cropping households, thereby choosing only those farmers who had taken advantage of the irrigation scheme to increase their yield. Altogether 403 farm households were included, and these were then divided about equally into households having one year, two years, or three or more years of experience in double cropping. This study focuses on one agricultural cycle for which complete records were available: the second yearly crop between April/May and August/September of 1973. A more detailed discussion of the survey and the data can be found in Barnum and Squire (1979, chapter 2).

The survey had only two questions dealing with education, one on the schooling of the head of household and one on the highest educational level of any male member of the household. As the responses were designated as one of twelve categories rather than number of grades for years, dummy variables were used in the regression equations to capture the effect of education. Religious education as reported consisted of Koranic teachings sponsored by the local mosque. It usually included reading and writing in Malay and some Arabic.

The variables used in the study of the agricultural production function in Malaysia are defined in Table 4–10. Table 4–11 presents the means and standard deviations of these variables.

PART TWO

Empirical Analysis

CHAPTER 5

Education and Productivity

IN THIS CHAPTER WE EXAMINE the effects of formal education and nonformal education (agricultural extension) on the technological levels of farmers. Data on farm outputs and inputs collected from individual farms are used to determine whether farmers with higher levels of education or agricultural extension or exposure (or both) exhibit a higher level of technology; that is, whether these farmers are able to obtain a higher output from the same measured quantities of inputs. Each individual farm, given its level of technology, which may depend on the quantity of education or agricultural extension, is assumed to be technically efficient. In other words, it operates on the frontier of its set of production possibilities. Thus, all variations in productivity across farms are attributed to variations in the technological level.

The chapter begins with an explanation of the empirical methods used to measure the effects of education, extension, and other characteristic variables. The results of the empirical analyses of the effects of education on productivity in Thailand, Korea, and Malaysia are then reported. These analyses assume that the effects of education on productivity are neutral, that is, that education does not affect the productivity of labor, chemical inputs, capital, or land differentially. A concluding section reports on statistical tests of the adequacy of this neutrality assumption.

Empirical Methodology

The basic concept used in the analysis of productivity is the production function. It is assumed that each farm has a set of production possibilities: the set of all feasible combinations of input and output from which the farm can choose. This set can be described by a production function

(5.1) $$Y = F(X, Z, E)$$

where Y is the quantity of output, X is a vector of quantities of variable inputs, Z is a vector of quantities of fixed inputs, and E is a vector of characteristic variables of the farm household, which includes location, education, age, sex, availability of agricultural extension services, and availability of credit. By assuming an algebraic form for the production function, it can be econometrically estimated from data on the quantities of output, variable and fixed inputs, and characteristic variables.

Functional form

The hypotheses maintained in this study on the production function are that, first, all the physical inputs of production (capital, labor, land, fertilizers, and so forth) are always included in the production function; and, second, the effect of education (or agricultural extension services) or any other characteristic variable on the agricultural production function is neutral, that is, it changes the whole production function by a multiplicative scalar factor. This is a substantive specialization of the production function because it does not allow, for example, different rates of factor augmentation for different inputs, nor does it allow, in the context of the Cobb-Douglas production function, the possibility that the elasticities of production may depend on the effect of education. Under the neutrality assumption, the production function may be written as

(5.2) $$Y = A(E)F(X, Z).$$

For the empirical analysis the production function is further specialized to the Cobb-Douglas form, so that

(5.3) $$Y = A \, \Pi_{i=1}^{m} X_i^{\alpha_i} \, \Pi_{i=1}^{n} Z_i^{\beta_i} \, \Pi_{i=1}^{p} e^{\gamma_i E_i}.$$

Taking the natural logarithms of both sides of equation (5.3), we have

(5.4) $$\ln Y = \ln A + \Sigma_{i=1}^{m} \alpha_i \ln X_i + \Sigma_{i=1}^{n} \beta_i \ln Z_i + \Sigma_{i=1}^{p} \gamma_i E_i.$$

Equation (5.4) is the basic estimating form used in the production function analysis, although subsequently we also allow the possibility that there may be interaction effects among the E_i's. The α_i's and the β_i's in equation (5.4) have the usual interpretation of production elasticities. The γ_i's have the interpretation of the percentage changes in output in response to unit changes in the E_i's, other inputs, and characteristics variables being held constant, that is,

$$(5.5) \qquad \gamma_i = \partial \ln Y_i / \partial E_i.$$

If the E_i variable is measured in terms of years of, say, education, then γ_i is approximately the percentage change in output in response to an increase of one year of education at the margin, other things being equal.

To assess the restrictiveness of the assumption that the effect of education on the agricultural production function is neutral for Thai farms, we performed Chow tests on the equality of the coefficients of the physical inputs between the production functions of the educated and the uneducated farmers. If education actually affects the production function in a nonneutral manner, for example, if it enhances the marginal product of chemical fertilizers more than that of labor, then the coefficients of the physical inputs of production should differ for both the educated and uneducated farms. To assess the restrictiveness of the neutrality assumption for Korean farms, we performed tests on the absence of interaction effects between education variables and physical input variables. The results of these tests are reported in the last section of this chapter.

Estimation procedure

The production functions are estimated by ordinary least squares. The basic assumption is that the independent variables and the stochastic disturbance term are uncorrelated and that the variance of the vector of stochastic disturbance terms is equal to a scalar times an identity matrix. Although such an assumption is standard in this kind of work, it is open to at least two criticisms. First, it is often argued that the quantities of output and variable inputs are simultaneously determined through the conditions for profit maximization, and hence the stochastic disturbance term in the production function may be correlated with the observed quantities of the variable inputs. This implies that the ordinary least-squares estimator will be subject to possible simultaneous equations bias. The conventional response to this argument is to suppose that the farm household maximizes expected profit, rather than actual profit.[1] Second, it is argued that farms in a given region are subject to the same climatic and other influences, and hence their stochastic disturbance terms will be correlated. This implies that ordinary least squares will not in general be efficient, but will, under the standard assumptions, be unbiased and consistent. In this study, we have not experimented with alternative estimators of the production function parameters. The results therefore may be sensitive to the above criticisms. The profit function analysis in Chapter 6, however, is immune from the simultaneous equations bias problem and indicates the robustness of the substantive findings.

As pointed out earlier, we use a Cobb-Douglas production function and maintain the hypotheses that, first, all the physical inputs of production should be included in the production function, and, second, education and the characteristic variables affect the production function in a neutral manner. Since the primary focus of this study is on the effects of education and the characteristic variables on the production function, we are concerned about possible sensitivity of the estimates to the choice of characteristic variables included in a particular specification of the production function. In order to assess the degree of robustness of the estimated effects of education and other characteristics, we have departed from the traditional procedure of reporting regression results for only one or a few selected specifications. Instead, we have run regressions of alternative specifications representing all possible distinct combinations of the independent variables corresponding to education, availability of agricultural extension, and other farm characteristics.[2] In all these regressions, the quantities of the physical inputs of production are always included as independent variables. Thus, for example, there will be one regression including an

1. See, for example, Zellner, Kmenta, and Drèze (1966).
2. The results are reported in technical annexes which, because of their bulk, are not included in the published monograph. They are available from the authors on request.

education variable, another regression including education and age variables, and another regression including only an age variable. It is entirely possible, given this empirical procedure, that the estimated effects may fluctuate all over, in both sign and magnitude, in which case we would be forced to conclude that the data are insufficient to identify the effects of education and other characteristic variables unambiguously, and we need to proceed no further. Fortunately, as we shall see, the regression results are quite robust to the choice of education and characteristic variables included in the regression. Given the regression results on all the alternative specifications, some choice needs to be made as to which ones should be analyzed in depth. In principle, since the estimates are rather robust, it does not matter which one is used. In practice, it is preferable to choose a specification that in some sense provides a best fit. For this purpose a brief discussion of measures of goodness of fit is given below. A more technical discussion of these measures is included as Appendix C.

This empirical procedure is superior to the traditional one of comparing several specifications informally and then choosing and reporting only one specification. With this procedure we know whether a given estimated effect is likely to be sustained by another researcher working with the same body of data, regardless of the education and characteristic variables used. Thus, to the extent that the estimated effects are robust, our confidence in them is correspondingly increased.

Measures of goodness of fit

Consider a standard linear regression model,

$$y = X\beta + \varepsilon$$

where y is a vector of observations on the dependent variable, X is a fixed matrix of observations on the independent variables with full rank, and ε is a vector of stochastic disturbances with expectation equal to zero and variance-covariance matrix equal to $\sigma^2 I$. Under these assumptions, the ordinary least-squares estimator $(X'X)^{-1}X'y$ is the unique, minimum variance, linear, and unbiased estimator of β.

In general, however, we do not know whether the set of independent variables contained in the matrix X is the correct one. Very often, there will be more than one set of independent variables that

seems equally plausible. One way to compare these different specifications is to use a summary statistic that provides a scalar measure of the degree to which the variations in the independent variables explain the variations in the dependent variable. In general
the higher the value of the summary statistic, the better, in some
sense, is the regression. Many such summary statistics are available. In this study three such summary statistics are used: the
coefficient of multiple determination, R^2; the coefficient of multiple
determination, adjusted for the degrees of freedom, $\bar{R}^2$; and the
prediction criterion, R^{*2}. The last criterion is due to Amemiya
(1980).

The summary statistic R^2 is probably the most well known measure of the goodness of fit of a regression. It is defined as the proportion of the total sum of squares of the dependent variable around its
mean that is explained by the regression. It is measured by the
formula

$$R^2 = 1 - [e'e/(y - \bar{y})'(y - \bar{y})]$$

where e is the vector of residuals from the regression, y is the vector
of independent variables, and $\bar{y}$ is a vector of units times the average
value of the dependent variable.[3] The difficulty with using R^2 as a
summary statistic for comparing regressions is that it can be increased by simply adding more independent variables.

The summary statistic $\bar{R}^2$ is proposed by Theil (1961) as a criterion for choosing between two competing regression models. $\bar{R}^2$ is
referred to as the coefficient of multiple determination adjusted for
degrees of freedom. $\bar{R}^2$ can decrease if the additional independent
variable does not increase the goodness of fit substantially. Thus, it
offers some protection against choosing a regression that includes
indiscriminately a large number of independent variables.

The summary statistic R^{*2} is proposed by Amemiya and is based
on minimizing the unconditional mean square error of prediction.
R^{*2} is even more conservative in guarding against the increase in
the number of included independent variables than is $\bar{R}^2$. Appendix C discusses the theoretical basis for using each of the summary
statistics.

---

3. R^2 may become negative if the regression does not include a vector of units as an
independent variable.

Empirical implementation

One frequent problem that arises in this kind of exploratory study is that the empirical results may be very sensitive to the particular regression that happens to be run and reported. In this study we protect against the possibility of statistical accidents by running regressions for every possible combination of education and characteristic variables, such as education, age, sex, availability of agricultural extension, and availability of credit, and so forth. We maintain, however, that the independent variables indicated by economic theory, such as quantities of inputs or prices of inputs, and locational dummy variables, are always part of the regression model. The resulting estimates are, on the whole, quite consistent across the regressions, which suggests that our conclusions are likely to be quite robust. It may be argued, quite justifiably, that in running all the regressions on the same body of data, we have in fact used up the degrees of freedom that we have, or at any rate we should alter the levels of significance used for the test statistics. Although we are not unconcerned about this problem, the fact that the results all seem to point in one direction is certainly reassuring. In addition, we consider this study partly also as a device to generate hypotheses to be examined in our more extensive surveys of the effect of education in the agricultural economy of Nepal and Thailand that are being currently conducted. In any case, our procedure is superior to the more conventional one of simply reporting one or several regressions selected from the many attempted.

Estimates of Production Functions

To facilitate the discussion of the results we have constructed summary tables of the best-fitting regressions. There is of course no general agreement about the definition of a best fit. The commonly used criterion of R^2 can always be increased simply by increasing the number of independent variables. The choice between the other two criteria, $\bar{R}^2$ and R^{*2}, is also not clear-cut. We do not wish to emphasize one criterion over another arbitrarily. Thus the summary of the regression results presents the three regressions that maximize, respectively, the R^2, $\bar{R}^2$, and R^{*2} criteria. In addition, we present for each coefficient the minimum and maximum estimates that are found in the regressions. Finally, we also present for each coefficient the value of the estimate that has the highest absolute value of the t ratio in the regressions. It is hoped that the summary will provide an adequate picture of the robustness of the empirical findings. The interested reader is encouraged to examine the technical annexes (see note 2 above).

Thai farms

As discussed in Chapter 4, the Thai farms are classified into two groups: the 91 farms that used chemical inputs and the 184 farms that did not. The regression results for each group of farms will be discussed separately.

The regression results for the chemical farms are summarized in Table 5–1. The first column of the table contains the values of the minimum estimates of the particular parameters for all the regressions. The second column contains the values of the maximum estimates of the particular parameters for all the regressions. Thus, between the first and second columns lie all the estimated values that have been found for any particular parameter in any one of the regressions. Altogether 160 regressions, representing all possible distinct combinations of independent variables, have been run for each group of farms. If the minimum value and the maximum value of the estimates of any particular parameter are fairly close together, it implies that the estimate for that parameter is rather robust, that is, it does not depend on the choice of a particular specification.

The third column contains the regression with the highest R^2. The fourth column contains the regression with the highest $\bar{R}^2$, that is, R^2 adjusted for the degrees of freedom. The fifth column contains the regression with the highest R^{*2}, which is a further adjustment of the $\bar{R}^2$. The sixth column contains the individual estimates of the parameters with the highest absolute value of the t ratio among all the regressions.

Several observations can be made about chemical farms from the data in Table 5–1. First, the estimates for the labor elasticity range from 0.22 to 0.41, indicating a substantial variability. For the best-fitting regressions, however, the range is narrowed to between 0.28 and 0.30. The estimates for the land elasticity range from 0.39 to

0.58, again reflecting a substantial variability. For the best-fitting regressions, however, the range is narrowed to between 0.50 and 0.52. The estimates for the chemical inputs and capital elasticities do not seem to be very stable and are always statistically insignificant. This may be due partly to multicollinearity among the various inputs of production. The estimates of the coefficients corresponding to the regional dummy variables appear to be quite robust across regressions.

The effects of the education variables, however, are the primary concerns of this study. The maximum education of either head of household has a positive and statistically significant effect of approximately 3 percent a year. If the formal education of the head of household variable is introduced in the form of the dummy variable $E5$ ($= 1$ if some formal education; 0 otherwise), the estimated effects range from a low of 10 percent to a high of 21 percent. These estimated effects, however, are not always statistically significant. If the formal education variable is introduced in the form of dummy variables $E2$ (less than 4 years), $E3$ (4 years), and $E4$ (more than 4 years), the precision of the estimates deteriorates, although the magnitudes of the estimates remain positively related to the level of education, as expected. What is most surprising is that the availability of agricultural extension services always has a negative, although not statistically significant, effect.[4]

There is a possible explanation of the negative effect of agricultural extension services on the productivity of chemical farms. On the one hand, if a farm voluntarily chose to use chemical inputs in the absence of agricultural extension service, the head of the farm probably knew what he or she was doing. On the other hand, the agricultural extension service might have prematurely coaxed some farmers into adopting chemical inputs, whether they were ready or not. Overall then, a negative correlation between output and availability of agricultural extension service may be expected,

4. Agricultural extension services are available in villages 2, 6, 7, 8, 9, 11, 12, 13, 14, 16, and 22. The variable used in the regression analysis to represent agricultural extension is only an indicator variable, indicating whether it is available in a given locality. The nature of the agricultural extension activity varies substantially even within the same region of a country. Such factors as organization, prior training of personnel, availability of other services, and budget all determine the effectiveness of agricultural extension. Thus, our findings here with respect to agricultural extension should be regarded as tentative and based on a very crude measure of its availability.

Table 5–1. Regressions of Production Functions for Thai Chemical Farms
(sample = 91)

Independent variable	Minimum estimate	Maximum estimate	Maximum R^2 (0.804)	Maximum $\bar{R}^2$ (0.778)	Maximum R^{*2} (0.755)	Estimate with highest t ratio
Labor	0.217	0.409	0.300	0.297	0.278	0.408
	(2.112)	(4.458)	(2.690)	(2.798)	(2.652)	(4.471)
Chemical inputs	-0.009	0.111	0.081	0.080	0.073	0.111
	(-0.118)	(1.442)	(0.952)	(1.019)	(0.933)	(1.442)
Capital	-0.016	0.049	0.026	0.037	0.027	0.022
	(-0.308)	(0.902)	(0.440)	(0.681)	(0.497)	(0.984)
Land	0.390	0.577	0.503	0.512	0.517	0.573
	(4.446)	(6.353)	(5.212)	(5.539)	(5.592)	(6.358)
Region 1	5.301	5.744	5.372	5.416	5.471	5.617
	(12.81)	(15.54)	(12.94)	(17.10)	(17.46)	(18.03)
Region 2	5.029	5.527	5.138	5.187	5.262	5.343
	(11.83)	(14.38)	(11.99)	(16.49)	(17.10)	(17.16)
Region 3	5.204	5.725	5.294	5.332	5.373	5.456
	(14.36)	(14.93)	(13.24)	(17.64)	(17.88)	(17.96)
Region 4	5.470	5.828	5.515	5.548	5.583	5.703
	(13.54)	(15.08)	(13.57)	(16.51)	(16.66)	(16.93)

A5 (education of head of household) (years)	0.022 (1.194)	0.042 (2.830)	—	—	—	0.042 (2.830)
A6 (average education) (years)	-0.004 (-0.137)	0.036 (1.506)	—	0.026 (1.683)	0.031 (2.098)	0.036 (1.516)
E2 (education, 0 < A5 < 4)	0.030 (0.208)	0.134 (0.935)	0.030 (0.208)	—	—	0.134 (0.935)
E3 (education, A5 = 4)	0.122 (1.256)	0.210 (2.383)	0.124 (1.341)	—	—	0.210 (2.383)
E4 (education, A5 > 4)	0.271 (1.280)	0.447 (2.246)	0.280 (1.549)	—	—	0.443 (2.639)
E5 (education, A5 > 0)	0.095 (0.931)	0.215 (2.495)	—	—	—	0.215 (2.495)
EXT (1 if extension services available; 0 otherwise)	-0.139 (-1.700)	-0.011 (-0.133)	-0.096 (-1.116)	-0.123 (-1.527)	—	-0.138 (-1.708)
A7 (age of head of household) (years)	-0.004 (-1.441)	0.001 (1.183)	—	—	—	-0.004 (-1.441)
CR (1 if credit taken or available; 0 otherwise)	-0.131 (-1.420)	0.224 (0.227)	0.010 (0.104)	—	—	-0.130 (-1.429)
HM (1 if male; 0 if female)	-0.144 (-0.558)	0.182 (0.695)	0.076 (0.284)	—	—	0.176 (0.695)

Note: Numbers in parentheses are t ratios. The variables are defined in Table 4–4.
— Not applicable.

109

given that a farm has chosen to use chemical inputs. This negative effect from premature adoption may confound any true positive effect to yield a negative and statistically insignificant estimate.

Findings of no statistically significant effect of specific character-istic variables are also of interest. The maximum age of either head of household does not seem to matter. Nor does the sex of the head of household. Of greater interest is the fact that the average level of education, in years, of all adults on the farm between 17 and 60 years of age does not seem to make a difference. This suggests that it is the educational level of the manager of the farm that is important, rather than the educational level of the work force. Finally, the availability of agricultural credit for the farm household does not seem to have any statistically significant direct effect on the produc-tivity of the household.

The effects of some of the characteristic variables such as educa-tion and age may be nonlinear, and there may be interaction effects between education and age, education and agricultural extension, or age and agricultural extension. To test these possibilities, addi-tional regressions with such nonlinear and interaction effects were also run. The results of the regressions are summarized in Table 5–2 in the same format as in Table 5–1.

First, Table 5–2 shows that neither age nor education has statisti-cally significant nonlinear effects. Second, there is some evidence of interaction between education and extension. The maximum education of the head of household variable ($A5$) had a statistically significant effect only in the absence of agricultural extension. Several hypotheses may be consistent with this finding, including the hypothesis that agricultural extension tends to narrow the dif-ferences in the level of practices among farms. In any case, there is evidence that the availability of agricultural extension has a nega-tive and occasionally statistically significant effect on productivity, consistent with the results in Table 5–1. Third, there is also some evidence of interaction between age and extension. The availability of agricultural extension seems to mitigate against the negative effect that the age of the head of household may have on agricultural productivity.

The regression results of the nonchemical farms are summarized in Table 5–3. Several observations can be made from the data in the table. First, the estimates of the production elasticities for labor and land are quite robust. The estimates for the labor elasticity range from 0.25 to 0.28, a much narrower spread than that of the chemical farms. The two labor elasticities are of comparable magnitude, however. The estimates for the land elasticity range from 0.58 to 0.64—again, a much narrower spread than that of the chemical farms. The land elasticity estimates for the nonchemical farms are on the whole higher than those for the chemical farms. Both of these estimates are statistically significant and have the correct signs. They also do not differ appreciably among the regressions that maximize R^2, $\bar{R}^2$, and R^{*2}. (The latter two regressions are actually the same one.) The estimates for the capital elasticity, however, range from a very small negative number, -0.00 to 0.02. In any case they are small and always statistically insignificant. The estimates of the parameters corresponding to the regional dummy variables are also quite robust for all the different regressions.

As for the effect of the educational variables, the maximum education of either head of the household has a substantial and statistically significant positive effect. Roughly speaking, each additional year of education for the head of household adds approximately 2.5 percent to the output, other things being equal, which is comparable to the corresponding effect on chemical farms. If the formal education of the head of the household variable is introduced in the form of the dummy variable, $E5$, the estimated effects range from a low of more than 7 percent to a high of less than 13 percent. As in the case of the chemical farms, they are not always statistically significant. Given that the heads of households in the sample had an average of more than four years of formal education, the magnitudes of these estimated effects are quite consistent with the effects measured through the $A5$ variable. If the variable for the formal education of the head of household is introduced in the form of dummy variables $E2$ (less than 4 years), $E3$ (4 years), and $E4$ (more than 4 years), it is found that 4 years of education have a positive and statistically significant effect of approximately 10 percent on output, other things being equal. This amounts to 2.5 percent a year, which is comparable to the estimates of the coefficient on $A5$. The effect is correspondingly reduced for less schooling and is correspondingly enhanced for more schooling. The estimates of the coefficients for $E2$ and $E4$ are not, however, statistically significant although they do have the expected signs and relative magnitudes.

The availability of agricultural extension services also has a substantial (8.5 percent) and statistically significant positive effect on output. The range of alternative estimates is quite narrow, between

Table 5–2. Regressions of Production Functions with Interactions for Thai Chemical Farms
(sample = 91)

Independent variable	Minimum estimate	Maximum estimate	Maximum R^2 (0.816)	Maximum $\bar{R}^2$ (0.782)	Maximum R^{*2} (0.753)	Estimate with highest t ratio
Labor	0.190	0.295	0.271	0.271	0.238	0.294
	(1.778)	(2.755)	(2.508)	(2.508)	(2.225)	(2.779)
Chemical inputs	0.076	0.133	0.113	0.113	0.087	0.133
	(0.945)	(1.681)	(1.401)	(1.401)	(1.099)	(1.681)
Capital	0.002	0.041	0.002	0.002	0.013	0.041
	(0.034)	(0.742)	(0.040)	(0.040)	(0.249)	(0.742)
Land	0.505	0.571	0.506	0.506	0.520	0.571
	(5.446)	(6.284)	(5.526)	(5.526)	(5.656)	(6.284)
Region 1	4.048	5.885	5.446	5.446	4.468	5.380
	(5.068)	(6.535)	(5.695)	(5.695)	(6.624)	(16.61)
Region 2	3.868	5.671	5.270	5.270	4.304	5.163
	(4.906)	(6.281)	(5.557)	(5.557)	(6.591)	(16.10)
Region 3	3.935	5.793	5.385	5.385	4.379	5.304
	(4.919)	(6.376)	(5.634)	(5.634)	(6.606)	(17.29)
Region 4	4.157	6.025	5.597	5.597	4.596	5.510
	(5.147)	(6.658)	(5.847)	(5.847)	(6.801)	(16.14)
A5 (education of head of household) (years)	0.021	0.040	0.023	0.023	0.036	0.035
	(1.234)	(0.752)	(1.318)	(1.318)	(2.191)	(2.191)
A7 (age of head of household) (years)	0.001	0.055	—	—	0.044	0.055
	(0.230)	(1.962)			(1.745)	(1.962)
$A7^2$	–0.001	–0.004	—	—	–0.001	–0.001
	(–1.737)	(–1.685)			(–1.737)	(–1.737)

EXT (1 if extension services available; 0 otherwise)	-2.239 (-1.773)	-0.472 (-1.542)	-1.918 (-1.498)	-1.918 (-1.498)	—	-0.587 (-2.007)
A5EX1	0.015 (0.718)	0.015 (0.718)	—	—	—	0.015 (0.718)
A5EX0	0.036 (2.316)	0.036 (2.316)	—	—	—	0.036 (2.316)
A6EX1	0.004 (0.154)	0.019 (0.772)	—	—	—	0.019 (0.772)
A6EX0	0.025 (0.756)	0.048 (0.772)	—	—	—	0.048 (0.772)
A7EX1	-0.002 (-0.829)	0.073 (2.079)	0.073 (2.079)	0.073 (2.079)	—	0.073 (2.079)
A7EX0	-0.007 (-1.583)	0.045 (1.779)	0.008 (0.240)	0.008 (0.240)	—	0.045 (1.779)
A7SE1	-0.001 (-2.000)	-0.000 (-1.027)	-0.001 (-2.000)	-0.001 (-2.000)	—	-0.001 (-2.000)
A7SE0	-0.000 (-1.868)	-0.000 (-0.140)	-0.000 (-0.385)	-0.000 (-0.385)	—	-0.000 (-1.868)
A7A5	-0.002 (-1.033)	-0.000 (-0.160)	—	—	—	-0.002 (-1.033)
$A5^2$	-0.003 (-0.748)	-0.000 (-0.044)	—	—	—	-0.003 (-0.748)

Note: Numbers in parentheses are t ratios. The variables are defined in Table 4-4.
— Not applicable.

Table 5–3. Regressions of Production Functions for Thai Nonchemical Farms
(sample = 184)

Independent variable	Minimum estimate	Maximum estimate	Maximum R^2 (0.824)	Maximum $\bar{R}^2$ (0.813)	Maximum R^{*2} (0.804)	Estimate with highest t ratio
Labor	0.253	0.282	0.260	0.265	0.265	0.282
	(4.956)	(5.793)	(5.338)	(5.523)	(5.523)	(5.793)
Capital	−0.001	0.019	0.013	0.012	0.012	0.019
	(−0.027)	(0.591)	(0.407)	(0.383)	(0.383)	(0.591)
Land	0.576	0.644	0.604	0.598	0.598	0.641
	(11.67)	(12.23)	(12.13)	(12.22)	(12.22)	(12.33)
Region 1	5.413	5.867	5.413	5.691	5.691	5.741
	(17.32)	(29.24)	(17.32)	(30.69)	(30.69)	(30.81)
Region 2	5.176	5.630	5.176	5.459	5.459	5.503
	(16.45)	(28.42)	(16.45)	(29.88)	(29.88)	(29.94)
Region 3	5.288	5.762	5.288	5.575	5.575	5.595
	(16.45)	(28.42)	(16.45)	(29.01)	(29.01)	(29.01)
Region 4	5.211	5.664	5.211	5.494	5.494	5.494
	(16.43)	(27.51)	(16.43)	(29.35)	(29.35)	(29.35)

		(1)	(2)	(3)	(4)	(5)	(6)
A5	(education of head of household) (years)	0.020 (1.271)	0.031 (2.678)	—	0.024 (2.268)	0.024 (2.268)	0.031 (2.678)
A6	(average education) (years)	0.001 (0.046)	0.019 (1.185)	—	—	—	0.019 (1.185)
E2	(education, 0 < A5 < 4)	0.059 (0.760)	0.097 (1.170)	0.066 (0.909)	—	—	0.096 (1.229)
E3	(education, A5 = 4)	0.885 (1.278)	0.137 (1.990)	0.108 (2.316)	—	—	0.130 (2.592)
E4	(education, A5 > 4)	0.091 (0.517)	0.136 (0.802)	0.132 (0.856)	—	—	0.131 (0.852)
E5	(education, A5 > 0)	0.077 (1.219)	0.126 (2.562)	—	—	—	0.126 (2.562)
EXT	(1 if extension services available; 0 otherwise)	0.082 (2.124)	0.106 (2.635)	0.086 (2.201)	0.085 (2.222)	0.085 (2.222)	0.106 (2.635)
A7	(age of head of household) (years)	−0.003 (−1.729)	0.001 (0.398)	—	—	—	−0.003 (−1.737)
CR	(1 if credit taken or available; 0 otherwise)	0.001 (0.030)	0.064 (1.325)	0.020 (0.467)	—	—	0.062 (1.341)
HM	(1 if male; 0 if female)	0.029 (0.105)	0.269 (1.052)	0.269 (1.052)	—	—	0.269 (1.052)

Note: Numbers in parentheses are *t* ratios. The variables are defined in Table 4–4.
— Not applicable.

8.2 and 10.6 percent. This is in direct contrast to the case of the chemical farms, in which the availability of agricultural extension has a consistently negative, although not statistically significant, effect. Unfortunately, the data do not indicate the kind of agricultural extension service available. Thus, a more detailed analysis of the relation between agricultural extension activities and agricultural productivity will have to await the results of a follow-up study in which the agricultural extension practices are more closely examined.

As in the case of chemical farms, neither average education, nor age of the head of household, nor sex, nor availability of agricultural credit seem to have a statistically significant effect on the agricultural productivity of the nonchemical farms.

There may be possible nonlinear and interaction effects of the characteristic variables for nonchemical farms. The interaction regressions are summarized in Table 5–4. As in the case of the chemical farms, no significant nonlinear effects can be found for age and education. In addition, none of the best-fitting regressions have statistically significant interaction effects. There is some evidence, however, that the availability of agricultural extension enhances the effect of education on agricultural productivity. With agricultural extension, 1 year of schooling is worth approximately a statistically significant 3.2 percent. Without agricultural extension, 1 year of schooling is worth approximately a statistically insignificant 1.5 percent. None of the other interaction effects are statistically significant. Finally, the estimates of the labor and land elasticities and the coefficients of the regional dummy variables remain rather stable, despite the introduction of the interaction variables.

Korean farms

As discussed in Chapter 4 the Korean farms are also classified into two groups—the 1,363 farms that used mechanical power and the 541 farms that did not. The two groups of farms are analyzed separately.

In this Korean sample two alternative average education variables are used: $A6$, which is the average number of years of education of all farm household members 17 to 60 years old; and $A6*$, which is the average number of years of education of all farm household members 17 to 60 years old other than the head of the household. Thus, *A6** attempts to measure the quality of the work force as distinct from the quality of the manager.

In the empirical analysis of the Korean farms we follow the same procedure used in the analysis of the Thai farms. As before, we run regressions of the production function for all distinct combinations of the education and characteristic variables. The regressions for the mechanical farms with the average education variable *A6* are summarized in Table 5–5. All the production elasticities of the mechanical farms, except for the elasticity of capital, are statistically significant and have the correct expected signs. Moreover, the statistically significant elasticity estimates vary little across the regressions. The difference between the maximum and minimum estimates of the land elasticity is less than 10 percent. The differences between the maximum and the minimum estimates of the elasticities of the other inputs—labor, animal power, and mechanical power—are even smaller. We conclude that these estimates of the elasticities are quite robust with respect to the alternative specifications of the characteristic variables. The returns to scale parameters may be computed, using the maximum R^{*2} regression, to be 0.88, indicating slightly decreasing returns.[5]

We next examine the effects of the education variables. The education of the head of household variable (*A5*) does not figure in the best-fitting regressions. It is, however, statistically quite significant in some regressions, with an estimated effect of up to 1.4 percent a year. The average education variable (*A6*) is featured in all three best-fitting regressions. It is consistently statistically significant and has the correct positive sign. Its estimated effect ranges from 2.2 to 3.1 percent a year. When the education of the head of household variable is disaggregated into the dummy variables *E2* (more than 0 but less than 6 years), *E3* (exactly 6 years), and *E4* (more than 6 years), it is occasionally statistically significant with the correct signs, and the estimated effects show the expected pattern of increases with increasing education.

Of the characteristic variables, only the dummy variable for the sex of the head of household, *HM* (1 if male, 0 otherwise), has a statistically significant estimated effect. Moreover, the effect is

---

5. The statistically insignificant and negative estimated capital elasticity is ignored in this computation.

Table 5–4. Regressions of Production Functions with Interactions for Thai Nonchemical Farms (sample = 184)

Independent variable	Minimum estimate	Maximum estimate	Maximum R^2 (0.825)	Maximum $\bar{R}^2$ (0.813)	Maximum $R*^2$ (0.803)	Estimate with highest t ratio
Labor	0.253 (5.179)	0.278 (5.782)	0.254 (5.222)	0.260 (5.408)	0.260 (5.408)	0.278 (5.782)
Capital	0.011 (0.347)	0.017 (0.528)	0.013 (0.433)	0.012 (0.394)	0.012 (0.394)	0.017 (0.528)
Land	0.580 (11.78)	0.612 (12.29)	0.608 (12.21)	0.605 (12.24)	0.605 (12.24)	0.612 (12.29)
Region 1	5.521 (9.173)	5.960 (28.03)	5.888 (15.56)	5.763 (25.91)	5.763 (25.91)	5.699 (30.51)
Region 2	5.279 (8.808)	5.722 (27.17)	5.652 (14.89)	5.532 (25.32)	5.532 (25.32)	5.468 (29.69)
Region 3	5.418 (8.999)	5.833 (26.55)	5.767 (14.88)	5.644 (24.91)	5.644 (24.91)	5.595 (28.95)
Region 4	5.305 (8.743)	5.758 (26.38)	5.688 (14.99)	5.569 (24.70)	5.569 (24.70)	5.495 (29.12)
A5 (education of head of household) (years)	-0.033 (-0.316)	0.027 (0.945)	0.020 (1.372)	0.022 (1.553)	0.022 (1.553)	0.023 (1.963)
A7 (age of head of household) (years)	-0.002 (-0.477)	0.010 (0.949)	—	—	—	0.010 (0.949)
$A7^2$	-0.000 (-1.183)	-0.000 (-0.715)	—	—	—	-0.000 (-1.183)

EXT (1 if extension services available; 0 otherwise)	-0.483 (-0.983)	-0.092 (-0.635)	-0.483 (-0.984)	—	—	-0.483 (-0.984)
A5EX1	0.032 (2.695)	0.032 (2.695)	—	—	—	0.032 (2.695)
A5EX0	0.016 (1.291)	0.016 (1.291)	—	—	—	0.016 (1.291)
A6EX1	0.004 (0.154)	0.019 (0.772)	—	—	—	0.019 (0.772)
A6EX0	0.025 (0.756)	0.048 (1.873)	—	—	—	0.048 (1.873)
A7EX1	-0.001 (-0.911)	0.017 (1.199)	0.016 (1.095)	0.001 (0.322)	0.001 (0.322)	0.017 (1.199)
A7EX0	-0.004 (-0.307)	0.007 (0.701)	-0.004 (-0.307)	-0.001 (-0.647)	-0.001 (-0.647)	0.007 (0.701)
A7SE1	-0.000 (-1.241)	-0.000 (-0.453)	-0.000 (-0.989)	—	—	-0.000 (-1.241)
A7SE0	-0.000 (-1.059)	0.000 (0.141)	0.000 (0.141)	—	—	-0.000 (-1.059)
A7A5	-0.000 (-0.055)	0.001 (0.552)	—	—	—	0.001 (0.552)
$A5^2$	-0.001 (-0.267)	-0.001 (-0.271)	—	—	—	-0.001 (-0.271)

Note: Numbers in parentheses are t ratios. The variables are defined in Table 4–4.
— Not applicable.

Table 5–5. Regressions of Production Functions for Korean Mechanical Farms, with Education Measured by the Household Average (sample = 1,363)

Independent variable	Minimum estimate	Maximum estimate	Maximum R^2 (0.669)	Maximum $\bar{R}^2$ (0.665)	Maximum R^{*2} (0.660)	Estimate of highest t ratio
Land	0.128	0.135	0.128	0.128	0.130	0.135
	(10.01)	(10.62)	(10.05)	(10.11)	(10.24)	(10.62)
Capital	-0.006	0.003	-0.005	-0.004	-0.004	-0.006
	(-0.526)	(0.323)	(-0.473)	(-0.412)	(-0.415)	(-0.526)
Labor	0.352	0.368	0.354	0.353	0.355	0.367
	(12.46)	(13.21)	(12.58)	(12.58)	(12.65)	(13.25)
Animal power	0.084	0.086	0.085	0.085	0.085	0.086
	(5.577)	(5.711)	(5.667)	(5.683)	(5.665)	(5.720)
Mechanical power	0.104	0.108	0.106	0.106	0.104	0.108
	(7.933)	(8.219)	(8.067)	(8.080)	(8.000)	(8.219)
Fertilizer	0.205	0.210	0.206	0.206	0.206	0.210
	(13.39)	(13.71)	(13.49)	(13.53)	(13.51)	(13.73)
Region 1	6.404	6.531	6.496	6.531	6.536	6.531
	(30.21)	(32.19)	(30.81)	(32.19)	(32.16)	(32.19)
Region 2	6.003	6.122	6.087	6.122	6.122	6.122
	(27.21)	(28.93)	(27.78)	(28.93)	(28.91)	(28.93)
Region 3	6.221	6.336	6.299	6.335	6.334	6.336
	(29.48)	(31.44)	(30.03)	(31.50)	(31.48)	(31.44)
Region 4	6.395	6.522	6.488	6.522	6.516	6.522
	(30.78)	(32.76)	(31.36)	(32.76)	(32.72)	(32.76)
Region 5	6.103	6.237	6.200	6.237	6.231	6.237
	(29.15)	(31.17)	(29.73)	(31.17)	(31.14)	(31.17)

Region 6	6.202 (29.32)	6.336 (31.30)	6.300 (29.91)	6.336 (31.30)	6.328 (31.26)	6.336 (31.30)
Region 7	5.991 (29.03)	6.121 (31.03)	6.085 (29.59)	6.121 (31.03)	6.116 (30.99)	6.121 (31.03)
Region 8	5.950 (28.89)	6.074 (30.97)	6.037 (29.46)	6.074 (30.97)	6.073 (30.96)	6.074 (30.97)
Region 9	5.787 (27.09)	5.935 (28.89)	5.900 (27.69)	5.935 (28.89)	5.926 (28.85)	5.935 (28.89)
A5 (education of head of household) (years)	-0.009 (-1.497)	0.014 (2.925)	-0.007 (-0.989)	-0.009 (-1.497)	—	0.014 (2.925)
A6 (average education) (years)	0.022 (4.224)	0.031 (3.992)	0.030 (3.851)	0.031 (3.992)	0.022 (4.224)	0.026 (4.665)
A7 (age of head of household) (years)	-0.000 (-0.287)	0.002 (1.457)	0.001 (0.619)	—	—	0.002 (1.457)
E2 (education, 0 < A5 < 4)	-0.006 (-0.129)	0.074 (1.709)	—	—	—	0.074 (1.709)
E3 (education, A5 = 4)	-0.037 (-0.733)	0.119 (2.607)	—	—	—	0.119 (2.607)
E4 (education, A5 > 4)	-0.073 (-1.085)	0.166 (3.031)	—	—	—	0.166 (3.031)
HM (1 if male; 0 if female)	0.082 (1.915)	0.111 (2.716)	0.101 (2.414)	0.104 (2.482)	0.091 (2.216)	0.111 (2.716)

Note: Numbers in parentheses are t ratios. The variables are defined in Table 4–7.
— Not applicable.

positive and quite substantial: on average, the output of a mechanical farm is enhanced by between 9 and 10 percent if the head
of household is male rather than female. The precise reason for this
phenomenon is not known, although certain special skill or strength
requirements may be associated with the use of mechanical power.
The finding is quite robust across regressions and cannot be explained away as a statistical happenstance.

To better isolate the effect of education of the head of household
on agricultural productivity, the same set of regressions was rerun
but with the average education variable $A6$ replaced by $A6*$, which
is the average number of years of schooling of all adult household
members other than the head of household. These regressions are
summarized in Table 5–6. The average education variable (as represented by $A6*$) continues to be statistically highly significant. Its
estimated effect now lies within the much narrower range of between 2.0 to 2.2 percent a year. The education of the head of household variable is occasionally statistically significant, whether represented by $A5$ or by $E2, E3$, and $E4$, but not always so. It does have
the correct expected signs. For the mechanical farms, one cannot,
on the basis of the regression results summarized in Table 5–6,
reject the possibility that education of the head of household may
enhance productivity. Although this is not a very strong conclusion,
it is consistent with the expectation that mechanical farms may
benefit more from a high level of managerial ability of the head of
household, which in turn depends on his or her education. Thus,
education of the head of household should be expected to have a
greater effect on mechanical farms than on nonmechanical farms;
that is, if there were to be an effect at all. The sex dummy variable
continues to have a robust and statistically significant positive
effect.

The regressions for the nonmechanical farms with the average
education variable $A6$ are summarized in Table 5–7. All the production elasticities are statistically significant and have the correct
expected signs. Their magnitudes are broadly comparable to the
corresponding estimates for the mechanical farms, although, of
course, in this case there is no estimate for the mechanical power
elasticity. The returns to scale parameter may be computed, using
the maximum R^{*2} regression, to be 0.78, indicating an even more
sharply decreasing returns to scale than in the case of the mechanical farms.

As for the effects of the education and characteristic variables, only those of the education variables are statistically significant. The sex of the head of household variable, in contrast to the case of mechanical farms, does not have a statistically significant effect. However, it also appears that the education of the head of household affects the output of the nonmechanical farm negatively, to the extent of -2.5 percent per year of education, contrary to our expectation. This negative effect is borne out when A5 is disaggregated into E2, E3, and E4 educational dummy variables, with E3 representing exactly 6 years of education. The effects remain negative and increasing in absolute magnitude with more and more education. In some regressions, the dummy variable E4, more than 6 years of education, has an almost statistically significant negative coefficient. In contrast, the average education variable is consistently statistically significant and has the expected positive sign. Its value ranges between 2.5 and 5.1 percent per year of average education, which is comparable to that of the mechanical farms. In the best-fitting regressions, its value ranges between 4.8 and 5.1 percent, higher than the corresponding estimates for the mechanical farms.

To complete this analysis, the same set of regressions was rerun but with the average education variable A6 replaced by A6*. These regressions are summarized in Table 5–8. The most interesting (and the only noteworthy) difference between Tables 5–7 and 5–8 is that the education of the head of household variable A5 is no longer statistically significant in any one of the regressions. The average education variable, however, remains positive and statistically significant. Its value, as in the case of the mechanical farms, becomes much less variable across regressions and fluctuates within a narrow range between 2.2 and 2.3 percent a year, comparable to the corresponding estimates for mechanical farms. This finding is consistent with the hypothesis that in Korea the education of the head of household does not matter for nonmechanical farms; only average education matters. And the reason a statistically significant negative effect is found for the education of the head of household variable in Table 5–7 is that it is incorrectly included in the A6 variable. Hence, to compensate for the inclusion, the A5 variable picks up a negative coefficient. When A6 is replaced by A6*, A5 is no longer included in the average education variable, and hence no compensation is necessary. We conclude that only the average

Table 5–6. *Regressions of Production Functions for Korean Mechanical Farms, with Education Measured by the Household Average, Excluding the Head of the Household* (sample = 1,363)

Independent variable	Minimum estimate	Maximum estimate	Maximum R^2 (0.670)	Maximum $\bar{R}^2$ (0.666)	Maximum R^{*2} (0.662)	Estimate of highest t ratio
Land	0.128	0.135	0.128	0.129	0.129	0.135
	(10.04)	(10.62)	(10.09)	(10.20)	(10.20)	(10.62)
Capital	–0.005	0.003	–0.005	–0.004	–0.003	–0.005
	(–0.487)	(0.323)	(–0.462)	(–0.395)	(–0.325)	(–0.487)
Labor	0.352	0.368	0.350	0.349	0.347	0.368
	(12.46)	(13.21)	(12.38)	(12.44)	(12.41)	(13.21)
Animal power	0.084	0.086	0.085	0.085	0.085	0.087
	(5.577)	(5.711)	(5.691)	(5.681)	(5.684)	(5.760)
Mechanical power	0.102	0.108	0.104	0.104	0.104	0.108
	(7.833)	(8.219)	(7.902)	(7.926)	(8.099)	(8.219)
Fertilizer	0.205	0.210	0.205	0.206	0.206	0.210
	(13.43)	(13.71)	(13.43)	(13.54)	(13.59)	(13.71)
Region 1	6.404	6.580	6.534	6.578	6.579	6.579
	(30.21)	(31.50)	(30.82)	(32.40)	(32.40)	(32.40)
Region 2	6.003	6.171	6.125	6.168	6.167	6.169
	(27.21)	(29.11)	(27.80)	(29.14)	(29.13)	(29.14)
Region 3	6.221	6.392	6.340	6.386	6.386	6.386
	(29.48)	(30.78)	(30.08)	(31.73)	(31.73)	(31.73)
Region 4	6.395	6.574	6.528	6.570	6.570	6.570
	(30.78)	(32.05)	(31.39)	(32.95)	(32.96)	(32.96)
Region 5	6.103	6.284	6.237	6.282	6.281	6.282
	(29.15)	(30.41)	(29.77)	(31.36)	(31.36)	(31.36)

Region 6	6.202	6.389	6.341	6.385	6.386	6.386
	(29.32)	(30.63)	(29.93)	(31.50)	(31.51)	(31.51)
Region 7	5.991	6.170	6.126	6.170	6.169	6.170
	(29.03)	(31.23)	(29.65)	(31.23)	(31.23)	(31.23)
Region 8	5.950	6.121	6.077	6.121	6.119	6.121
	(28.89)	(31.19)	(29.50)	(31.19)	(31.18)	(31.19)
Region 9	5.787	5.990	5.945	5.989	5.990	5.990
	(27.09)	(29.11)	(27.73)	(29.10)	(29.11)	(29.11)
A5 (education of head of household) (years)	0.033	0.014	—	0.003	—	0.014
	(0.810)	(2.925)		(0.810)		(2.925)
A6* (average education) (years)	0.020	0.022	0.020	0.021	0.022	0.022
	(4.452)	(5.172)	(4.457)	(4.605)	(4.974)	(5.172)
A7 (age of head of household) (years)	−0.000	0.002	0.001	—	—	0.002
	(−0.287)	(1.457)	(0.652)			(1.457)
E2 (education, 0 < A5 < 4)	0.029	0.074	0.032	—	—	0.074
	(0.669)	(1.709)	(0.735)			(1.709)
E3 (education, A5 = 4)	0.033	0.119	0.047	—	—	0.119
	(0.766)	(2.607)	(0.974)			(2.607)
E4 (education, A5 > 4)	0.048	0.166	0.067	—	—	0.166
	(0.948)	(3.031)	(1.146)			(3.031)
HM (1 if male; 0 if female)	0.082	0.111	0.082	0.087	0.095	0.111
	(1.915)	(2.716)	(1.929)	(2.097)	(2.326)	(2.716)

Note: Numbers in parentheses are *t* ratios. The variables are defined in Table 4–7.
— Not applicable.

Table 5-7. Regressions of Production Functions for Korean Nonmechanical Farms, with Education Measured by the Household Average
(sample = 541)

Independent variable	Minimum estimate	Maximum estimate	Maximum R^2 (0.623)	Maximum $\bar{R}^2$ (0.611)	Maximum R^{*2} (0.599)	Estimate of highest t ratio
Land	0.112	0.130	0.113	0.112	0.114	0.130
	(4.806)	(5.645)	(4.848)	(4.806)	(4.893)	(5.645)
Capital	0.043	0.060	0.044	0.045	0.045	0.060
	(1.945)	(2.802)	(2.017)	(2.034)	(2.056)	(2.802)
Labor	0.357	0.376	0.358	0.357	0.364	0.373
	(8.439)	(8.808)	(8.365)	(8.439)	(8.681)	(8.843)
Animal power	0.065	0.069	0.069	0.066	0.066	0.068
	(2.123)	(2.275)	(2.270)	(2.200)	(2.191)	(2.275)
Fertilizer	0.192	0.196	0.195	0.193	0.194	0.196
	(8.420)	(8.746)	(8.623)	(8.631)	(8.689)	(8.746)
Region 1	6.051	6.340	6.279	6.340	6.327	6.349
	(15.82)	(17.59)	(16.32)	(17.59)	(17.55)	(17.59)
Region 2	5.788	6.078	6.032	6.078	6.067	6.078
	(15.10)	(16.75)	(15.60)	(16.75)	(16.72)	(16.75)
Region 3	5.332	5.649	5.582	5.649	5.635	5.649
	(14.09)	(15.79)	(14.63)	(15.79)	(15.75)	(15.79)
Region 4	5.962	6.274	6.211	6.274	6.261	6.274
	(15.50)	(17.13)	(16.01)	(17.13)	(17.09)	(17.13)
Region 5	5.772	6.089	6.023	6.089	6.067	6.089
	(15.28)	(17.04)	(15.81)	(17.04)	(16.98)	(17.04)

	(1)	(2)	(3)	(4)	(5)	(6)
Region 6	5.940	6.259	6.199	6.259	6.241	6.259
	(15.72)	(17.47)	(16.23)	(17.47)	(17.42)	(17.47)
Region 7	5.780	6.105	6.045	6.105	6.088	6.105
	(15.59)	(17.37)	(16.12)	(17.37)	(17.33)	(17.37)
Region 8	5.791	6.068	6.012	6.068	6.059	6.068
	(15.59)	(17.38)	(16.10)	(17.38)	(17.35)	(17.38)
Region 9	5.392	5.729	5.674	5.729	5.702	5.729
	(13.87)	(15.52)	(14.42)	(15.52)	(15.47)	(15.52)
A5 (education of head of household) (years)	−0.026	0.011	—	−0.026	−0.022	−0.026
	(−2.344)	(1.358)		(−2.344)	(−2.095)	(−2.344)
A6 (average education) (years)	0.025	0.051	0.048	0.051	0.050	0.051
	(2.762)	(3.572)	(3.422)	(3.572)	(3.467)	(3.572)
A7 (age of head of household) (years)	0.000	0.002	0.000	0.002	—	0.002
	(0.117)	(1.406)	(0.117)	(1.406)		(1.406)
E2 (education, 0 < A5 < 4)	−0.026	0.082	−0.026	0.082	—	0.082
	(−0.365)	(1.260)	(−0.352)	(1.260)		(1.260)
E3 (education, A5 = 4)	−0.134	0.082	−0.130	−0.134	—	−0.134
	(−1.602)	(1.180)	(−1.404)	(−1.602)		(−1.602)
E4 (education, A5 > 4)	−0.229	0.124	−0.222	−0.229	—	−0.229
	(−1.915)	(1.383)	(−1.670)	(−1.915)		(−1.915)
HM (1 if male; 0 if female)	0.045	0.083	0.076	0.083	—	0.083
	(0.706)	(1.266)	(1.120)	(1.266)		(1.266)

Note: Numbers in parentheses are *t* ratios. The variables are defined in Table 4–7.
— Not applicable.

127

Table 5–8. *Regressions of Production Functions for Korean Nonmechanical Farms, with Education Measured by the Household Average, Excluding the Head of the Household* (sample = 541)

Independent variable	Minimum estimate	Maximum estimate	Maximum R^2 (0.621)	Maximum $\bar{R}^2$ (0.608)	Maximum R^{*2} (0.597)	Estimate of highest t ratio
Land	0.117 (5.026)	0.130 (5.645)	0.118 (5.055)	0.118 (5.089)	0.118 (5.089)	0.130 (5.645)
Capital	0.047 (2.185)	0.060 (2.802)	0.048 (2.192)	0.049 (2.237)	0.049 (2.237)	0.060 (2.802)
Labor	0.351 (8.231)	0.376 (8.808)	0.354 (8.177)	0.357 (8.452)	0.357 (8.452)	0.376 (8.808)
Animal power	0.065 (2.123)	0.071 (2.321)	0.070 (2.313)	0.069 (2.275)	0.069 (2.275)	0.071 (2.321)
Fertilizer	0.192 (8.420)	0.196 (8.663)	0.190 (8.405)	0.193 (8.589)	0.193 (8.589)	0.196 (8.663)
Region 1	6.051 (15.82)	6.362 (17.48)	6.296 (16.16)	6.350 (17.46)	6.350 (17.46)	6.362 (17.48)
Region 2	5.788 (15.10)	6.102 (16.64)	6.039 (15.43)	6.092 (16.62)	6.092 (16.62)	6.102 (16.64)
Region 3	5.332 (14.09)	5.668 (15.68)	5.595 (14.45)	5.654 (15.65)	5.654 (15.65)	5.668 (15.68)
Region 4	5.962 (15.50)	6.283 (16.99)	6.220 (15.82)	6.272 (16.97)	6.272 (16.97)	6.283 (16.99)
Region 5	5.772 (15.28)	6.109 (16.90)	6.039 (15.62)	6.090 (16.88)	6.090 (16.88)	6.109 (16.90)

Region 6	5.940	6.277	6.214	6.262	6.262	6.277
	(15.72)	(17.30)	(16.03)	(17.28)	(17.28)	(17.30)
Region 7	5.783	6.115	6.055	6.099	6.099	6.115
	(15.59)	(17.23)	(15.92)	(17.20)	(17.20)	(17.23)
Region 8	5.791	6.096	6.032	6.086	6.086	6.096
	(15.59)	(17.29)	(15.93)	(17.27)	(17.27)	(17.29)
Region 9	5.392	5.732	5.681	5.713	5.713	5.732
	(13.87)	(15.37)	(14.25)	(15.34)	(15.34)	(15.37)
A5 (education of head of household) (years)	−0.002	0.011	—	—	—	0.011
	(−0.265)	(1.358)				(1.358)
A6* (average education) (years)	0.022	0.024	0.023	0.023	0.023	0.023
	(2.648)	(2.886)	(2.796)	(2.947)	(2.947)	(2.962)
A7 (age of head of household) (years)	0.000	0.002	0.000	—	—	0.002
	(0.189)	(1.058)	(0.189)			(1.058)
E2 (education, 0 < A5 < 4)	0.052	0.082	0.053	—	—	0.824
	(0.771)	(1.260)	(0.779)			(1.260)
E3 (education, A5 = 4)	−0.000	0.082	0.001	—	—	0.821
	(−0.004)	(1.180)	(0.081)			(1.180)
E4 (education, A5 > 4)	0.005	0.124	0.014	—	—	0.124
	(0.063)	(1.383)	(0.146)			(1.383)
HM (1 if male; 0 if female)	0.050	0.076	0.059	—	—	0.076
	(0.747)	(1.185)	(0.871)			(1.185)

Note: Numbers in parentheses are t ratios. The variables are defined in Table 4–7.
— Not applicable.

129

education of the work force matters in Korean nonmechanical farms.

One proposed explanation of why the education of the head of household (as opposed to the average education of all adult members of the household) does not appear to affect the productivity of Korean farms is based on the hypothesis that the educated heads of households had greater off-farm employment opportunities than those who were uneducated. Thus, the argument goes, the educated heads of households were likely to spend less of their time on their farms and consequently had less of a discernible effect on farm productivities. An examination of the data on nonfarm income for our Korean sample reveals that among mechanical farms, those with educated heads of households had an average off-farm income (including side business receipts, nonagricultural wages, salaries, rents and interest, gifts, and other income, but excluding agricultural wages) of 110,389 wons, whereas those with uneducated heads had an average off-farm income of 47,312 wons. Among nonmechanical farms, however, those with educated heads of households had an average off-farm income of 88,188 wons, compared with 74,286 wons for those with uneducated heads. These figures suggest that although the off-farm opportunities were much greater for educated than for uneducated heads of mechanical farm households, they did not differ significantly between educated and uneducated heads of nonmechanical farm households. For mechanical farms, the proposed explanation seems sufficient to account for the absence of a strong positive observable effect of the education of the heads of household on farm productivity. For nonmechanical farms, however, the proposed explanation does not seem to be sufficient, given that the off-farm employment opportunities appeared to be the same for both educated and uneducated heads of households. An alternative explanation will have to be sought.

It is of interest to compare the Korean results with the Thai results. The two groups of farms that seem most comparable are the Korean nonmechanical farms and the Thai chemical farms because they have, aside from animal power, approximately the same set of distinguished inputs. The relative magnitudes of the estimates of the production elasticities of Korean farms, however, are quite different from those of Thai farms. The estimated land elasticity of Korean nonmechanical farms is between 0.12 and 0.14 and is only one-third of the estimated labor elasticity, which ranges between

0.35 and 0.37. In contrast, the estimated land elasticity for Thai chemical farms is between 0.39 and 0.58 and is generally larger than the estimated labor elasticity, which ranges between 0.22 and 0.41. The estimated fertilizer elasticity is also higher in Korea than in Thailand. In addition, the estimated Korean production function exhibits rather significant decreasing returns to scale, whereas the estimated Thai production function exhibits constant or even slightly increasing returns to scale.

Finally, the one significant contrast between the Korean non-mechanical farms and the Thai chemical farms is in the effect of education. For Korean nonmechanical farms, it is found that the education of the head of household does not have a statistically significant effect on productivity. Rather, it is the average education of the adult household members 17 to 60 years old other than the head of household that has a consistently statistically significant positive effect. In contrast, for Thai chemical farms, the education of the head of household has a statistically significant positive effect on productivity, whereas average education of the adult household members 17 to 60 years old never has a statistically significant effect. We do not have a satisfactory explanation of these opposite findings in the two countries, but the key may lie in the different rice cultivation practices used, which possibly reflect the different natural factor endowments of the two countries.

Malaysian farms

The Malaysian sample consists of farm households that all had some experience in double cropping. As discussed in Chapter 4, however, these farm households can be further classified into three groups: those with 1 year of double-cropping experience, those with 2 years of double-cropping experience, and those with 3 or more years of double-cropping experience.

The production function regressions results for Malaysian farms are reported in Table 5–9. Regressions were run for the pooled sample—regressions 1, 2, and 3. Two facts stand out immediately. First, except for the capital elasticity, the production elasticities are all statistically significant and have the correct signs. They are also broadly comparable in order of magnitude to the production elasticity estimates for Thai farms. Second, prior double-cropping experience has a strong and statistically significant negative effect on

Table 5–9. Regressions of Production Functions for Malaysian Farms

Independent variable	Equations					
	1	2	3	Within STR4 (1 year's experience) 4	Within STR6 (2 years' experience) 5	Within STR8 (3 or more years' experience) 6
Constant	2.986	2.918	2.954	3.478	2.642	2.295
L Labor	0.305	0.307	0.308	0.162	0.358	0.381
	(4.55)	(4.606)	(4.582)	(1.464)	(2.991)	(3.334)
V Other variable inputs	0.075	0.075	0.082	0.010	0.039	0.142
	(2.811)	(2.802)	(3.024)	(0.219)	(0.860)	(3.108)
K Capital	0.019	0.023	0.011	0.043	0.062	−0.014
	(0.652)	(0.811)	(0.381)	(0.939)	(1.139)	(−0.283)
T Land	0.619	0.601	0.618	0.712	0.553	0.558
	(9.332)	(9.032)	(9.289)	(6.034)	(4.850)	(4.95)
Double-cropping dummy variables						
STR6 2 years' experience	−0.122	−0.103	−0.114	—	—	—
	(−2.018)	(−1.699)	(1.858)			
STR8 3 or more years' experience	−0.264	−0.230	−0.257	—	—	—
	(−4.482)	(−3.799)	(4.334)			

Education dummy variables

LIT	Literate	—	-0.109 (1.614)	-0.161 (1.072)	0.186 (1.424)	0.123 (1.003)	0.104 (1.007)
EDS	Some primary, 1–3 years' religious	—	0.071 (1.139)	0.025 (0.249)	0.212 (1.813)	0.151 (1.479)	-0.085 (-0.812)
EDL	Finished primary, more than 3 years' religious	—	0.186 (2.599)	0.064 (0.612)	0.397 (3.434)	0.065 (0.550)	0.178 (1.221)
EDA	Attended adult class	—	0.237 (1.733)	-0.379 (-0.789)	0.333 (1.288)	-0.175 (-0.802)	0.618 (2.639)
EDB	Some secondary school or beyond	—	—	0.003 (0.032)	—	—	—
	Sample	403	403	403	109	137	157
	R^2	0.687	0.694	0.831	0.765	0.685	0.696

Note: Numbers in parentheses are t ratios.
— Not applicable.

133

output, and the effect is stronger the longer the prior experience.[6] One possible explanation for this phenomenon is the depletion of the natural fertility of the soil as a result of more intense double cropping. Another possible explanation is the change in the procedure of selecting new migrants for settlement in the Muda River area. The selection process might have been tightened up so that later settlers were screened more carefully than the earlier ones. Moreover, these changes in the selection standards were not reflected in the observed characteristic variables.[7] If data were available on the soil fertility and settlement date of individual farms, both of these explanations could be tested.

In the second pooled regression, equation (2), the education of the head of household has large and statistically significant positive effects on output. Completion of primary education (or more than 3 years of religious education) increases output by almost 19 percent. Translated to a yearly basis, this amounts to a gain of approximately 4.5 percent per year of additional education. This is comparable to the magnitude of the estimated effect of education for Thai farms.

In the third pooled regression, equation (3), another education variable, the highest level of education achieved by any male member of the farm household, is used instead of the education of the head of household. This education variable has no statistically significant estimated effect whatsoever. An examination of the data indicates that 60 percent of these male members were not the heads of their respective households. This is consistent with the finding in Thailand that it is the educational level of the head of household, the decisionmaker, that makes a difference. But it is directly opposite to the finding in Korea.

When the farms are divided into three groups according to their experience with double cropping (1 year, 2 years, and 3 or more years), a more complex pattern of effects emerges. With only 1 year's experience, education has a substantial and statistically significant positive effect. Completion of primary education (or more than 3 years of religious education) increases output by almost 40 percent. Translated to a yearly basis, this amounts to a gain of 10 percent per year of additional education. With 2 years of experience, however, education is no longer statistically significant. With 3

6. The same phenomenon has been observed by Barnum and Squire (1978), pp. 189–93; see also Barnum and Squire (1979), pp. 48–53.
7. This is due to Robert Evenson.

years of experience, only adult classes make a statistically significant difference. But the effect is enormous: attendance of adult classes makes a difference of 60 percent in the productivity of the three-year group. Unfortunately, information is not available on the exact content and duration of these adult classes. If they were in fact agricultural extension and farm management classes, this result would indicate that they were tremendously effective in raising the productivity of even experienced farmers.[8]

Our interpretation of the difference between farmers with 1 year of experience and 2 or more years of experience is based on the speed of learning and adaptation to a new environment. With 1 year of experience, there may still be a substantial quantity of knowledge to be acquired, and formal education enhances the ability of the head of household to acquire that knowledge and therefore increases his productivity. Even farmers without formal education, however, can learn through experience, although probably at a slower rate. By the end of the second year of experience, it is possible that whatever advantages that formal education confers on a head of household in his learning process have been exhausted and that further progress no longer depends on the quantity of past formal education, but on the availability of specific agricultural knowledge, which can be acquired through adult classes. This is indeed consistent with Schultz's argument that education tends to be much more important in a "modernizing environment," that is, an environment of innovative change.

Our results here are also consistent with the notion that a minimum quantity of formal education, a threshold, must be exceeded before education becomes useful. It appears that completion of primary education (or more than 3 years of religious education) is the critical dividing line. In Thailand, 4 years of formal education seems to be the critical dividing line.

Restrictiveness of the Neutrality Assumption

The empirical results reported above for Thai, Korean, and Malaysian farms are all conditional on the maintained hypothesis that given the choice of a technology (using chemical inputs or not

---

8. An alternative explanation of this productivity differential can be based on self-selection.

using chemical inputs, using mechanical power or not using mechanical power), educated and uneducated farms differ in their technological levels only by a scalar multiplier depending on the values of the education variables. To assess the restrictiveness of this neutrality assumption for the Thai farms, farms that chose the same technology, say, those using chemical inputs, were subdivided further into educated and uneducated farms. A Chow (1960) test was performed on the hypothesis that the production elasticities of the educated and uneducated farms are the same. Since the only characteristic variables that have been found to have consistently statistically significant effects are formal education of the head of household and the availability of agricultural extension services, the other characteristic variables were dropped from the Chow test regressions. Thus, separately for educated and uneducated farms, production functions of the form

$$\ln Y^i = \alpha_L^i \ln L + \alpha_C^i \ln C + \beta_K^i \ln K + \beta_T^i \ln T$$
$$+ \Sigma_{l=1}^4 \delta_{R_l}^i R_l + \delta_{EXT}^i EXT, \qquad (i = E, NE)$$

were estimated, where the superscripts E and NE stand for the educated and uneducated farms, respectively. The educated and uneducated farms are then pooled, and new regressions are estimated in which the restrictions corresponding to hypotheses (5.6), (5.7), and (5.8), below, are successively imposed. Given a technology, the first Chow test is the following null hypothesis:

(5.6)
$$\alpha_L^E = \alpha_L^{NE}$$
$$\alpha_C^E = \alpha_C^{NE}$$
$$\beta_K^E = \beta_K^{NE}$$
$$\beta_T^E = \beta_T^{NE}.$$

An alternative Chow test that is more stringent requires not only that the production elasticities be the same, but also that the coefficients corresponding to the regional dummy variables be the same, that is,

(5.7)
$$\alpha_L^E = \alpha_L^{NE}$$
$$\alpha_C^E = \alpha_C^{NE}$$
$$\beta_K^E = \beta_K^{NE}$$
$$\beta_T^E = \beta_T^{NE}$$
$$\delta_{Rl}^E = \delta_{Rl}^{NE}. \qquad (l = 1, \ldots, 4).$$

Another alternative Chow test that is even more stringent requires that the coefficients corresponding to the extension variable be equal as well:

(5.8)
$$\alpha_L^E = \alpha_L^{NE}$$
$$\alpha_C^E = \alpha_C^{NE}$$
$$\beta_C^E = \beta_K^{NE}$$
$$\beta_T^E = \beta_T^{NE}$$
$$\delta_{Rl}^E = \delta_{Rl}^{NE} \qquad (l = 1, \ldots, 4)$$
$$\delta_{EXT}^E = \delta_{EXT}^{NE}.$$

The test statistics are computed from the sum of squares of residuals of the separate regressions and the pooled regressions, under the three alternative hypotheses. This process is repeated for the nonchemical farms in Thailand. The results of the Chow tests are presented in Table 5–10.

It is evident from Table 5–10 that, at a significance level of 0.05, one cannot reject the hypothesis that education has a neutral effect on productivity in Thailand. That is, the sole effect of education is to raise or lower the technological level and not to change the form of the production function. It does not have a statistically significant effect on the production elasticities, the coefficients of the regional dummy variables, or the coefficient of agricultural extension. We conclude that the hypothesis of neutrality we maintained is consistent with the empirical evidence for Thailand.

Table 5–10. *Tests of the Neutrality Hypotheses, for Thai Chemical and Nonchemical Farms*

Hypothesis	Degrees of freedom	Test statistic	Critical values at given levels of significance		
			0.10	0.05	0.01
Chemical farms					
(1)	(4,71)	1.64	2.02	2.50	3.58
(2)	(8,71)	1.33	1.75	2.07	2.75
(3)	(9,71)	1.26	1.71	2.01	2.69
Nonchemical farms					
(1)	(3,166)	0.39	2.10	2.65	3.90
(2)	(7,166)	1.81	1.75	2.06	2.74
(3)	(8,166)	1.62	1.70	1.99	2.61

To assess the restrictiveness of the neutrality assumption for the Korean farms, interaction effects between the educational variables (education of the head of household and average education of the adult members of the household) on the one hand and the physical inputs, regional dummy, and sex dummy variables on the other were estimated. Statistical tests were performed to ascertain whether these estimated effects are statistically significant. Thus, separately for mechanical and nonmechanical farms, production functions of the form:

$$\ln Y = \Sigma_{i=1}^{4} \alpha_i \ln X_i + \Sigma_{i=1}^{2} \beta_i \ln Z_i + \Sigma_{l=1}^{9} \delta_{R_l} R_l$$
$$+ \delta_1 A5 + \delta_2 A6 + \delta_3 HM$$
$$+ \Sigma_{i=1}^{4} \Sigma_{j=5}^{6} \varepsilon_{ij} \ln X_i \cdot A_j + \Sigma_{i=1}^{2} \Sigma_{j=5}^{6} \eta_{ij} \ln Z_i \cdot A_j$$
$$+ \Sigma_{l=1}^{9} \Sigma_{j=5}^{6} \xi_{lj} R_l \cdot A_j + \Sigma_{j=5}^{6} \tau_j HM \cdot A_j$$

were estimated. As in the case of Thai farms, there are three alternative hypotheses of neutrality of different degrees of stringency which can be tested. Given a technology, the first hypothesis is

(5.9)
$$\varepsilon_{ij} = 0 \qquad (i = 1, \ldots, 4: j = 5, 6)$$
$$\eta_{ij} = 0. \qquad (i = 1, 2; j = 5, 6)$$

This null hypothesis implies that the education variables do not interact with the physical input variables although they may interact with the regional and sex dummy variables. An alternative and more stringent hypothesis requires neutrality not only with respect to the physical input variables, but also with respect to the regional dummy variables, that is,

(5.10)
$$\varepsilon_{ij} = 0 \qquad (i = 1, \ldots, 4; j = 5, 6)$$
$$\eta_{ij} = 0 \qquad (i = 1, 2; j = 5, 6)$$
$$\xi_{lj} = 0. \qquad (l = 1, \ldots, 9; j = 5, 6)$$

This null hypothesis implies that the education variables do not interact with the physical input or the regional dummy variables although they may interact with the sex dummy variable. Finally, the most stringent hypothesis requires that the education variables be neutral with respect to the effect of the sex dummy variable as well, that is,

$$\varepsilon_{ij} = 0 \qquad\qquad (i = 1, \ldots, 4; j = 5, 6)$$

(5.11)
$$\eta_{ij} = 0 \qquad\qquad (i = 1, 2; j = 5, 6)$$

$$\xi_{lj} = 0 \qquad\qquad (l = 1, \ldots, 9; j = 5, 6)$$

$$\tau_j = 0. \qquad\qquad (j = 5, 6)$$

This null hypothesis implies that the education variables do not interact with any of the other independent variables. In other words, the neutrality assumption holds.

Table 5–11. *Tests of the Neutrality Hypotheses,*
for Korean Mechanical and Nonmechanical Farms

Hypothesis	Degrees of freedom	Test statistic		Critical values at given levels of significance		
		A6	A6*	0.10	0.05	0.01
Mechanical farms						
(1)	(12,1317)	1.076	1.079	1.55	1.75	2.18
(2)	(30,1317)	0.619	0.704	1.34	1.46	1.70
(3)	(32,1317)	0.617	0.723	1.33	1.45	1.69
Nonmechanical farms						
(1)	(10,498)	0.945	0.900	1.60	1.83	2.32
(2)	(28,498)	1.407	1.244	1.35	1.47	1.71
(3)	(30,498)	1.460	1.403	1.34	1.46	1.70

The test statistics for these hypotheses for mechanical and nonmechanical farms and for both choices of the average education variable are presented in Table 5–11. It is evident from Table 5–11 that, at a significance level of 0.05, one cannot reject any of the hypotheses that the effect of education on productivity is also neutral for Korea. This is particularly true for the cases in which the variable A6* is used as the average education variable. We conclude that our maintained hypothesis of neutrality is also consistent with the empirical evidence for Korea.

CHAPTER 6

Education and Profitability

ALLOCATIVE EFFICIENCY REFERS to a farmer's ability to maximize profit given his production function, the quantity of fixed inputs, and the prices of output and variable inputs. A farm household is said to be allocatively efficient if the marginal product of every variable input is equal to the price of the variable input normalized by the price of output, that is,

$$(6.1) \qquad \partial F/\partial X_i \,(X, Z, E) = q_i^*/p_0, \;\; \forall\, i$$

where $F(X, Z, E)$ is the production function of the farm, X is the vector of quantities of variable inputs, Z is the vector of quantities of fixed inputs, E is a vector of characteristic variables, which includes the quantity of education of the head of household, q_i^* is the price of the ith variable input, and p_0 is the price of output. We include the education variable explicitly in the production function to emphasize that the production function—the level of technology itself— may depend on education.

One way to ascertain whether education improves allocative efficiency is to separate the farms into groups with different educational levels and test, for each group, whether the marginal conditions for profit maximization are satisfied. If these conditions are not satisfied for one or more groups, one can then proceed to examine if the ability to maximize profit depends on the quantity of education of each group. This is the approach taken in this study. The methodology used depends on the concept of a profit function and is described below for the case of one input and in Appendix D for the case of multiple inputs. The empirical implementation of the profit function approach requires observed variations for all farms in the prices of output and variable inputs.

There are at least two other ways to study the effect of education on allocative efficiency using data on prices for individual farms.[1] First, suppose that the marginal conditions in equation (6.1) do not hold. Instead, the marginal products of the variable inputs are equal to some functions of the prices of output and variable inputs. Specifically, they are equal to homogeneous linear functions of the prices of variable inputs normalized by the price of output. Thus, in vector notation,

(6.2) $$\partial F/\partial X \, (X, Z, E) = Kq^*/p_0$$

where $\partial F/\partial X(\cdot)$ is the vector of marginal products, K is a square matrix of parameters, and q^* is the vector of prices of variable inputs. The matrix K indicates the degree to which profit is maximized. If $K = I$, the identity matrix, then we are back in the profit maximization case. The matrix of parameters K can be made a function of the quantity of education, and then the dependence of K on E can be studied. Lau and Yotopoulos (1971) have analyzed a special case of equation (6.2) with K equal to a constant diagonal matrix.[2]

Second, again in equation (6.1), suppose that a farm household cannot respond instantaneously to a change in the prices of output and variable inputs, but takes time to adjust to a new equilibrium. One may hypothesize that the speed of adjustment depends on the quantity of education.

The above two models can be combined, so that both the equilibrium conditions of equation (6.2) and the speed of adjustment toward this nonprofit-maximizing equilibrium may depend on the quantity of education.

In Chapter 3 the concept of market efficiency was introduced to describe the extent of an agent's capacity to influence prices, in imperfect markets, in a direction favorable to himself. Market efficiency is then, like allocative efficiency, a concept of efficiency defined in terms of prices. In this chapter the application of the profit function approach to measure allocative efficiency is de-

1. If data on prices are available only for regions, it is possible to insert those prices into equation (6.1) with an estimated production function and examine the extent to which each farm in the sample maximizes profit. Previous studies that lacked data on prices for individual farms have typically found the effect of education on allocative efficiency, assessed in this way, to be more substantial than its effect on the level of technology.

2. See Lau and Yotopoulos (1971) and Yotopoulos and Lau (1973).

scribed, then the empirical findings from Thailand on allocative efficiency are discussed followed by the findings on market efficiency from Thailand.

Allocative Efficiency and the Normalized Restricted Profit Function

In this section we introduce the concept of a normalized restricted profit function and formulate a model within which questions of allocative efficiency can be studied. We largely follow the approach developed by Lau and Yotopoulos. For the sake of simplicity, the concept of a normalized restricted profit function is presented primarily within the context of a technology having one output and one variable input. A complete technical exposition of the concept of a normalized restricted profit function is presented in Appendix D for the case of a technology in which an arbitrary but finite number of variable inputs is allowed.

Normalized restricted profit function

We begin with the familiar concept of a production function with one output and one variable input. Let the production function of a farm be given by

$$Y = F(X)$$

where Y is the quantity of output, X is the quantity of variable input, and the quantities of fixed inputs are suppressed for convenience. It is assumed that zero variable input implies zero output, that is, $F(0) = 0$. Restricted profit for the farm, defined as revenue less variable cost, is given by

$$P^* = p_0 F(X) - q^* X$$

where P_0 is the price of output, and q^* is the price of the variable input. It is assumed that the farm operator maximizes profit, that is, he selects the quantity of the variable input, X, for which the profit of the farm is at the maximum, taking the prices of output and the variable input and the quantities of the fixed inputs as given. Whatever value of X maximizes profit, P^*, also maximizes normalized profit, P, which is defined as

(6.3) $$P \equiv P^*/p_0 = F(X) - qX$$

where $q \equiv q^*/p_0$ is the normalized price of the variable input. As a result, the maximization of normalized profit may be considered equivalently in the analysis of the production behavior of the farm.

The first-order condition for maximizing normalized profit is given by the usual rule that equates marginal product of a variable input to its opportunity cost:

(6.4) $$dF/dX = q.$$

Under mild regularity conditions equation (6.4) may be solved for X as a function of q, say,

$$X = D(q).$$

$D(q)$ then gives the quantity of the variable input needed to maximize profit as a function of its normalized price, q. Substituting the demand function back into equation (6.3) gives

(6.5) $$P = F[D(q)] - qD(q),$$

so that the maximized normalized profit can be expressed as a function of q alone. Equation (6.5) thus gives the maximized value of normalized profit at normalized price, q. In other words, given any normalized input price, q, if the farm maximizes profit, then its maximized normalized profit will be given by equation (6.5). Of course, to the extent that the farm fails to maximize profit, its actual normalized profit will be less than the maximized normalized profit. The function on the right-hand side of equation (6.5) will be referred to as the normalized profit function and denoted by Π, so that

(6.6) $$\Pi(q) \equiv F[D(q)] - qD(q).$$

$\Pi(q)$ has several remarkable properties. First, differentiating equation (6.6) with respect to q gives

$$d\Pi(q)/dq = dF/dX \, dD(q)/dq - D(q) - q \, dD(q)/dq.$$

But $dF/dX = q$ by virtue of the assumption of profit maximization, hence

(6.7) $$-d\Pi(q)/dq = D(q).$$

In other words, the negative of the derivative of the normalized profit function is the demand function. This result is sometimes referred to as the Hotelling-Shephard lemma.[3] There are two aspects of the plausibility of this result. First, the demand function $D(q)$ must be positive, and intuition suggests that as the price of an input increases, profit should fall, which implies that $d\Pi/dq$ is negative. Second, if input demand is small, then profit cannot be too sensitive to changes in the input price, that is, $d\Pi/dq$ should be small also. If input demand is large, then $d\Pi/dq$ should be large. Equation (6.7) generalizes to the case of m multiple variable inputs, in which the negative of the vector of partial derivatives of the normalized profit function is the vector of demand functions for the variable inputs:

$$- \partial\Pi/\partial q_i\,(q) = D_i(q) \qquad (i = 1, \ldots, m).$$

Not any arbitrary function $\Pi(q)$ can be admissible as a normalized profit function. It must be nonnegative, monotonically decreasing, and convex in the normalized price. To see that a normalized profit function must be nonnegative for all normalized prices, one need only observe that the farm always has the option of simply shutting down, thus using zero variable input, and producing zero output, resulting in zero profit. A firm that maximizes profit will therefore never operate with negative profit. To see that a normalized profit function must be nonincreasing in the normalized price, consider two normalized prices, q, q', such that $q > q'$. Let X^* and X'^* be the quantities of the variable inputs needed to maximize profit at q and q', respectively. Then

$\Pi(q') = F(X'^*) - q'X'^*$, by the definition of a profit function,

$\qquad \geqq F(X^*) - q'X^*$, since X'^* maximizes profit at q',

$\qquad \geqq F(X^*) - qX^*$, since $q > q'$,

$\qquad = \Pi(q)$.

One implication of the monotonicity of $\Pi(q)$ is that the derivative of the normalized profit function is less than or equal to zero:

$$d\Pi/dq\,(q) \leqq 0.$$

Finally a function $\Pi(q)$ is convex in q if

$$(1 - \lambda)\,\Pi\,(q) + \lambda\,\Pi(q') \geqq \Pi((1 - \lambda)q + \lambda q') \qquad (\forall\,\lambda,\ 1 \geqq \lambda \geqq 0).$$

3. See Hotelling (1935) and Shephard (1953).

To see that a normalized profit function must be convex in the normalized price, again consider two normalized prices, q, q', and their convex combination, $q_\lambda = (1 - \lambda)q + \lambda q'$, $1 \geq \lambda \geq 0$. Let X_λ^* be the quantity of the variable input needed to maximize profit at normalized price q_λ. Then

$$\Pi(q) \geq F(X_\lambda^*) - qX_\lambda^*, \text{ since } \Pi(q) \text{ is maximum profit at } q,$$

$$\Pi(q') \geq F(X_\lambda^*) - q'X_\lambda^*, \text{ since } \Pi(q') \text{ is maximum profit at } q'.$$

If the first inequality is multiplied by $(1 - \lambda)$ and the second inequality by λ, and then they are added together,

$$(1 - \lambda)\Pi(q) + \lambda \Pi(q') \geq F(X_\lambda^*) - ((1 - \lambda)q + \lambda q') \cdot X_\lambda^*$$
$$= \Pi(q_\lambda).$$

One implication of the convexity of the normalized profit function is that the second derivative of the normalized profit function is nonnegative:

$$d^2 \Pi (q)/dq^2 \geq 0.$$

It can be proved, under mild regularity conditions, that there is a one-to-one correspondence between production functions on the one hand and normalized profit functions on the other, so that given a production function, the normalized profit function is uniquely determined and vice versa. This one-to-one correspondence implies that if the assumption of profit maximization is maintained, the analysis can just as well start with a normalized profit function as a production function, because a production function must exist that gives rise to the normalized profit function. The advantage of starting with a normalized profit function lies in the fact that the demand function can be obtained simply by differentiation. If one starts with a production function, the demand function can be obtained only by solving an optimization problem as, for example, in equation (6.4). If one starts with a normalized profit function, however, one should verify that it is indeed nonnegative, monotonically decreasing, and convex in the normalized price in the range of normalized prices of interest.

Having obtained the demand function from the normalized profit function, the supply function can be readily derived. Revenue is given by the product of the price of output, p_0, and supply, y. Profit, however, is given by revenue minus cost, so that nonnormalized profit is equal to

$$p_0 \, \Pi \, (q) = p_0 \, Y(q) - p_0 q D(q),$$

which, by dividing through by p_0 and solving for $Y(q)$, yields

(6.8) $$Y(q) = \Pi(q) + q \cdot D(q)$$
$$= \Pi(q) - q \cdot d \, \Pi \, (q)/dq \, .$$

Thus, by specifying a normalized profit function $\Pi \, (q)$, the demand and supply functions can be obtained immediately by equations (6.7) and (6.8), that is, as functions of q above. Equation (6.8) also generalizes to the case of multiple variable inputs with the supply function given by:

(6.9) $$Y(q) = \Pi \, (q) - \Sigma_{i=1}^{m} \, q_i \, \partial \, \Pi \, (q)/\partial q_i \, .$$

Test of profit maximization

The normalized profit function not only is useful in modeling farms that maximize profit, but it also provides an analytical framework within which the hypothesis of profit maximization can be statistically tested. This idea is illustrated again with reference to the case of one output and one variable input. Suppose that the normalized profit and the input demand of a farm are observed at different normalized prices. In addition, for the purpose of illustration, assume that the normalized profit function takes the form

(6.10) $$\Pi \, (q) = Aq^{\alpha} \qquad\qquad (\alpha < 0).$$

Then input demand is given by equation (6.7) as

$$D(q) = - \, d \, \Pi \, /dq = - \, A\alpha q^{(\alpha - 1)}$$

which implies that

(6.11) $$- \, q \, D(q)/ \Pi = \alpha$$

that is, the ratio of the cost of variable input to profit is a constant equal to α.

By taking natural logarithms of equation (6.10),

(6.12) $$\ln \Pi = \ln A + \alpha \ln q \, .$$

Equations (6.11) and (6.12) form a pair. Given observations of normalized profits and input demands at different normalized prices, the parameters of these equations can be estimated. But there are two possible estimates for α: one from equation (6.11), the factor share function, and one from equation (6.12), the normalized profit function. For any particular sample of observations the two estimates are not necessarily identical. If indeed the farm maximizes profit, however, then the parameter α in the two equations must be identical. Thus, a test of the hypothesis of profit maximization consists of verifying whether the two alternative estimates are in fact equal.

More generally, let the normalized profit function be

$$(6.13) \qquad\qquad \Pi(q) = G(q)$$

where $G(q)$ is a nonnegative, monotonically decreasing, and convex function. Then the input demand function is given by

$$(6.14) \qquad\qquad D(q) = -\,dG(q)/dq\,.$$

Since $D(q)$ is the negative of the derivative of $G(q)$, its parameters must be a subset of the parameters of $\Pi(q)$, which is equal to $G(q)$. Again, given an algebraic form for $G(q)$ and observations of normalized profits and input demands at different normalized prices, the parameters of $G(q)$ can be estimated. A subset of such parameters will appear in both equations (6.13) and (6.14) and hence can be estimated in two different ways: one from equation (6.13) and the other from equation (6.14). If indeed the farm maximizes profit, then the two estimates should coincide. This then provides the basis for a test of the hypothesis of profit maximization in general. The same consideration for the case of multiple variable inputs leads to an analogous conclusion, with

$$\Pi(q) = G(q)$$
$$D_i(q) = -\,\partial G(q)/\partial q_i \qquad\qquad (i = 1, \ldots, m).$$

Differences in the levels of technology

Next, the effect of differences in the levels of technology between two farms on their normalized profit functions is considered. The differences in the technological levels are assumed to be neutral. The production functions of the two farms are then given by

$$Y_1 = A_1 F(X); \; Y_2 = A_2 F(X)$$

where the only difference lies in the scalar factor A_i.

The normalized profit functions of the two farms are given, respectively, by

$$\Pi_i(q) = \underset{x}{\text{Max}} \{A_i F(X) - qX\} \qquad (i = 1, 2).$$

Let $G(q) \equiv \underset{x}{\text{Max}} \{F(X) - qX\}$, that is, the normalized profit function of a farm with a production function $Y = A_i F(X)$. Then it follows that the normalized profit function of a farm with a production function $Y_i = A_i F(X)$ is given by

$$\Pi_i(q) = A_i \underset{x}{\text{Max}} \{F(X) - q/A_i X\}.$$

But $\underset{x}{\text{Max}} \{F(X) - (q/A_i)X\}$ is precisely the same as the maximized normalized profit of a farm with production function $Y = F(X)$ and facing normalized price equal to q/A_i, that is, $G(q/A_i)$. Thus,

$$\Pi_i(q) = A_i G(q/A_i) \qquad (i = 1, 2).$$

What is the effect of changes in the level of technology on the normalized profit function? It may be noted that

$$d\,\Pi_i(q)/dA_i = G(q/A_i) - q/A_i\, dG/dq\, (q/A_i).$$

Since A_i is nonnegative and $G(q)$ is nonnegative and monotonically decreasing, the effect of an increase in the technological level parameter A_i is to increase normalized profit. Thus, the farm with a higher technological level parameter will have a higher normalized profit function, that is, will have higher maximized normalized profit for all possible normalized prices.

Moreover, the relative profitability of the two farms is not necessarily proportional to the relative productivity. The relative productivity of the two farms is given by

$$Y_1/Y_2 = A_1 F(X)/A_2 F(X)$$

$$= A_1/A_2.$$

The relative profitability, however, is given by

$$\Pi_1(q)/\Pi_2(q) = A_1 G(q/A_1)/A_2 G(q/A_2).$$

Suppose that the first farm is on a higher technological level than the second farm, so that $A_1 > A_2$. Then $q/A_1 < q/A_2$, which by monotonicity of $\Pi(\cdot)$ implies that

$$G(q/A_1) > G(q/A_2)$$

so that

$$\Pi_1(q)/\Pi_2(q) > A_1/A_2.$$

In other words, differences in the levels of technology will lead to more than proportional differences in profits. For example, if $G(q) = q^\alpha$, then relative profitability is given by

$$\Pi_1(q)/\Pi_2(q) = A_1/A_2 \cdot (q/A_1)^\alpha/(q/A_2)^\alpha$$

$$= (A_1/A_2)^{1-\alpha} = (A_1/A_2)^{1+|\alpha|}$$

$$> A_1/A_2, \qquad\qquad \text{since } \alpha < 0.$$

Allocative inefficiency

Farms may, however, fail to maximize profit perfectly. Following the terminology of Chapter 3, a technically efficient farm is said to be allocatively efficient if it does maximize profit, that is, equates the marginal product of every variable input to its corresponding opportunity cost. A farm that fails to do so is said to be allocatively inefficient. The normalized profit function can also be used to assess relative allocative efficiency.

Again let there be two farms whose production functions are identical up to a multiplicative technological level parameter. Instead of equating the marginal product of the variable input to its normalized price, we assume that each of the farms equates the marginal product to a constant, not necessarily equal to one, times the normalized price, that is,

(6.15) $\qquad\qquad dY_1/dX_1 = A_1 \, dF(X_1)/dX_1 = k_1 q;$

$\qquad\qquad dY_2/dX_2 = A_2 \, dF(X_2)/dX_2 = k_2 q.$

The parameters k_1 and k_2 will be referred to as allocative efficiency parameters. Under profit maximization,

(6.16) $\qquad\qquad\qquad k_1 = k_2 = 1.$

From equation (6.15) one can, under mild regularity conditions, solve for the demand functions of the variable inputs of the two farms. In particular, since the production functions are identical up to a constant multiplicative technological level parameter, the marginal conditions are given by

$$dF/dX \, (X_1) = k_1 q/A_1; \; dF/dX \, (X_2) = k_2 q/A_2$$

which implies that farms 1 and 2 equate the marginal products of the variable input to $k_1 q/A_1$ and $k_2 q/A_2$, respectively, that is, they act as if they maximize profit, taking as given $k_1 q/A_1$ and $k_2 q/A_2$ as their respective normalized prices. If $D(q)$ is the demand function of a farm that maximizes profit with production function $F(X)$ and facing normalized price q, then the demand functions for the variable inputs for farms 1 and 2 are given by

(6.17) $$D_1(q) = D(k_1 q/A_1); \quad D_2(q) = D(k_2 q/A_2).$$

It is possible that $k_1/A_1 = k_2/A_2$, in which case the demand functions of the two farms will be identical, but that will be purely fortuitous. By equation (6.7), $D(q) = - [d\Pi(q)/dq] = - [dG(q)/dq]$, where $G(q)$ is the normalized profit function corresponding to the production function $Y = F(X)$.

The output supply function for a farm that maximizes profit with a normalized profit function $\Pi(q)$ is given in equation (6.8) as a function of q. The output supply functions of two farms with different levels of technology and allocative efficiency, as in equation (6.17), may be written as

$$Y_1(q) = A_1 F(X_1^*) \qquad\qquad Y_2(q) = A_2 F(X_2^*)$$
$$= A_1 F[D(k_1 q/A_1)] \qquad = A_2 F[D(k_2 q/A_2)]$$

where X_1^* and X_2^* are the quantities of the variable input used at normalized price, q by farms 1 and 2, respectively.

But, by definition, from equation (6.8), the output supply function is given by

$$F[D(q)] = G(q) - q\, dG/dq\,(q).$$

Thus,

$$F[D(k_i q/A_i)] = G(k_i q/A_i) - k_i q/A_i\, dG/dq\,(k_i q/A_i) \quad (i = 1, 2)$$

which leads to the output supply functions of the two farms:

(6.18) $$Y_i(q) = A_i G(k_i q/A_i) - k_i q\, dG/dq\,(k_i q/A_i) \qquad (i = 1, 2).$$

Actual normalized profit is given by

(6.19)
$$\Pi_i^a(q) = Y_i(q) - q D_i(q)$$
$$= A_i G(k_i q/A_i) - k_i q\, dG/dq\,(k_i q/A_i) + q\, dG/dq\,(k_i q/A_i)$$
$$= A_i G(k_i q/A_i) + (1 - k_i)\, q\, dG/dq\,(k_i q/A_i) \qquad (i = 1, 2).$$

This is in general not equal to $A_i G(k_i q/A_i)$. But if $k_i = 1$, that is, the ith farm is allocatively efficient, then actual normalized profit becomes

$$\Pi_i^a(q) = A_i G(q/A_i)$$

as before.

What is the effect of differences in the level of technology on the actual normalized profit function? Differentiating equation (6.19) with respect to A_i,

$$dП_i^a(q)/dA_i = G(k_iq/A_i) - dG/dq \ (k_iq/A_i) \ k_iq/A_i$$
$$- (1 - k_i) \ q \ d^2G/dq^2 \ (k_iq/A_i) \ k_iq/A_i^2$$

which by equation (6.18) may be rewritten as

$$= Y_i(q)/A_i - (1 - k_i) \ q \ d^2G/dq^2 \ (k_iq/A_i) \ k_iq/A_i^2 \ .$$

$Y_i(q)/A_i$ is nonnegative, and d^2G/dq^2 is nonnegative by virtue of convexity of $G(q)$, but $(1 - k_i)$ is indefinite in sign, and hence $dП_i^a(q)/dA_i$ is indefinite in sign. If $k_i \geq 1$, however, that is, if the ith farm overvalues the opportunity cost of the variable input, then $(1 - k_i) \leq 0$, and an increase in the level of technology increases the actual normalized profit function.

If the additional assumption is made that $\Pi(q)$ has the form

$$\Pi(q) = q^\alpha \qquad\qquad (\alpha < 0)$$

then the demand functions may be derived as

$$D_i(q) = - d\Pi/dq \ (k_iq/A_i)$$
$$= - \alpha \ (k_iq/A_i)^{\alpha - 1} \qquad\qquad (i = 1, 2)$$

where $d\Pi/dq(\cdot)$ is understood to be the first derivative function of $\Pi(\cdot)$ with respect to its argument, and the actual normalized profit functions as

$$\Pi_i^a(q) = A_i(k_iq/A_i)^\alpha + (1 - k_i)^\alpha q \ (k_iq/A_i)^{\alpha - 1}$$
$$= [A_i \ k_i^\alpha/A_i^\alpha + (1 - k_i) \ k_i^{\alpha - 1}\alpha/A_i^{\alpha - 1}] \ q^\alpha$$
$$= (k_i/A_i)^{\alpha - 1} \ [k_i + (1 - k_i)\alpha]q^\alpha$$
$$\equiv A_i^* q^\alpha \qquad\qquad (i = 1, 2)$$

so that in this case an increase in the level of technology increases the actual normalized profit function. Finally, the ratio of expenditure on the variable input to profit is given by

$$qD_i(q)/\Pi_i^a(q) = - \alpha/[k_i + (1 - k_i)\alpha] \equiv - \alpha_i^* \qquad (i = 1, 2).$$

Combining these results produces the logarithmic actual normalized profit function,

(6.20) $$\ln \Pi_i^a (q) = \ln A_i^* + \alpha \ln q$$

and the factor share function,

(6.21) $$- qD_i(q)/\Pi_i^a(q) = \alpha_i^* . \qquad (i = 1, 2)$$

$A_1^* = A_2^*$ implies equal relative economic efficiency as defined in Chapter 3. The parameters of technological level and allocative efficiency are equal for the two farms, that is, $A_1 = A_2$ and $k_1 = k_2$, if and only if $A_1^* = A_2^*$ and $\alpha_1^* = \alpha_2^*$. $k_i = 1$, that is, perfect allocative efficiency obtains for the ith farm, if and only if $\alpha_i^* = \alpha$. These results and their analogs for the case of multiple variable inputs then form the basis of the tests of relative economic efficiency between two farms.

Cobb-Douglas production function

In the empirical applications several variable inputs and fixed inputs are distinguished. The production function is assumed to be Cobb-Douglas in form:

$$Y = A \prod_{i=1}^m X_i^{\alpha_i} \sum_{j=1}^n Z_j^{\beta_j}$$

where X_i's are the quantities of the variable inputs, and Z_j's are the quantities of the fixed inputs, $\alpha_i > 0$, $\beta_j > 0$, $\forall_{i, j}$, and $\sum_{i=1}^m \alpha_i < 1$. The last restriction implies decreasing returns to scale in the variable inputs.

The normalized restricted profit function corresponding to the Cobb-Douglas production function takes the form[4]

$$
\begin{aligned}
(6.22) \quad \Pi(q, Z) = G(q, Z) &= Y^* - \sum_{i=1}^m q_i X_i^* \\
&= A^{(1 - \mu)^{-1}} (1 - \mu) \prod_{i=1}^m (q_i/\alpha_i)^{-\alpha_i/(1 - \mu)} \\
&\quad \prod_{j=1}^n Z_j^{\beta_j/(1 - \mu)}
\end{aligned}
$$

where q is the vector of normalized prices of the variable inputs, Z is the vector of the quantities of the fixed inputs, and

$$\mu \equiv \sum_{i=1}^m \alpha_i .$$

---

4. For a detailed derivation, see Lau (1978), pp. 190–91.

Given the functional form of $G(q, Z)$, the actual normalized profit function and the demand functions can be derived for a farm with technological level parameter, A_i, and vector of allocative efficiency parameter, k_i, as

$$(6.23) \quad \Pi_i^a = A_i^{(1-\mu)^{-1}} (1 - \Sigma_{j=1}^m \alpha_j/k_{ij})$$
$$[\Pi_{j=1}^m k_{ij}^{-\alpha_j (1-\mu)^{-1}}] [\Pi_{j=1}^m \alpha_j^{\alpha_j (1-\mu)^{-1}}]$$
$$[\Pi_{j=1}^m q_{ij}^{-\alpha_j (1-\mu)^{-1}}] [\Pi_{j=1}^n Z_{ij}^{\beta_j (1-\mu)^{-1}}] \qquad (i = 1, 2)$$

and

$$(6.24) \quad X_{ij} = A_i^{(1-\mu)^{-1}} \alpha_j/k_{ij}q_{ij}$$
$$[\Pi_{j=1}^m k_{ij}^{-\alpha_j (1-\mu)^{-1}}] [\Pi_{j=1}^m \alpha_j^{\alpha_j (1-\mu)^{-1}}]$$
$$[\Pi_{j=1}^m q_{ij}^{-\alpha_j (1-\mu)^{-1}}] [\Pi_{j=1}^n Z_{ij}^{\beta_j (1-\mu)^{-1}}]$$
$$(i = 1, 2; j = 1, \ldots, m).$$

From these two equations, the factor share functions can be derived:

$$(6.25) \quad q_{ij}X_{ij}/\Pi_i^a = \alpha_j/k_{ij}(1 - \Sigma_{l=1}^m \alpha_l/k_{il}) \quad (i = 1, 2; j = 1, \ldots, m)$$

so that the ratio of expenditure on the jth input to the actual restricted profit is a constant. Moreover, this constant depends only on the vector of allocative efficiency parameters, k_i, and on the elasticities of production of the variable inputs (and in particular is independent of A_i, the parameter of the technological level).

Taking natural logarithms of the actual normalized restricted profit function:

$$(6.26) \quad \ln \Pi_i^a = \ln A_i^* + \Sigma_{j=1}^m \alpha_j^* \ln q_{ij} + \Sigma_{j=1}^n \beta_j^* \ln Z_{ij}$$

where

$$\ln A_i^* = (1 - \mu)^{-1} \ln A_i + \ln (1 - \Sigma_{j=1}^m \alpha_j/k_{ij})$$
$$- \Sigma_{j=1}^m \alpha_j (1 - \mu)^{-1} \ln k_{ij} + \Sigma_{j=1}^m \alpha_j (1 - \mu)^{-1} \ln \alpha_j$$
$$\alpha_j^* \equiv - \alpha_j (1 - \mu)^{-1} \qquad\qquad (i = 1, \ldots, m)$$
$$\beta_j^* \equiv \beta_j (1 - \mu)^{-1} \qquad\qquad (j = 1, \ldots, n)$$

so that the actual normalized restricted profit function of two farms differ only by a multiplicative constant A_i^*. The ith farm is said to be relatively more economically efficient than the jth farm if the ith actual normalized restricted profit function is greater than the jth actual normalized restricted profit function. In the present Cobb-Douglas case, this implies $A_i^* > A_j^*$, which is also sufficient for the ith farm to be globally (for all normalized prices and fixed inputs) relatively more economically efficient than the jth farm. Further, for the Cobb-Douglas case, $\partial \Pi_i^a/\partial A_i > 0$, $\forall\ i$, so that an increase in the technological level of the ith farm always increases the actual normalized restricted profit function of the ith farm.

The ratio of expenditures on the jth variable input to actual profit may be written as

$$(6.27) \qquad - q_{ij}X_{ij}/\Pi_i^a \equiv \alpha_{ij}^{**} \qquad (i = 1, 2\,; j = 1, \ldots, m)$$

where

$$\alpha_{ij}^{**} \equiv (-\alpha_j/k_{ij})/(1 - \Sigma_{l=1}^m \alpha_l/k_{il}) \quad (i = 1, 2\,; j = 1, \ldots, m).$$

These are referred to as the factor share functions. Four observations may be made. First, two farms are equally allocatively (in)efficient ($k_1 = k_2$) if and only if $\alpha_{1j}^{**} = \alpha_{2j}^{**}$, $j = 1, \ldots, m$. Second, a farm is allocatively efficient ($k_{ij} = 1$, $\forall\ j$) if and only if $\alpha_{ij}^{**} = \alpha_j^*$, $j = 1, \ldots, m$. Third, two farms are of equal relative economic efficiency if and only if $\ln A_1^* = \ln A_2^*$. Fourth, two farms are equal in technological level and in allocative efficiency if and only if $\ln A_1^* = \ln A_2^*$ and $\alpha_{1j}^{**} = \alpha_{2j}^{**}$, $j = 1, \ldots, m$. These four observations form the basis of the empirical tests of relative efficiency between different groups of farms.

Finally, if $\ln A_1^*$ is greater than $\ln A_2^*$, then the marginal product of the actual normalized restricted profit function with respect to the kth fixed input will be greater in the first farm than in the second farm, holding the normalized prices and the fixed inputs constant. To the extent that the latter variables are different, the marginal products, or quasi-rents, will be different. By the Hotelling-Shephard lemma, the marginal profit of the profit function with respect to the kth fixed input is precisely the marginal product of the production function with respect to the kth fixed input. The marginal products of the fixed inputs may be compared by comparing the partial derivatives of the actual normalized restricted profit functions with respect to the fixed inputs. Such a comparison may have important implications for the relative desirability of alternative distributions of the fixed inputs among the farms.

Indirect estimates of the parameters
of the production function

Given the parameter estimates of the actual normalized re-
stricted profit function, α_j^*, $(j = 1, \ldots, m)$ and β_j^*, $(j = 1, \ldots, n)$, the
implicit estimates of the parameters of the production function can
be computed through the identities

$$\alpha_j^* = -\alpha_j (1 - \mu)^{-1} \qquad\qquad (j = 1, \ldots, m)$$
$$\beta_j^* = \beta_j (1 - \mu)^{-1} \qquad\qquad (j = 1, \ldots, n)$$

where

$$\mu \equiv \Sigma_{j=1}^m \alpha_j .$$

Summing the first identity across the variable inputs gives

$$\Sigma_{j=1}^m \alpha_j^* = -\mu (1 - \mu)^{-1} .$$

Let

$$\mu^* \equiv \Sigma_{j=1}^m \alpha_j^*$$

then

$$\mu^* \equiv -\mu (1 - \mu)^{-1}$$

which leads to

$$(1 - \mu)\mu^* = -\mu$$

or

$$\mu = -\mu^*(1 - \mu^*)^{-1}, (1 - \mu) = (1 - \mu^*)^{-1} .$$

Thus,

(6.28) $$\alpha_j = -\alpha_j^*(1 - \mu^*)^{-1} \qquad\qquad (j = 1, \ldots, m)$$

(6.29) $$\beta_j = \beta_j^*(1 - \mu^*)^{-1} \qquad\qquad (j = 1, \ldots, n).$$

Since $(1 - \mu) > 0$ by assumption, and $\mu > 0$ by monotonicity, the
value $(1 - \mu)$ lies strictly between zero and one. It follows that the
value of $(1 - \mu^*)$ must be strictly greater than one, or that μ^* must
be strictly negative. It also follows that the production elasticities
α_j's and β_j's are always smaller in magnitude than the correspond-

ing profit elasticities with respect to the normalized prices, α_j^*, and the fixed inputs, β_j^*.

These implicit estimates of the production function parameters computed from the estimates of the normalized profit function parameters are referred to as indirect estimates to distinguish them from the direct estimates obtained from the direct estimation of the production function. The indirect estimates are consistent if and only if the estimator of the normalized profit function parameters is consistent.

Profit Functions of Thai Farms

In this section agricultural production in Thailand is analyzed using the profit function approach under the hypothesis that the production function, and hence the normalized restricted profit function, is Cobb-Douglas in form. The basic estimating equations are therefore equation (6.26), the actual normalized restricted profit function, and equation (6.27), the factor share functions. Comparison of the values of the coefficients estimated separately from these two equations constitutes the test of profit maximization. It is also possible to identify differences in the levels of technology, if there are any, between two or more groups of farms with different levels of education.

Estimates of profit functions

As before, the Thai farms are divided into two groups: those which used chemical inputs, and those which did not. The members of each group are assumed to have identical production functions, $F(X, Z, E)$, and actual normalized profit functions, $\Pi(q, Z, E)$, where the vector E includes the characteristic variables of the individual farms such as age and sex of the head of household in addition to education. First, the actual normalized restricted profit function (equation (6.26)) is estimated alone, that is, without using the information provided by the factor shares, for each group. It is assumed that there is an additive stochastic disturbance term in equation (6.26), so that a typical estimating equation takes the form:

$$\ln \Pi_{ik}^a = \ln A_i^* + \Sigma_{j=1}^m \alpha_j^* \ln q_{ijk}$$
$$+ \Sigma_{j=1}^n \beta_j^* \ln Z_{ijk} + \beta_E^* E_{ik} + \varepsilon_{ik}$$

where the subscript k denotes the kth farm in the ith group, and E_{ik} is a measure of the educational level of the kth farm in the ith group. It is further assumed that the farms take the normalized prices, q, and the quantities of fixed inputs and their characteristic variables as given and fixed during the short run. In addition, it is assumed that $E(\varepsilon_i) = 0$, $i = 1, 2$, and $V(\varepsilon_i) = \sigma_i^2 I$. The ordinary least squares estimator, which is unbiased and consistent under these assumptions, is used to estimate the unknown parameters. The profit function approach implies a different stochastic specification from the production function approach. The two approaches are not necessarily equivalent.

For the chemical farms, there are two variable inputs—labor and chemical inputs—and two fixed inputs—capital and land. The regression results are summarized in Table 6–1. Profit is positively and statistically significantly related to the maximum number of years of formal education of either head of household (A5) to the extent of approximately 5 percent a year. The estimated effect ranges between 3 and 8 percent a year. When the years of formal education variable is represented by three dummy variables—E2 (more than 0 and less than 4 years), E3 (exactly 4 years), and E4 (more than 4 years)—they yield estimated coefficients that increase with successively higher levels of education. The dummy variable corresponding to less than 4 years of formal education, however, does not have a statistically significant effect. The dummy variable corresponding to 4 years of formal education is occasionally statistically significant, and its estimated effect on profit ranges from 16 to 35 percent, relative to 0 year of education. The dummy variable corresponding to more than 4 years of formal education is also occasionally statistically significant, and its estimated effect on profit ranges from 39 to 83 percent, more than double the estimated effect of exactly 4 years of formal education. It is hypothesized that this may reflect the higher level of education that may be required for effective utilization of the chemical inputs. When the years of formal education variable is represented by a single dummy variable, E5 (more than 0 year of education), it yields estimated coefficients that are occasionally statistically significant. The overall picture that these results convey is that each year of formal education has a statistically significant positive effect of approximately 5 percent on the level of profit, and that there is evidence that a minimum threshold of about 4 years of education is needed before education has any discernible effect.

Table 6–1. Regressions of Profit Functions for Thai Chemical Farms
(sample = 91)

Independent variable	Minimum estimate	Maximum estimate	Maximum R^2 (0.654)	Maximum R^2 (0.600)	Maximum R^{*2} (0.556)	Estimate of highest t ratio
Constant	7.525	9.409	8.907	8.980	8.980	8.980
	(8.984)	(9.022)	(9.154)	(9.921)	(9.921)	(9.921)
Labor	−0.523	−1.160	−1.115	−1.107	−1.107	−1.160
	(−1.785)	(−3.793)	(−3.596)	(−3.438)	(−3.438)	(−3.793)
Chemical inputs	−0.197	−0.432	−0.431	−0.387	−0.387	−0.432
	(−2.209)	(−4.835)	(−4.833)	(−4.388)	(−4.388)	(−4.835)
Capital	−0.003	0.100	0.056	0.080	0.080	0.100
	(−0.031)	(1.239)	(0.695)	(0.962)	(0.962)	(1.239)
Land	0.621	0.900	0.831	0.833	0.833	0.886
	(6.761)	(9.328)	(9.222)	(9.149)	(9.149)	(9.948)
Region 2	−0.593	−0.739	−0.722	−0.670	−0.670	−0.731
	(−3.753)	(−3.966)	(−4.198)	(−3.835)	(−3.835)	(−4.301)
Region 3	−0.135	−0.265	−0.195	−0.213	−0.213	−0.265
	(−0.590)	(−1.183)	(−0.918)	(−0.980)	(−0.980)	(−1.183)
Region 4	−0.794	0.098	0.065	−0.012	−0.012	0.098
	(−0.346)	(0.401)	(0.285)	(−0.050)	(−0.050)	(0.401)

		(1)	(2)	(3)	(4)	(5)	(6)
A5	(education of head of household) (years)	0.038 (1.305)	0.082 (3.064)	—	0.051 (2.062)	0.051 (2.062)	0.079 (3.074)
A6	(average education) (years)	0.011 (0.211)	0.085 (2.227)	0.037 (0.843)	—	—	0.085 (2.227)
E2	(education, 0 < A5 < 4)	-0.041 (-0.187)	0.153 (0.658)	-0.024 (-0.116)	—	—	0.153 (0.658)
E3	(education, A5 = 4)	0.158 (1.049)	0.349 (2.271)	0.198 (1.282)	—	—	0.347 (2.273)
E4	(education, A5 > 4)	0.386 (1.152)	0.831 (2.654)	0.420 (1.247)	—	—	0.809 (2.701)
E5	(education, A5 > 0)	0.105 (0.737)	0.323 (2.174)	—	—	—	0.323 (2.174)
EXT	(1 if extension services available; 0 otherwise)	-0.275 (-2.039)	0.043 (0.326)	-0.205 (-1.594)	-0.194 (-1.429)	-0.194 (-1.429)	-0.274 (-2.053)
A7	(age of head of household) (years)	-0.005 (-1.004)	0.004 (0.773)	0.001 (0.251)	—	—	-0.005 (-1.005)
CR	(1 if credit taken or available; 0 otherwise)	-0.234 (-1.488)	0.142 (0.853)	0.136 (0.882)	—	—	-0.234 (-1.488)
HM	(1 if male; 0 if female)	-0.675 (-1.593)	0.065 (1.612)	—	—	—	0.065 (1.612)

Note: Numbers in parentheses are *t* ratios. The variables are defined in Table 4–4.
— Not applicable.

Availability of agricultural extension services, however, has mostly negative effects on profit. Sometimes these effects are statistically significant. This contrasts (but is not inconsistent) with the production function results, which found extension to be statistically insignificant for the chemical farms. The estimated effect of agricultural extension ranges from 4 to -27 percent, with -20 percent being approximately the modal value. The negative relation between profit and availability of agricultural extension is somewhat counter to intuition. One possible explanation may lie in the fact that agricultural extension service personnel tend to be agronomists rather than agricultural economists and hence may be more prone to recommend practices that maximize output rather than profit. Thus, farmers who do not have the benefit of agricultural extension but have to follow their own instincts as to the best economic practice (rather than the best technical practice recommended by the agricultural extension services) may actually achieve a higher level of profit with possibly a lower level of output. Another possible explanation is that in localities where agricultural extension is available some farmers may have been coaxed into adopting chemical inputs before either they or the objective circumstances are ready, thus resulting in lower profit relative to those farmers who adopt chemical inputs on their own in the absence of agricultural extension. Shortcomings of this sort in the quality of extension advice can often result, as Schultz (1965) has suggested, from lack of sufficient research to provide appropriate inputs into the agricultural extension service.

The average level of formal education of members of the household (as distinct from the head of the household) shows a slight and positive and occasionally statistically significant effect for some regressions, but not generally. The other variables such as age, sex, and credit availability do not seem to affect profitability of the farms in a statistically significant manner at all.

The estimated price of labor and land coefficients are both statistically significant and have the correct signs. The estimated capital coefficients are statistically insignificant.

For the nonchemical farms, there is only one variable input—labor—and two fixed inputs—capital and land. The regression results are summarized in Table 6–2. The effect of education, as indicated by the single dummy variable, $E5$ (more than 0 year of education), is quite statistically significant. Whether the head of household had some formal education makes an average difference of 17 percent on profit. The lower and upper bounds are 16 and 24 percent, respectively. Given that the average number of years of schooling for those heads of households who had some formal education is approximately 4, this works out to between 4 and 5 percent per year of schooling. This is consistent with the estimates obtained for the coefficient of years of formal schooling, *A5*, which range between 4 and 6 percent. The estimated coefficient for *A5* is frequently statistically significant, although not as significant as the estimated coefficient for *E5*. The same result is borne out by disaggregating the education variable into *E2*, *E3*, and *E4*. *E3*, which represents 4 years of schooling, makes a difference of 18 percent, which amounts to 4.5 percent a year on the average. Neither *E2* nor *E4* have statistically significant estimated coefficients, however, suggesting perhaps that 4 years of formal education may be the locally optimum quantity of education.

Profit is positively and statistically significantly related to availability of agricultural extension, in contrast to what is observed for the chemical farms. The availability of agricultural extension services makes a difference of between 14 and 18 percent, with 14.5 percent being the most probable value. This is comparable in order of magnitude to the effect of 4 years of formal education.

The average level of formal education has positive effects (approximately 4 percent per year per person) in some regressions, which are on the borderline of being significant. None of the other variables—age, sex, and credit availability—have any statistically significant effect.

The estimated price of labor and land coefficients are both statistically significant and have correct signs. The estimated capital coefficients are almost always insignificant, as in the case of the chemical farms. On the whole, however, the estimates of the profit function parameters for both the chemical and the nonchemical farms seem to have a higher variability than the corresponding estimates of the parameters of the production function.

The possible existence of various interaction effects in the profit function regressions were also explored. The regression results for the chemical farms are summarized in Table 6–3. It is evident that profitability is positively related to education and negatively related to agricultural extension as before. Moreover, it appears that without agricultural extension, the effect of education on profit can be estimated to be a statistically significant 7 percent a year. But with agricultural extension, the effect of education can be estimated

Table 6–2. Regressions of Profit Functions for Thai Nonchemical Farms
(sample = 184)

Independent variable	Minimum estimate	Maximum estimate	Maximum R^2 (0.656)	Maximum $\bar{R}^2$ (0.636)	Maximum R^{*2} (0.618)	Estimate of highest t ratio
Constant	6.383	8.460	7.881	8.167	8.167	8.282
	(11.49)	(20.12)	(12.75)	(20.26)	(20.26)	(20.50)
Labor	–0.701	–0.918	–0.906	–0.912	–0.912	–0.916
	(–4.384)	(–6.028)	(–5.839)	(–6.031)	(–6.031)	(–6.192)
Capital	–0.026	0.013	–0.002	0.000	0.000	–0.026
	(–0.491)	(0.252)	(–0.040)	(0.009)	(0.009)	(–0.491)
Land	0.767	0.867	0.792	0.789	0.789	0.855
	(12.97)	(13.98)	(13.08)	(13.31)	(13.31)	(14.25)
Region 2	–0.416	–0.442	–0.424	–0.424	–0.424	–0.442
	(–5.286)	(–5.494)	(–5.324)	(–5.425)	(–5.425)	(–5.624)
Region 3	–0.187	–0.251	–0.233	–0.230	–0.230	–0.248
	(–1.455)	(–1.890)	(–1.754)	(–1.764)	(–1.764)	(–1.923)
Region 4	–0.351	–0.419	–0.357	–0.357	–0.357	–0.419
	(–3.039)	(–3.510)	(–2.989)	(–3.033)	(–3.033)	(–3.510)

Variable	(1)	(2)	(3)	(4)	(5)	(6)
A5 (education of head of household) (years)	0.038 (1.916)	0.058 (2.013)	—	—	—	0.052 (2.156)
A6 (average education) (years)	-0.003 (-0.107)	0.044 (1.841)	—	—	—	0.044 (1.841)
E2 (education, $0 < A5 < 4$)	0.146 (1.182)	0.207 (1.443)	0.156 (1.212)	—	—	0.205 (1.466)
E3 (education, $A5 = 4$)	0.162 (1.948)	0.254 (2.146)	0.181 (2.270)	—	—	0.217 (2.536)
E4 (education, $A5 > 4$)	0.153 (0.542)	0.265 (0.905)	0.210 (1.212)	—	—	0.265 (0.905)
E5 (education, $A5 > 0$)	0.160 (1.992)	0.241 (2.147)	—	0.168 (2.190)	0.168 (2.190)	0.214 (2.558)
EXT (1 if extension services available; 0 otherwise)	0.140 (2.119)	0.179 (2.584)	0.143 (2.150)	0.147 (2.267)	0.147 (2.267)	0.179 (2.584)
A7 (age of head of household) (years)	-0.004 (-1.478)	0.003 (0.710)	—	—	—	-0.004 (-1.478)
CR (1 if credit taken or available; 0 otherwise)	0.020 (0.270)	0.118 (1.493)	0.053 (0.701)	—	—	0.118 (1.512)
HM (1 if male; 0 if female)	-0.122 (-0.256)	0.235 (0.556)	0.235 (0.535)	—	—	0.235 (0.556)

Note: Numbers in parentheses are *t* ratios. The variables are defined in Table 4–4.
— Not applicable.

163

Table 6–3. *Regressions of Profit Functions with Interactions for Thai Chemical Farms* (sample = 91)

Independent variable	Minimum estimate	Maximum estimate	Maximum R^2 (0.667)	Maximum $\bar{R}^2$ (0.607)	Maximum R^{*2} (0.559)	Estimate of highest t ratio
Constant	7.013 (4.917)	10.57 (6.100)	9.741 (5.497)	9.741 (5.497)	8.688 (9.857)	8.688 (9.857)
Labor	-0.839 (-2.649)	-1.171 (-3.538)	-1.171 (-3.538)	-1.171 (-3.538)	-1.026 (-3.280)	-1.171 (-3.538)
Chemical inputs	-0.326 (-3.629)	-0.415 (-4.554)	-0.401 (-4.447)	-0.401 (-4.447)	-0.395 (-4.485)	-0.411 (-4.589)
Capital	0.030 (0.338)	0.081 (0.928)	0.030 (0.338)	0.030 (0.338)	0.075 (0.913)	0.080 (0.944)
Land	0.793 (8.383)	0.880 (9.714)	0.835 (8.807)	0.835 (8.807)	0.838 (9.176)	0.880 (9.714)
Region 2	-0.539 (-3.032)	-0.689 (-3.924)	-0.605 (-3.369)	-0.605 (-3.369)	-0.630 (-3.750)	-0.689 (-3.924)
Region 3	-0.124 (-0.543)	-0.223 (-1.017)	-0.150 (-0.679)	-0.150 (-0.679)	-0.164 (-0.754)	-0.233 (-1.017)
Region 4	-0.033 (-0.136)	0.063 (0.265)	0.005 (0.019)	0.005 (0.019)	0.015 (0.062)	0.063 (0.265)
A5 (education of head of household) (years)	0.035 (1.163)	0.195 (1.112)	0.051 (1.779)	0.051 (1.779)	—	0.074 (2.772)
A7 (age of head of household) (years)	0.021 (0.495)	0.048 (1.134)	—	—	—	0.062 (1.363)
A7²	-0.000 (-0.552)	-0.000 (-1.054)	—	—	—	-0.000 (-1.225)

Variable	(1)	(2)	(3)	(4)	(5)	(6)
EXT (1 if extension services available; 0 otherwise)	-3.988 (-1.935)	-0.882 (-1.836)	-3.323 (-1.607)	-3.323 (-1.607)	—	-1.103 (-2.340)
A5EX1	0.025 (0.759)	0.025 (0.759)	—	—	0.025 (0.759)	0.025 (0.759)
A5EX0	0.071 (2.888)	0.071 (2.888)	—	—	0.071 (2.888)	0.071 (2.888)
A6EX1	0.029 (0.636)	0.053 (1.284)	—	—	—	0.053 (1.284)
A6EX0	0.075 (1.412)	0.112 (2.630)	—	—	—	0.112 (2.630)
A7EX1	-0.003 (-0.699)	0.098 (1.688)	0.098 (1.688)	0.098 (1.688)	—	0.098 (1.688)
A7EX0	-0.036 (-0.655)	0.051 (1.207)	-0.011 (-0.195)	-0.011 (-0.195)	—	-0.012 (-1.633)
A7SE1	-0.001 (-1.556)	-0.000 (-0.230)	-0.001 (-1.556)	-0.001 (-1.556)	—	-0.001 (-1.556)
A7SE0	-0.000 (-1.267)	0.000 (0.425)	0.000 (0.074)	0.000 (0.074)	—	-0.000 (-1.267)
A7A5	-0.002 (-0.830)	-0.001 (-0.570)	—	—	—	-0.002 (-0.830)
$A5^2$	-0.002 (-0.295)	0.002 (0.417)	—	—	—	0.002 (0.417)
D35	-0.305 (-1.210)	-0.305 (-1.210)	—	—	—	-0.305 (-1.210)
D35A5	0.078 (1.906)	0.078 (1.906)	—	—	—	0.078 (1.906)
D35PA5	0.056 (2.177)	0.056 (2.177)	—	—	—	0.056 (2.177)

Note: Numbers in parentheses are t ratios. The variables are defined in Table 4–4.
— Not applicable.

to be only a statistically insignificant 2.5 percent. Without agricultural extension, the estimated effect of average education is statistically insignificant. But with agricultural extension, the average education effect is positive and statistically significant in some regressions. The estimated coefficient ranges between 7.5 and 11 percent. These results suggest the possible existence of a negative interaction effect between formal education and agricultural extension. In other words, the measured effect of education is diminished by the presence of agricultural extension. One possible explanation may be that agricultural extension personnel work more with the poorly educated farmers. Thus, in a region with agricultural extension, the effect of agricultural extension is compensatory, and hence will lower the measured effect of years of formal education in that region. The validity of this explanation, however, has yet to be empirically verified. It also appears that education enhances profitability much more for younger heads of household than for older heads of household: 8 percent a year for the former compared with 6 percent a year for the latter.

The regression results with interaction effects for the nonchemical farms are summarized in Table 6–4. There is some evidence that agricultural extension enhances the effect of education and vice versa, as indicated by the estimated coefficient for $A5EX1$. This suggests that for nonchemical farms they may be complements rather than substitutes. With agricultural extension, 1 year of formal schooling appears to make a difference of 5.5 percent in profit, as compared with 2.0 percent without agricultural extension. This positive interaction effect is exactly the reverse of what is observed for the chemical farms. There is also some evidence of positive interaction between age and education. The positive effect of education (4 percent a year) on profit for farms with household heads 35 years or older is statistically significant, whereas the same effect is not statistically significant for farms with household heads 35 years or younger. The magnitude of the effect also seems to be higher for the former group. Again, this interaction between age and education is precisely the opposite of what is observed for the chemical farms. Age and extension seem to have a marginally statistically significant negative interaction effect. None of the remaining variables have statistically significant coefficient estimates.

Test of profit maximization

From the point of view of this study, we are most interested in whether formal education makes a difference in the ability of a farmer to maximize profit. To test this hypothesis, the farm households are divided further by whether the heads of household had formal education. In other words, the farm households are classified into four groups: chemical farms with educated heads, chemical farms with uneducated heads, nonchemical farms with educated heads, and nonchemical farms with uneducated heads.

The chemical farms and the nonchemical farms are analyzed separately, on the grounds that the technology is different for the two kinds of farms. Only variables of farm household characteristics that have been previously statistically significant are included. Thus, in addition to the prices of variable inputs, the quantities of fixed inputs, and the regional dummy variables, the only other independent variables that are included are education and the availability of agricultural extension.

The model used here is based on the one developed by Lau and Yotopoulos that was discussed in some detail in the first section of this chapter. The profit function as well as the factor share functions are estimated for the chemical and nonchemical farms. The factor share functions are allowed to differ between the educated and the uneducated farms. The estimating equations for the chemical farms take the form

$$\ln \Pi_{ik}^{a} = \ln A_{i}^{*} + \alpha_{L}^{*} \ln W_{ik} + \alpha_{C}^{*} \ln PCN_{ik} + \beta_{K}^{*} \ln K_{ik}$$
$$+ \beta_{T}^{*} \ln T_{ik} + \Sigma_{l=2}^{4} \delta_{l} R_{ikl} + \delta_{EXT} EXT_{ik} + \varepsilon_{E5} E5_{ik}$$
$$- W_{ik} L_{ik} / \Pi_{ik}^{a} = \alpha_{L, E5}^{*} E5_{ik} + \alpha_{L, E6}^{*} E6_{ik}$$
$$- PCN_{ik} XCN_{ik} / \Pi_{ik}^{a} = \alpha_{C, E5}^{*} E5_{ik} + \alpha_{C, E6}^{*} E6_{ik} \qquad (\forall\ i,\ k)$$

where W_{ik} and PCN_{ik} are, respectively, the normalized wage rate and the normalized price of chemical inputs of the kth farm in the ith group; K_{ik} and T_{ik} are, respectively, the quantities of capital and land operated by the kth farm in the ith group; and R_{ikl}, EXT_{ik}, $E5_{ik}$, and $E6_{ik}$ are, respectively, the values of the dummy variables corresponding to each region, availability of agricultural extension, and levels of education for the kth farm in the ith group. $E5$ takes the value 1 for a farm the head of which is educated, and otherwise is 0. $E6$ takes the value 1 for a farm the head of which is uneducated, and otherwise is 0. The coefficient $\alpha_{L, E5}^{*}$ on the $E5$ variable in the wage share function is the negative of the average ratio of total labor cost to restricted profit for all educated farms. The coefficient $\alpha_{L, E6}^{*}$ on the $E6$ variable in the wage share function is the negative of the

Table 6–4. *Regressions of Profit Functions with Interactions for Thai Nonchemical Farms* (sample = 184)

Independent variable	Minimum estimate	Maximum estimate	Maximum R^2 (0.655)	Maximum $\bar{R}^2$ (0.636)	Maximum $R*^2$ (0.617)	Estimate of highest t ratio
Constant	7.283 (6.776)	8.446 (20.34)	8.161 (12.12)	8.146 (18.16)	8.217 (19.97)	8.446 (20.34)
Labor	-0.880 (-5.802)	-0.904 (-5.832)	-0.887 (-5.700)	-0.880 (-5.802)	-0.888 (-5.840)	-0.902 (-5.928)
Capital	-0.002 (-0.040)	0.013 (0.248)	-0.002 (-0.031)	-0.001 (-0.023)	-0.003 (-0.052)	0.013 (0.248)
Land	0.770 (12.80)	0.799 (13.29)	0.789 (13.03)	0.791 (13.20)	0.788 (13.15)	0.799 (13.29)
Region 2	-0.417 (-5.295)	-0.452 (-5.615)	-0.423 (-5.240)	-0.417 (-5.295)	-0.424 (-5.390)	-0.452 (-5.615)
Region 3	-0.188 (-1.428)	-0.245 (-1.852)	-0.223 (-1.672)	-0.219 (-1.669)	-0.214 (-1.634)	-0.245 (-1.852)
Region 4	-0.350 (-2.947)	-0.416 (-3.482)	-0.357 (-2.963)	-0.350 (-2.947)	-0.352 (-2.965)	-0.416 (-3.482)
A5 (education of head of household) (years)	0.036 (0.335)	0.192 (1.074)	0.039 (1.540)	0.042 (1.710)	0.038 (1.892)	0.038 (1.892)
A7 (age of head of household) (years)	0.001 (0.107)	0.028 (0.912)	—	—	—	0.028 (0.912)
$A7^2$	-0.000 (-0.836)	-0.000 (-0.467)	—	—	—	-0.000 (-1.019)
EXT (1 if extension services available; 0 otherwise)	-0.243 (-0.286)	0.055 (0.220)	-0.243 (-0.286)	—	—	-0.243 (-0.286)

	Col 1	Col 2	Col 3	Col 4	Col 5	Col 6
A5EX1	0.056 (2.788)	0.056 (2.788)	—	—	—	0.056 (2.788)
A5EX0	0.020 (0.994)	0.020 (0.994)	—	—	—	0.000 (0.994)
A6EX1	0.020 (0.682)	0.041 (1.559)	—	—	0.020 (0.682)	0.041 (1.559)
A6EX0	-0.018 (-0.616)	0.003 (0.110)	—	—	-0.018 (-0.616)	0.003 (0.110)
A7EX1	-0.002 (-0.592)	0.017 (0.672)	0.014 (0.559)	0.002 (0.642)	—	0.013 (0.743)
A7EX0	-0.005 (-1.811)	0.008 (0.474)	-0.000 (-0.019)	-0.001 (-0.239)	—	-0.005 (-1.811)
A7SE1	-0.000 (-0.771)	-0.000 (-0.410)	-0.000 (-0.497)	—	—	-0.000 (-0.860)
A7SE0	-0.000 (-0.695)	-0.000 (-0.006)	-0.000 (-0.006)	—	—	-0.000 (-0.695)
A7A5	-0.002 (-0.724)	0.000 (0.077)	—	—	—	0.000 (0.077)
A5^2	-0.007 (-0.889)	-0.005 (-0.636)	—	—	—	-0.007 (-0.889)
D35	0.018 (0.211)	0.018 (0.211)	—	—	—	0.018 (0.211)
D35A5	0.034 (1.344)	0.034 (1.344)	—	—	—	0.034 (1.344)
D35PA5	0.041 (2.155)	0.041 (2.155)	—	—	—	0.041 (2.155)

Note: Numbers in parentheses are t ratios. The variables are defined in Table 4–4.
— Not applicable.

average ratio of total labor cost to restricted profit for all unedu-
cated farms. The coefficients $\alpha^*_{C, E5}$ and $\alpha^*_{C, E6}$ on $E5$ and $E6$ in the
chemical inputs share function may be similarly interpreted. The
estimating equations for the nonchemical farms are similar:

$$\ln \Pi^a_{ik} = \ln A^*_i + \alpha^*_L \ln W_{ik} + \beta^*_K \ln K_{ik} + \beta^*_T \ln T_{ik}$$

$$+ \Sigma^4_{l=2} \delta_l R_{ikl} + \delta_{EXT} EXT_{ik} + \varepsilon_{E5} E5_{ik}$$

$$- W_{ik} L_{ik} / \Pi^a_{ik} = \alpha^*_{L, E5} E5_{ik} + \alpha^*_{L, E6} E6_{ik} \qquad (\forall \ i, k).$$

Given the assumption of price-taking behavior on the part of the
farm households and the short-run fixity of the quantities of capital
and land, the farm's decision variables are the quantity of output
and the quantities of the variable inputs. The price of output and the
prices of the variable inputs as well as the quantities of the fixed
inputs are predetermined and are not affected by the action of any
one farm in the short run. Consequently, the quantities of output
and variable inputs are jointly dependent variables, and the prices
of output and variable inputs and the quantities of fixed inputs are
the predetermined variables in the model. Because of the profit
identity, namely, that profit is equal to current revenue less current
variable costs, an alternative set of jointly dependent variables
consists of normalized profit and expenditures on each of the variable factors of production. It is clear that, given the predetermined
variables, there is a one-to-one correspondence between normalized profit and expenditures on each variable factor of production,
and the quantities of output and of each of the variable factors of
production. Thus, in the estimating equations, the variables on the
left-hand side are the jointly dependent variables, and those on the
right-hand side include only the predetermined variables.

Under these conditions, ordinary least squares applied to each of
the equations separately will be consistent. These estimates may in
general not be efficient, however. Little is known about how the
stochastic disturbance terms in general should be introduced into
economic relations, although Hoch (1958), Mundlak and Hoch
(1965), and subsequently Zellner, Kmenta, and Drèze (1966) have
proposed one assumption that is compatible with the Cobb-Douglas
case. Here, an additive error with zero expectation and finite
variance is assumed for the normalized profit equation and for each
of the factor share equations. In his pioneering study of cost func-

tions, Nerlove (1960) derives an additive error to the natural logarithm of the cost function. The same can be done here for the profit function, using similar assumptions: namely, that farms maximize profits subject to unknown exogenous disturbances. The additive error in the factor share equations may arise from different abilities to maximize profits or divergence between expected and realized prices. A similar stochastic specification is used by Arrow, Chenery, Minhas, and Solow (1961) in their equation for estimating the elasticity of substitution. Here it is assumed that for the same farm the covariance of the errors of any two of the equations is permitted to be nonzero. However, the covariances of the errors of any two equations corresponding to different farms are assumed to be identically zero. Given this specification of errors, Zellner's estimator for seemingly unrelated regressions is asymptotically efficient and is used here. These equations are estimated first without any prior restrictions on the parameters. Then additional restrictions are successively imposed corresponding to the following three hypotheses:

a. The educated farmers maximize profits.
b. The uneducated farmers maximize profits.
c. Both the educated and the uneducated farmers maximize profits.

The regressions for the chemical farms are reported in Table 6–5. The regressions for the nonchemical farms are reported in Table 6–6. For both groups of farms, profit maximization by the educated farmers implies that the wage coefficient in the profit function should be equal to the $E5$ coefficient in the wage share function. If the two coefficients are not equal, it implies that the educated farmers have not maximized profits. Profit maximization by the uneducated farmers implies that the wage coefficient in the profit function should be equal to the $E6$ coefficient in the wage share function. If the two coefficients are not equal, it implies that the uneducated farmers have not maximized profits. Profit maximization on the part of all farmers, educated and uneducated, within each group, implies that all three coefficients are equal. In addition, for the chemical farms, profit maximization by the educated and uneducated farmers further implies that the chemical input price coefficient in the profit function should be equal to, respectively, the $E5$ and $E6$ coefficients in the chemical input share function. Profit

Table 6–5. Regressions of Profit Functions for Thai Chemical Wet Season Rice Farms (sample = 91)

$$\ln \Pi = \ln A^* + \alpha_L^* \ln W + \alpha_C^* \ln PCN + \beta_K^* \ln K + \beta_T^* \ln T + \sum_{i=2}^{4} \delta_i R_i + \delta_{EXT} EXT + \epsilon_{E5} E5$$

$$-WL/\Pi = \alpha_{L,E5}^* E5 + \alpha_{L,E6}^* E6; \quad -PCN.XCN/\Pi = \alpha_{C,E5}^* E5 + \alpha_{C,E6}^* E6$$

Independent variable	Single equation OLS	Unrestricted estimates	Restricted		
			$\alpha_L^* = \alpha_{L,E5}^*$ $\alpha_C^* = \alpha_{C,E5}^*$	$\alpha_L^* = \alpha_{L,E6}^*$ $\alpha_C^* = \alpha_{C,E6}^*$	$\alpha_L^* = \alpha_{L,E5}^* = \alpha_{L,E6}^*$ $\alpha_C^* = \alpha_{C,E5}^* = \alpha_{C,E6}^*$
Profit function					
Constant (ln A)	8.911 (10.29)	7.550 (10.74)	7.465 (20.13)	7.483 (17.65)	7.402 (23.06)
Labor wage (α_L^*)	-1.081 (-3.504)	-0.594 (-2.379)	-0.581 (-5.785)	-0.609 (-4.200)	-0.576 (-6.444)
Chemical input price (α_C^*)	-0.355 (-4.294)	-0.179 (-2.672)	-0.116 (-5.108)	-0.087 (-2.550)	-0.103 (-5.088)
Capital (β_K^*)	0.082 (1.036)	0.058 (0.901)	0.052 (0.857)	0.052 (0.854)	0.052 (0.847)
Land (β_T^*)	0.853 (9.845)	0.804 (11.46)	0.787 (12.08)	0.781 (11.86)	0.784 (12.03)

R_2	-0.693	-0.413	-0.375	-0.383	-0.367
	(-4.159)	(-3.062)	(-3.282)	(-3.195)	(-3.238)
R_3	-0.259	-0.181	-0.223	-0.277	-0.227
	(-1.236)	(-1.067)	(-1.498)	(-1.824)	(-1.527)
R_4	-0.012	0.083	0.076	0.063	0.077
	(-0.054)	(0.456)	(0.475)	(0.383)	(0.488)
$E5$ (education, $A5 > 0$)	0.180	0.175	0.174	0.208	0.223
	(1.431)	(1.424)	(1.434)	(1.753)	(2.327)
EXT (1 if extension services available; 0 otherwise)	-0.252	-0.109	-0.093	-0.097	-0.091
	(-2.007)	(-1.078)	(-0.991)	(-1.015)	(-0.973)
Wage share function					
$E5$ (education, $A5 > 0$)	-0.576	-0.576	-0.581	-0.576	-0.576
	(-5.047)	(-5.047)	(-5.785)	(-5.046)	(-6.444)
$E6$ (education, $A5 = 0$)	-0.548	-0.548	-0.548	-0.609	-0.576
	(-2.794)	(-2.794)	(-2.794)	(-4.200)	(-6.444)
Chemical input share function					
$E5$ (education, $A5 > 0$)	-0.112	-0.112	-0.116	-0.112	-0.103
	(-4.640)	(-4.640)	(-5.108)	(-4.294)	(-5.088)
$E6$ (education, $A5 = 0$)	-0.061	-0.061	-0.061	-0.087	-0.103
	(-1.460)	(-1.460)	(-1.390)	(-2.550)	(-5.088)
R^2	0.635	—	—	—	—

Note: Numbers in parentheses are t ratios. The variables are defined in Table 4-4.
— Not applicable.

Table 6-6. *Regressions of Profit Functions for Thai Nonchemical Wet Season Rice Farms* (sample = 184)

$$\ln \Pi = \ln A + \alpha_L^* \ln W + \beta_K^* \ln K + \beta_T^* \ln T + \Sigma_{i=2}^4 \delta_i R_i + \delta_{EXT} EXT + \epsilon_{E5} E5$$

$$-WL/\Pi = \alpha_{LE5}^* E5 + \alpha_{LE6}^* E6$$

Independent variable	Single equation OLS	Unrestricted estimates	Restricted		
			$\alpha_L^* = \alpha_{LE5}^*$	$\alpha_L^* = \alpha_{LE6}^*$	$\alpha_L^* = \alpha_{LE5}^*$ $\alpha_L^* = \alpha_{LE6}^*$
Profit function					
Constant (ln A)	8.167	6.960	6.991	7.215	7.165
	(20.78)	(22.29)	(30.40)	(28.76)	(34.36)
Labor wage (α_L^*)	−0.912	−0.471	−0.496	−0.564	−0.543
	(−6.184)	(−4.058)	(−7.141)	(−5.999)	(−8.434)
Capital (β_K^*)	0.000	0.042	0.047	0.044	0.047
	(0.010)	(1.061)	(1.236)	(1.137)	(1.210)
Land (β_T^*)	0.789	0.812	0.811	0.807	0.808
	(13.65)	(17.82)	(18.65)	(18.06)	(18.48)

	(1)	(2)	(3)	(4)	(5)
R_2	−0.424	−0.306	−0.301	−0.313	−0.307
	(−5.562)	(−5.088)	(−5.281)	(−5.327)	(−5.366)
R_3	−0.230	−0.209	−0.213	−0.218	−0.217
	(−1.809)	(−2.089)	(−2.230)	(−2.218)	(−2.254)
R_4	−0.357	−0.284	−0.291	−0.304	−0.300
	(−3.110)	(−3.140)	(−3.428)	(−3.452)	(−3.520)
$E5$ (education, $A5 > 0$)	0.168	0.159	0.171	0.104	0.095
	(2.246)	(2.145)	(2.311)	(1.568)	(1.669)
EXT (1 if extension services available; 0 otherwise)	0.147	0.142	0.142	0.143	0.143
	(2.324)	(2.839)	(2.967)	(2.908)	(2.958)
Wage share function					
$E5$ (education, $A5 > 0$)	−0.540	−0.540	−0.496	−0.540	−0.543
	(−6.080)	(−6.080)	(−7.141)	(−6.080)	(−8.434)
$E6$ (education, $A5 = 0$)	−0.788	−0.788	−0.788	−0.564	−0.543
	(−4.752)	(−4.752)	(−4.751)	(−5.999)	(−8.434)
R^2	0.654	—	—	—	—

Note: Numbers in parentheses are t ratios. The variables are defined in Table 4-4.
— Not applicable.

175

maximization by all chemical farmers—educated and uneducated—implies that all three coefficients are equal.

F tests were used for each of the hypotheses, and the results are summarized in Table 6–7. It is evident from Table 6–7 that at any conventional level of significance, the hypothesis that all farms—chemical and nonchemical, educated and uneducated—maximize profits subject to their respective production functions cannot be rejected. In fact, to obtain a rejection, the level of significance has to be 0.25, which implies that there is one chance in four that a true hypothesis may be falsely rejected. For this sample of Thai farms we therefore conclude that differences in education do not lead to differences in the ability to maximize profits. In other words, the allocative efficiency of a farm does not appear to depend on its level of education.

We should add a caveat here that what we have analyzed is the ability of farmers to maximize profits, given that the farmers have chosen the traditional or the new technology. The individual levels of the technology may also depend on the characteristics of the farmers and the economic environment. We cannot reject the hypothesis that farmers do maximize profits given their individual

Table 6–7. *Tests of Profit Maximization*
for Thai Chemical and Nonchemical Farms

Hypothesis	Degrees of freedom	Computed F	Critical values at given levels of significance	
			0.25	0.1
Chemical farms (sample $=$ 91)				
(1) Profit maximization by educated farms	(2,259)	0.454	1.39	2.30
(2) Profit maximization by uneducated farms	(2,259)	1.251	1.39	2.30
(3) Profit maximization by all farms	(4,257)	1.431	1.35	1.94
Nonchemical farms (sample $=$ 184)				
(1) Profit maximization by educated farms	(1,357)	0.225	1.32	2.71
(2) Profit maximization by uneducated farms	(1,357)	2.500	1.32	2.71
(3) Profit maximization by all farms	(2,356)	1.288	1.39	2.30

technologies. We have not, however, analyzed whether farmers have chosen their technology—traditional or new—in a manner consistent with maximizing their profits. This latter question is examined in Chapter 7. There is in fact some indication that some of the farmers may not have chosen the technology that maximizes profits for them, although given their choice of technology, they do manage to maximize profits.

Returning now to Tables 6–5 and 6–6, the estimates are examined with the profit-maximization hypothesis maintained, that is, the estimates of the last columns. They suggest that for chemical farms, education enhances profitability by 22 percent and that the effect is statistically significant. Agricultural extension, which has a negative effect of approximately 9 percent, is no longer statistically significant. For nonchemical farms, education enhances profitability by 9 percent, and agricultural extension enhances profitability by 14 percent. The education coefficient, however, is statistically significant only at the 10 percent level of significance. The agricultural extension variable is quite statistically significant.

The estimated normalized profit functions should also be verified as being nonnegative, monotonically decreasing in the normalized prices, and convex in the normalized prices, that is, they satisfy all the requirements of a normalized profit function. This implies the following restrictions on the estimated parameters:

$$\alpha_L^* \leq 0$$

$$\alpha_C^* \leq 0.$$

The last columns of Tables 6–5 and 6–6 show that both estimated normalized profit functions have all of the required properties, providing further confirmation of the hypothesis of profit maximization.

These results based on restricted estimation are broadly consistent with our previous findings based on the estimation of the actual normalized profit function alone. There are, however, also significant differences. For the chemical farms, the estimated effect of education remains unchanged at approximately 20 percent. The estimated effect of agricultural extension is increased from −25 to −9 percent and becomes statistically insignificant in the process. For the nonchemical farms, the estimated effect of education is reduced from 17 to 9 percent. The estimated effect of agricultural extension remains essentially unchanged at between 14 and 15 percent.

We do not argue that the restricted estimates are necessarily better than the unrestricted estimates, although the restricted estimators are asymptotically more efficient than the unrestricted estimators if the maintained hypothesis is true. In any case, the differences in the estimates are not sufficiently strong to affect the broad conclusion that education and agricultural extension do matter, although their effects on different groups of farms may differ.

We also experimented with alternative groupings of the farm households based on different educational classifications, such as putting those with less than 4 years of education into one group and those with 4 or more years of education into another group. Since the regression results for these alternative groupings are not quantitatively very different, we shall not report them here. They are in the technical annex to this study, which is available from the authors.

What can one conclude from this analysis? First, the empirical results suggest that given the choice of technology—traditional (using nonchemical inputs) or new (using chemical inputs)—whether the head of household had any formal education does not affect the level of allocative efficiency. All farmers, educated or uneducated, appear to have maximized profits. Second, again given the choice of technology, educated farmers had on average higher profits than uneducated farmers, other things being equal, which suggests that educated farmers must have a higher level of technology than the uneducated farmers. And since both educated and uneducated farmers maximize profits, it also implies that the educated farmers have higher relative economic efficiency. Third, again given the choice of technology, the availability of agricultural extension has a positive effect on the profits of nonchemical farms but a negative albeit statistically insignificant effect on the profits of chemical farms.

Comparison of production and profit functions

It is useful to compare the estimated effects of education and agricultural extension on production and profit functions. Table 6–8 has been compiled from the results from the best-fitting regressions of Chapter 5 and the restricted profit function regressions from Tables 6–5 and 6–6 and gives the effects of education on a yearly basis. (The average number of years of education of the head of household for educated chemical farms is 4.20, and the corre-

Table 6–8. *Estimated Effects of Education and Agricultural Extension for Thai Chemical and Nonchemical Farms*
(percent)

Independent variable	Production function	Profit function (single equation)	Profit function (restricted)
Chemical farms (sample = 91)			
Education (per year)	0.026–0.031	0.043	0.053
		(1.431)	(2.327)
Agricultural extension	–0.12	–0.252	–0.091
		(–2.007)	(–0.973)
Nonchemical farms (sample = 184)			
Education (per year)	0.024	0.043	0.024
		(2.246)	(1.669)
Agricultural extension	0.085	0.147	0.143
		(2.324)	(2.958)

Note: Numbers in parentheses are *t* ratios.

sponding number for educated nonchemical farms is 3.87.) The magnitudes of the effects, however, are not directly comparable between the production function estimates and the profit function estimates. In general, as was shown earlier, a 1 percent change in productivity translates into a more than 1 percent change in profitability.

It is evident from Table 6–8 that the results are quite consistent in terms of the direction of effects between the production and profit function estimates, despite differences in the underlying assumptions on the nature of the stochastic disturbances. Education has a positive and statistically significant (at the 10 percent level) effect on both chemical and nonchemical farms, and its effect is higher for chemical than for nonchemical farms. This latter finding is consistent with Schultz's hypothesis on the importance of ability and knowledge in a changing environment. Agricultural extension, however, has a positive and statistically significant effect only on the nonchemical farms. Its effect on the chemical farms is consistently negative, but not statistically significant. Further, the effect of agricultural extension on nonchemical farms is at least three times that of 1 year of formal education—a surprisingly large difference indeed.

Given the parameters of the actual normalized restricted profit function, a unique set of estimates of the parameters of the underlying production function can be obtained as discussed in the beginning of this chapter. This has been done for Thailand separately for the chemical and the nonchemical farms using the estimates in the last columns of Tables 6–5 and 6–6. These indirect estimates are compared with the direct estimates in Table 6–9. The two sets of estimates are quite different: the indirect estimates imply a higher production elasticity for labor and lower production elasticities for the fixed inputs, especially land. Strictly speaking, the estimates are not directly comparable because the stochastic specifications that underlie the production and normalized profit function estimations are fundamentally different. On the one hand, it is assumed that the stochastic disturbances are additive in the logarithms to output. On the other hand, it is assumed that the stochastic disturbances are additive to the logarithms of normalized restricted profit and to the factor shares. Our results therefore suggest that the production elasticity estimates may be quite sensitive to the stochastic specification. The directions of the estimated effects of education and extension, however, do not appear to be as sensitive to the stochastic specification. For both the chemical and the nonchemical farms,

Table 6–9. *Production Elasticities*
for Thai Chemical and Nonchemical Farms

Independent variable	*Direct*	*Indirect*
Chemical farms (sample = 91) ⟩		
Labor	0.297	0.343
Chemical inputs	0.071	0.061
Capital	0.037	0.031
Land	0.524	0.467
Education (1, if educated; 0, otherwise)	0.124	0.133
Extension (1, if available; 0, otherwise)	–0.119	–0.054
Nonchemical farms (sample = 184)		
Labor	0.261	0.352
Capital	0.135	0.030
Land	0.601	0.524
Education (1, if educated; 0, otherwise)	0.098	0.061
Extension (1, if available; 0, otherwise)	0.085	0.092

the indirect estimates are the same as the direct estimates in terms of their signs. In magnitudes, the indirect estimates are comparable with the direct estimates, except for the extension coefficient for chemical farms. The indirect estimate of the extension coefficient for chemical farms is -0.05, which may be compared with a direct estimate of -0.12.

Tests of the neutrality of the effect of education

Our profit function analysis is based on the maintained hypothesis that the production function of the educated and uneducated farms differ by only a multiplicative technological level parameter:

$$Y_1 = A_1 F(X_1); \; Y_2 = A_2 F(X_2)$$

that is, the effect of education on productivity is neutral. This hypothesis implies that the normalized profit functions of the educated and uneducated farms will have the form

$$\Pi_1 = A_1 G(p_1/A_1); \; \Pi_2 = A_2 G(p_2/A_2).$$

Under the additional assumption that $F(\cdot)$ is Cobb-Douglas in form, then $\Pi_1(\cdot)$ and $\Pi_2(\cdot)$ differ only by a scalar multiplier, as shown in the beginning of this chapter. In other words, the profit elasticities with respect to the normalized prices of the variable inputs and the quantities of the fixed inputs will be the same for educated and uneducated farms, that is, the effect of education on profitability is also neutral.

To further assess the restrictiveness of this neutrality assumption for Thai farms, the farms that chose the same technology, say, those using chemical inputs, are subdivided into educated and uneducated farms. Chow (1960) tests are performed of the hypothesis that the profit elasticities of the educated and uneducated farms are the same. As in the case of Chapter 5, all characteristic variables, except the education of the head of household and the availability of agricultural extension, are dropped. Then separately for the educated and uneducated farms, profit functions of the form

$$\ln \Pi^i = \alpha_L^{*i} \ln W + \alpha_C^{*i} \ln PCN + \beta_K^{*i} \ln K + \beta_T^{*i} \ln T$$
$$+ \Sigma_{l=1}^4 \delta_{Rl}^{*i} R_l + \delta_{EXT}^{*i} EXT \qquad (i = E, NE)$$

where the superscripts E and NE stand for the educated and uneducated farms, respectively, are estimated. The educated and uneducated farms are then pooled, and new regressions are estimated. In these regressions, first, the profit elasticities with respect to the normalized prices of the variable inputs and quantities of the fixed inputs are constrained to be the same for educated and uneducated farms; second, all the elasticities and the coefficients corresponding to the regional dummy variables are constrained to be the same; and, third, all the elasticities and the coefficients of the regional dummy variables and the coefficients of the extension variable are constrained to be the same. This process is repeated for the nonchemical farms in Thailand.

The results of these Chow tests are presented in Table 6–10. It is apparent from Table 6–10 that at a level of significance of 0.05 the hypothesis that the effect of education on productivity is neutral for the chemical farms cannot be rejected on the basis of the estimated profit functions. For the nonchemical farms, however, the hypothesis of neutrality can be rejected at a level of significance of 0.05 (although not at 0.01). This finding is not completely consistent with our finding in Chapter 5, using estimated production functions, that the effect of education on productivity appears to be neutral. We thus conclude that for the nonchemical farms, our results may be sensitive with respect to our assumption of neutrality.

Table 6–10. *Tests of the Neutrality of Education's Effect on Productivity for Thai Chemical and Nonchemical Farms*

Hypothesis	Degrees of freedom	Test statistic	Critical values at given levels of significance		
			0.10	*0.05*	*0.01*
Chemical farms (sample = 91)					
(1)	(4,71)	1.07	2.02	2.51	3.58
(2)	(8,71)	1.33	1.75	2.07	2.75
(3)	(9,71)	1.43	1.71	2.01	2.69
Nonchemical farms (sample = 184)					
(1)	(3,166)	3.07	2.10	2.65	3.90
(2)	(7,166)	2.20	1.75	2.06	2.74
(3)	(8,166)	1.95	1.70	1.99	2.61

Note: Hypotheses are given in Table 6–7.

Summary

Our results from the production function and profit function analyses indicate that education has a positive effect on the technological levels of both chemical and nonchemical farms in Thailand equal to between 12 and 13 percent for chemical farms and between 6 and 9 percent for nonchemical farms. This finding lends further support to Schultz's thesis that the effect of education is more substantial in a changing environment. Since the average number of years of schooling among chemical and nonchemical farmers with formal education is, respectively, 4.2 and 3.9, the estimated effects may be approximately translated into 3 percent a year for chemical farms and 1.5 to 2.3 percent a year for nonchemical farms. Agricultural extension, however, is found to have a negative effect on the technological level of chemical farms of between −5 and −12 percent, but a positive effect on the technological level of nonchemical farms of 9 percent.

Market Efficiency of Thai Farms

Market efficiency is defined as the ability to obtain the highest net sale price for the outputs and the lowest net purchase price for the inputs (Chapter 3).[5] In any market there is usually a distribution of prices for essentially the same commodity, centered around some mean price. The dispersion of prices from the mean is attributable to differences in access to information, differences in the ability to use information, and differences in the qualities of the commodity. If every farm household has the same information and the same ability to use the information, and if there is no difference in quality, the price should be the same for all farm households, apart from transport costs.

To the extent that the market is not perfect, however, the access to and the ability to use information will make a difference. It is hypothesized that better educated farm households will on average

---

5. It is possible to consider a more generalized notion of market efficiency than one defined narrowly in terms of price advantage in the market; advantages of timing, convenience, and small gifts are other possible dimensions of gain. Belshaw (1965, p. 56) provides an engaging example of these practices within Haitian markets.

receive higher net prices for their outputs and pay lower net prices for their variable inputs. Education enhances a farmer's ability to know his alternatives, to know when and where to buy and sell. A better educated farmer is more likely to know what prices are likely to prevail in equilibrium, and can therefore become a better bargainer. He may also have a finer discrimination of quality differences and be able to judge quality more accurately.

Education is, however, not the only factor that may influence market efficiency. A farmer's age, prior experience in farming, sex, availability of storage, availability of agricultural extension, and availability of credit may all play a role in determining the prices received and paid by the farmer.

Education, and generally better information, may also affect market efficiency by narrowing the dispersion of prices received and paid by the farmers. If this were true, then one observable implication, in addition to higher net price received and lower net price paid on average, is that the net prices received and paid by the educated farmers as a group should vary less than those for uneducated farmers. This thus constitutes another dimension of market efficiency in which education may play a role.

Differences in individual market efficiency arise only because the market as a whole is not perfect. If the market were perfect, all commodities would be bought and sold at single prices. There would then not be a distribution of prices for the same commodity, and every farm household would have the same degree of market efficiency.

Table 6–11 shows the means and variances of the prices received and paid by the sample of Thai farmers, disaggregated by whether the head of household was educated. On the one hand, prices received by the educated farmers were on average higher than those received by uneducated farmers, but the prices paid by the educated farmers were also higher. On the other hand, the variances in the prices received and paid by the educated farmers do seem to be equal to or lower than the corresponding variances of the uneducated farmers. These initial findings are not completely in accord with our expectations. Thus, a more detailed analysis of the interfarm differences in prices is needed.

Empirical implementation

The empirical method used to further study market efficiency is multiple regression analysis. The three prices—price of output,

Table 6–11. *Prices Received and Paid by Thai Farmers*

Kind of farm	Mean	Variance
Price of output (bahts per kilogram)		
Educated farms	1.215	0.024
Uneducated farms	1.169	0.023
All farms	1.180	0.023
Price of labor (bahts per day)		
Educated farms	1.215	4.674
Uneducated farms	1.169	5.818
All farms	1.180	5.532
Price of chemical inputs (bahts per kilogram)		
Educated farms	6.076	13.435
Uneducated farms	5.538	15.863
All farms	5.940	13.935

price of labor, and price of chemical inputs—are regressed on independent variables such as regional dummies, education, chemical or nonchemical dummies, age, sex, availability of extension, and availability of credit.

It is hypothesized that the price of output should depend positively on education and positively on the use of chemicals (because the output will have higher quality). It should relate positively to age (reflecting experience), availability of credit, and possibly the availability of extension.

It is also hypothesized that the price of labor should be negatively related to education and positively related to the use of chemical inputs (because use of chemical inputs is likely to require higher quality labor). It should also relate negatively to age (again reflecting experience). The directions of the effects of the other independent variables cannot be unambiguously specified.

Finally, it is hypothesized that the price of chemical inputs should be negatively related to education. Age, however, will be less relevant because chemical inputs are essentially new inputs. Again, the directions of the effects of the other independent variables cannot be unambiguously specified.

PRICE OF OUTPUT. The regressions of the price of output are summarized in Table 6–12. On the one hand, the negative coefficients on the education dummy variable $E5$ (more than 0 year) indicate that the price received by a farmer is negatively related to whether he had formal education, contrary to our expectation.

Table 6–12. Regressions of the Price of Output for Thai Farms
(sample = 275)

Independent variable	Minimum estimate	Maximum estimate	Maximum R^2 (0.108)	Maximum $\bar{R}^2$ (0.077)	Maximum R^{*2} (0.048)	Estimate of highest t ratio
Region 1	0.871	1.212	0.884	0.899	0.898	1.158
	(8.163)	(47.11)	(8.352)	(9.831)	(9.808)	(60.06)
Region 2	0.859	1.212	0.870	0.885	0.885	1.158
	(7.984)	(58.66)	(8.168)	(9.502)	(9.495)	(82.31)
Region 3	0.936	1.286	0.944	0.959	0.962	1.226
	(8.489)	(37.70)	(8.651)	(9.970)	(10.00)	(40.67)
Region 4	0.861	1.200	0.872	0.887	0.888	1.154
	(8.049)	(39.20)	(8.188)	(9.566)	(9.569)	(41.62)
A5 (education of head of household) (years)	-0.080	-0.012	-0.009	-0.010	—	-0.012
	(-0.946)	(-1.342)	(-1.135)	(-1.211)		(-1.342)
A6 (average education) (years)	0.000	0.004	0.004	—	—	0.004
	(0.010)	(0.590)	(0.590)			(0.590)
A7 (age of head of household) (years)	0.000	0.001	0.000	—	—	0.001
	(0.242)	(2.017)	(0.289)			(2.017)

E5 (education, A5 > 0)	−0.009 (−1.055)	−0.056 (−2.562)	—	—	—	−0.056 (−2.562)
E7	0.002 (0.062)	0.054 (1.151)	0.051 (1.103)	0.048 (1.070)	0.007 (0.230)	0.054 (1.151)
E8	−0.025 (−0.892)	0.023 (0.532)	0.020 (0.474)	0.017 (0.407)	−0.021 (−0.809)	−0.024 (−0.900)
E9	0.093 (2.357)	0.126 (3.196)	0.124 (3.162)	0.124 (3.158)	0.124 (3.160)	0.126 (3.198)
EC	0.040 (2.021)	0.052 (2.691)	—	—	—	0.052 (2.691)
EXT (1 if extension services available; 0 otherwise)	0.017 (0.896)	0.029 (1.539)	—	—	—	0.029 (1.539)
CR (1 if credit taken or available; 0 otherwise)	0.008 (0.376)	0.025 (1.143)	—	—	—	0.025 (1.143)
HM (1 if male; 0 if female)	0.206 (2.326)	0.286 (3.228)	0.284 (3.195)	0.286 (3.229)	0.286 (3.223)	0.286 (3.229)

Note: Numbers in parentheses are t ratios. The variables are defined in Table 4-4.
— Not applicable.

Although this may seem paradoxical, we shall attempt to explain it below. On the other hand, the positive coefficients on the chemical inputs dummy variable *EC* indicate that the price received by a farmer is positively related to whether he used chemical inputs. This, as has been argued earlier, is consistent with the hypothesis of a higher quality of output produced by a farm that used chemical inputs. A further examination through dummy variables *E7*, *E8*, and *E9* reveals that the price of output received is on the average higher by 12 percent for a farm that used chemical inputs but whose head had no education compared with all other farms, including farms that used chemical inputs but whose heads had education. This may have resulted from a higher quality of output produced on farms using chemical inputs. In addition, educated farmers may be more likely to produce varieties that are perhaps less expensive per unit of output but that nevertheless result in higher profits.[6] There is strong evidence, however, that the price received by a male head of household is substantially and statistically significantly higher than that received by a female head of household. The other variables, such as education of the head of household, average education of the adult household members, agricultural extension, and credit availability do not seem to figure significantly. The age variable is statistically significant in some regressions and has the expected positive sign.

Our interpretation of the somewhat unexpected negative association between the price received for the output and the level of education is that it reflects the quality of the output. It is hypothesized that the farmers with higher education produced a quality of rice that, while more profitable at the existing price configurations, nevertheless was less preferred by the consumers. This phenomenon is not an uncommon one, since new varieties (which presumably require less input for a given quantity of output) are generally less willingly accepted by consumers. The proof of this hypothesis awaits further fieldwork to determine whether there are any objective differences in the quality of output.

PRICE OF LABOR. The regressions of the price of labor are summarized in Table 6–13. The price of labor paid by the farmers is positively and statistically significantly related to whether they

6. Alternatively, one may argue that education may inhibit bargaining, but the empirical evidence on this point is rather scanty.

used chemical inputs. This is probably due to the higher quality of labor that would be required to apply chemical inputs. Education does not seem to be a statistically significant factor overall, although the average education of the farm household occasionally has a marginally statistically significant negative effect. This is again consistent with the general hypothesis that the use of chemical inputs requires higher quality labor. When family labor is better educated, the price of labor paid can be lowered.

PRICE OF CHEMICAL INPUTS. The regressions of the price of chemical inputs are reported in Table 6–14. The price of chemical inputs paid by farmers appears to be marginally statistically significantly higher for educated farmers than for uneducated farmers on occasion. The explanation of this phenomenon is not known, although it is consistent with the effect of education on the price of output. (Are we to infer that educated farmers are too polite to bargain?) It may also have been caused by the differences in the composition of the chemical inputs used by the educated and uneducated farmers. It does seem, however, that male heads of households paid on average much less for chemical inputs than female heads of households, an effect consistent with what was found in the price of output regressions. The only persistently statistically significant effect is the substantial negative influence of the availability of agricultural extension. This is consistent with the earlier interpretation that the agricultural extension service is interested in promoting the use of chemical inputs. But another explanation is that the agricultural extension service has done such a successful job that the farmers know not to pay any more than necessary for their chemical inputs. The availability of credit is occasionally statistically significant and always has a positive sign. The reason is possibly that the availability of credit enhances a farmer's ability to use higher-priced—possibly also higher-quality—chemical inputs.

Explanatory power of price regressions

The explanatory power of these price regressions is very low compared with the production function and the profit function regressions. Only 10 percent of the variation in the prices of output, 18 percent of the variation in the price of labor, and 18 percent of the variation in the price of chemical inputs can be accounted for by these regressions. This implies that a substantial proportion of the

Table 6–13. Regressions of the Price of Labor for Thai Farms
(sample = 275)

Independent variable	Minimum estimate	Maximum estimate	Maximum R^2 (0.178)	Maximum $\bar{R}^2$ (0.150)	Maximum R^{*2} (0.134)	Estimate of highest t ratio
Region 1	10.16 (15.29)	11.39 (21.40)	10.90 (16.13)	10.28 (21.49)	10.73 (38.86)	10.73 (38.86)
Region 2	8.627 (6.211)	9.854 (20.20)	9.402 (15.35)	8.810 (22.31)	9.197 (45.66)	9.197 (45.66)
Region 3	9.068 (12.28)	10.32 (16.21)	9.780 (12.97)	9.186 (15.86)	9.626 (22.29)	9.626 (22.29)
Region 4	7.670 (10.90)	8.68 (15.80)	8.276 (13.80)	7.799 (15.71)	8.139 (20.49)	8.139 (20.49)
A5 (education of head of household) (years)	-0.052 (-0.387)	-0.139 (-1.124)	-0.053 (-0.410)	—	—	-0.138 (-1.126)
A6 (average education) (years)	-0.150 (-1.348)	-0.175 (-1.710)	-0.150 (-1.353)	—	—	-0.175 (-1.710)
A7 (age of head of household) (years)	-0.003 (-0.210)	0.009 (0.840)	—	—	—	0.009 (0.840)

	(1)	(2)	(3)	(4)	(5)	(6)
E5 (education, A5 > 0)	-0.072 (-0.179)	-0.230 (-0.710)	—	—	—	-0.229 (-0.712)
E7	0.987 (2.040)	1.574 (2.332)	1.388 (2.071)	—	—	1.214 (2.717)
E8	-0.132 (-0.278)	0.394 (0.650)	0.206 (0.338)	—	—	0.394 (0.650)
E9	1.098 (1.922)	1.267 (2.182)	1.111 (1.949)	—	—	1.267 (2.182)
EC	1.143 (4.065)	1.181 (4.173)	—	1.151 (4.132)	1.169 (4.198)	1.176 (4.202)
EXT (1 if extension services available; 0 otherwise)	-0.109 (-0.396)	0.123 (0.447)	—	—	—	0.123 (0.447)
CR (1 if credit taken or available; 0 otherwise)	0.279 (0.881)	0.408 (1.289)	—	—	—	0.408 (1.289)
HM (1 if male; 0 if female)	-0.019 (-0.014)	0.552 (0.419)	—	—	—	0.552 (0.419)

Note: Numbers in parentheses are *t* ratios. The variables are defined in Table 4–4.
— Not applicable.

Table 6–14. *Regressions of the Price of Chemical Inputs for Thai Farms* (sample = 91)

Independent variable	Minimum estimate	Maximum estimate	Maximum R^2 (0.183)	Maximum $\bar{R}^2$ (0.112)	Maximum R^{*2} (0.049)	Estimate of highest t ratio
Region 1	2.395	3.039	2.672	2.620	2.775	2.733
	(13.16)	(14.79)	(14.38)	(16.24)	(27.79)	(42.09)
Region 2	2.377	3.069	2.656	2.611	2.770	2.741
	(13.44)	(14.69)	(15.15)	(16.75)	(32.53)	(69.83)
Region 3	2.554	3.248	2.858	2.816	2.961	2.905
	(14.00)	(14.75)	(15.42)	(16.58)	(24.43)	(34.04)
Region 4	2.312	2.860	2.598	2.544	2.692	2.563
	(12.95)	(14.12)	(13.39)	(15.05)	(22.87)	(27.16)
A5 (education of head of household) (years)	-0.016	0.019	-0.010	—	—	0.019
	(-1.074)	(1.384)	(-0.561)			(1.384)
A6 (average education) (years)	0.022	0.038	0.035	0.027	0.023	0.038
	(0.947)	(1.677)	(1.526)	(1.483)	(1.282)	(1.677)
A7 (age of head of household) (years)	0.001	0.004	0.002	0.003	—	0.004
	(0.447)	(1.283)	(0.793)	(1.213)		(1.283)

E2 (education, 0 < A5 < 4)	-0.093 (-0.809)	-0.017 (-0.141)	—	—	—	-0.093 (-0.809)
E3 (education, A5 = 4)	-0.039 (-0.581)	0.033 (0.423)	—	—	—	-0.039 (-0.581)
E4 (education, A5 > 4)	0.084 (0.612)	0.263 (1.768)	—	—	—	0.263 (1.768)
E5 (education, A5 > 0)	-0.036 (-0.541)	0.034 (0.433)	—	—	—	-0.036 (-0.541)
EXT (1 if extension services available; 0 otherwise)	-0.172 (-2.638)	-0.203 (-3.104)	-0.196 (-2.988)	-0.185 (-2.953)	-0.183 (-2.902)	-0.203 (-3.104)
CR (1 if credit taken or available; 0 otherwise)	0.145 (1.737)	0.172 (2.173)	—	—	—	0.172 (2.173)
HM (1 if male; 0 if female)	-0.304 (-1.467)	-0.361 (-1.726)	—	—	—	-0.361 (-1.726)

Note: Numbers in parentheses are *t* ratios. The variables are defined in Table 4–4.
— Not applicable.

variation in prices for all farm households remains unexplained. It is possible that individual factors specific to each farm, such as location, might have been important.

Summary

Our results from the empirical analyses of market efficiency do not indicate that education has a strong effect on prices received and paid by Thai farmers in general. For chemical farms, there is some evidence that educated farmers received on average lower prices for their outputs than uneducated farmers. The precise reason for this phenomenon is unknown, although we had several alternative hypotheses. There is also some evidence that for educated farmers the variances of the prices received and paid are generally smaller. On the whole, however, we must conclude that the effect of education on market efficiency as we have defined it is rather weak.

The availability of agricultural extension services has a weak positive effect on the prices of output received by the farmers and a statistically significant negative effect on the prices of chemical inputs paid by the farmers. The latter effect may be partly due to greater availability of chemical inputs wherever agricultural extension is available.

CHAPTER 7

Education and the Adoption of Innovation

T. W. SCHULTZ HAS ARGUED that education is likely to make a more substantial contribution to agricultural productivity if the environment is changing rapidly. Education increases a person's awareness of his environment and his ability to acquire and process information about his environment and to detect changes in it. It also enhances his ability to identify alternatives and to assess and compare the benefits and costs associated with each of the alternatives, possibly under different states of nature. Education also in general increases the facility and speed with which new skills and techniques can be learned and new alternatives, when judged desirable, can be adopted and implemented. Thus, other things being equal, it is eminently reasonable to expect that education will enhance the probability of adopting a new, presumably superior, technology.

A number of previous studies have examined the effect of education on the willingness of farmers to adopt innovations. Roy, Waisanen, and Rogers (1969) made an early and important study in this area. Villaume (1977, chapter 2) provides a valuable review of this extensive literature as well as an assessment of the direct and indirect effect of literacy on the adoption of innovations in Brazil and India. Gerhart (1975) and Rosenzweig (1978) use empirical techniques similar to those of this chapter to identify factors influencing the probability of farmers' adopting new varieties. Gerhart found that in Kenya a farmer's level of education was positively associated with the probability that he would adopt hybrid maize varieties. Rosenzweig developed a model in which the time cost associated with acquiring and using information was an important factor influencing the decision to innovate. He applied the model to a sample of farmers in the Punjab, again finding that education was positively associated with the probability of a farmer's adopting new varieties.

In this chapter we analyze the determinants of Thai farmers' use of chemical inputs. In our sample of Thai farms, approximately 33 percent used chemical inputs, and the remaining 67 percent did not. We determine whether education and agricultural extension play a significant role in the decision to adopt the technology. In addition, other variables that may be relevant, such as the age and sex of the head of the household and the availability of credit, are included in the analysis.

Empirical Methods

To begin, a model of individual behavior in which the objects of choice are discrete and dichotomous is presented. Each farm household may be described by a vector of observable characteristics, such as location, maximum age of heads of household, sex of head of household, maximum education of heads of household, and average education of household members 17 to 60 years old.[1] These characteristics affect the ability and willingness of the farm household to adopt a new technology—in this case, a technology that uses chemical inputs.

In addition to the characteristics of the farm household, the economic environment also effects the potential benefits and costs to the farm households of adopting a new technology. The economic environment faced by a farm household may be described by the quantities of capital and land, location, prices of output and variable inputs, availability of agricultural extension services, and availability of credit.

Whether a farm household adopted a new technology depends on both its characteristics and on the economic environment it faced. This chapter assesses the importance of household characteristics, especially education, and public interventions in the economic environment, such as agricultural extension, in the decision to adopt technology. We abstract from an explicit consideration of the farm

---

1. The term maximum is used in cases in which more than one individual is listed as the head of household.

household's decisionmaking process under uncertainty and particularly its attitude toward risk. To the extent that the farm household's attitude toward risk is related to the characteristics of the farm household, it is taken into account through the characteristic variables.

The price of chemical inputs is also included as an independent variable even for the nonchemical farms, because it is expected to have a significant effect on the decision to adopt technology. If the price of chemical inputs is high, it will deter the adoption of a technology using chemical inputs. If the price of chemical inputs is low, it will encourage the adoption of a technology using chemical inputs. Since the prices of the chemical inputs faced by the nonchemical farms were not directly observed, it is assumed in the empirical analysis that they were equal to the average price of chemical inputs faced by the chemical farms within the same village.

A model of dichotomous choice

The farm household had to choose between two mutually exclusive and exhaustive alternatives: to adopt the new technology that uses chemical inputs or to continue to use the traditional technology. It is assumed that the net benefit accruing to the ith individual farm household from using the traditional technology can be written as a function of the characteristics of the farm household, variables representing the economic environment, and a specific household factor, in the form

$$U_{iT}(Z_i) = U_T(Z_i) + \varepsilon_{iT}$$

where Z_i is a vector of independent variables representing the household characteristics and the economic environment, and ε_{iT} is a variable representing the ith household's specific preference for the traditional technology. The function $U_T(\,\cdot\,)$ does not depend on the individual household. Similarly, the net benefit accruing to the ith individual farm household from using the new technology can be written as a function of the same independent variables, and a specific household factor, in the form

$$U_{iN}(Z_i) = U_N(Z_i) + \varepsilon_{iN}.$$

The variables ε_{iT} and ε_{iN} cannot be directly observed, but it is assumed that their joint distribution over the whole population can be described by a probability density function.

Figure 7–1. *Probability Distribution Function
for the Logistic Variate with* $\mu = 0$ *and* $\sigma = 1$

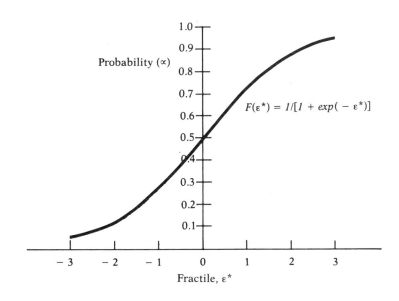

Figure 7–2. *Probability Density Function
for the Logistic Variate with* $\mu = 0$ *and* $\sigma = 1$

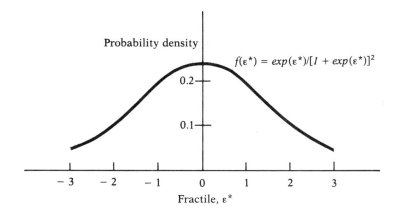

It is assumed that the individual farm household compared the net benefits accruing from the two alternatives, and chose the alternative that gave a higher level of net benefit.[2] Thus, the probability of an individual farm household drawn randomly from the population, with characteristics and environment represented by Z, would choose the new technology equals

$$P_i(N|Z) = P_i[U_{iN}(Z) > U_{iT}(Z)]$$
$$= P_i[U_N(Z) - U_T(Z) > \varepsilon_{iT} - \varepsilon_{iN}].$$

It is clear that this probability depends on the difference of the functions $U_N(Z)$ and $U_T(Z)$ and $\varepsilon_{iT} - \varepsilon_{iN}$. Even with an infinite number of observations on the discrete choice behavior of the individual farm households, these functions and random variables cannot be identified separately. Only their differences can be identified. The difference $U_N(Z) - U_T(Z)$ is specified to be a linear function of Z, that is,

(7.1) $$U_N(Z) - U_T(Z) = \gamma'Z$$

where γ is a vector of unknown parameters. The difference in the individual household factors

$$\varepsilon_{iT} - \varepsilon_{iN} \equiv \varepsilon^*$$

is assumed to be identically and independently distributed as the logistic distribution over the population. A large value of the random variable $\varepsilon_{iT} - \varepsilon_{iN}$ implies that there is a small probability, given Z, that the ith individual farm household will adopt the new technology.

The logistic distribution function is given by

$$F(\varepsilon^*) = 1 - \{1 + \exp[(\varepsilon^* - \mu)/\sigma]\}^{-1}$$
$$= \{1 + \exp[-(\varepsilon^* - \mu)/\sigma]\}^{-1}$$

where μ and σ are parameters of the distribution function. A typical distribution function for the logistic variate is plotted in Figure 7–1. The corresponding probability density function $f(\varepsilon^*)$ is plotted in Figure 7–2.

---

2. When the net benefits are equal, it is assumed that the individual farm household chooses the status quo—the traditional technology. But, as pointed out below, the probability of the net benefits being exactly equal is zero.

The probability of adopting a new technology under the assumption that ε^* is distributed as the logistic distribution is given by[3]

$$P(N|Z) = P(\gamma'Z > \varepsilon^*)$$
$$= P(\varepsilon^* \leqq \gamma'Z)$$
$$= \{1 + \exp[-(\gamma'Z - \mu)/\sigma]\}^{-1}.$$

Without loss of generality μ and σ may be absorbed into $\gamma'Z$ (by adding a constant term and rescaling of the parameters), so that the probability of adopting becomes

$$P(N \mid Z) = [1 + \exp - (\gamma'Z)]^{-1}.$$

The probability of not adopting is of course given by

$$P(T \mid Z) = 1 - P(NZ)$$
$$= [\exp - (\gamma'Z)]/[1 + \exp - (\gamma'Z)]$$
$$= [1 + \exp(\gamma'Z)]^{-1}.$$

This is the basic equation of the logit model. The relative probabilities of adopting versus not adopting are given by

$$P(N|Z)/P(T|Z) = [1 + \exp - (\gamma'Z)]^{-1}/\{[\exp - (\gamma'Z)]/[1 + \exp - (\gamma'Z)]\}$$
$$= \exp \gamma'Z$$

so that

$$\ln P(N \mid Z)/P(T \mid Z) = \gamma'Z.$$

In other words, the logarithm of the relative odds of adopting versus not adopting is equal to $\gamma'Z$, a linear function of Z. This is a standard feature of a dichotomous logit model.

Maximum likelihood estimation

The parameters γ represent the effect of the independent variables Z on the probability of adoption. Our objective is to estimate these parameters. The method of estimation used is maximum likelihood, which is described below.

---

3. For the logistic distribution,
$$P_i(\gamma'Z > \varepsilon_i^*) = P_i(\gamma'Z \geqq \varepsilon_i^*) \text{ where } P_i(\gamma'Z = \varepsilon_i^*) = 0.$$

Define a variable Y_i which takes the value 1 if the ith individual farm household adopted the new technology, and 0 if otherwise. Let Z_i be the vector of independent variables of the ith individual farm household. Then the probability of $Y_i = 1$, given Z_i, is

$$P(Y_i = 1 \mid Z_i) = [1 + \exp - (\gamma'Z_i)]^{-1}.$$

The probability of $Y_i = 0$, given Z_i, is

$$P(Y_i = 0 \mid Z_i) = [1 + \exp(\gamma'Z_i)]^{-1}.$$

Each variable Y_i may be regarded as the result of a single trial from a binomial distribution with the probability of success given by $P(Y_i = 1 \mid Z_i)$. Thus, the likelihood of the ith observation is given by

$$L_i = P(Y_i = 1 \mid Z_i)^{Y_i} P(Y_i = 0 \mid Z_i)^{(1 - Y_i)}$$
$$= [1 + \exp - (\gamma'Z_i)]^{-Y_i}[1 + \exp(\gamma'Z_i)]^{-(1 - Y_i)}.$$

The likelihood function for a sample of n independent observations is given by

$$L = \Pi_{i=1}^{n} P(Y_i = 1 \mid Z_i)^{Y_i}[1 - P(Y_i = 1 \mid Z_i)]^{(1 - Y_i)}$$
$$= \Pi_{i=1}^{n} [1 + \exp - (\gamma'Z_i)]^{-Y_i}\{[\exp - (\gamma'Z_i)]/$$
$$[1 + \exp - (\gamma'Z_i)]\}^{(1 - Y_i)}$$
$$= \Pi_{i=1}^{n} [\exp - (\gamma'Z_i)]^{(1 - Y_i)}[1 + \exp - (\gamma'Z_i)]^{-1}.$$

A value of γ is sought such that the sample likelihood function is maximized. Instead of maximizing the likelihood function itself, the natural logarithm of the likelihood function is maximized:

(7.2) $\ln L = - \Sigma_{i=1}^{n} (1 - Y_i)\gamma'Z_i - \Sigma_{i=1}^{n} \ln [1 + \exp - (\gamma'Z_i)].$

Differentiating $\ln L$ with respect to γ, and setting the derivative equal to zero, we obtain the maximum likelihood equations,

(7.3) $\partial \ln L/\partial \gamma = - \Sigma_{i=1}^{n} (1 - Y_i)Z_i$
$$+ \Sigma_{i=1}^{n} 1/[1 + \exp - (\gamma'Z_i)] Z_i$$
$$= \Sigma_{i=1}^{n} \{(Y_i - 1) + 1/[1 + \exp - (\gamma'Z_i)]\} Z_i = 0.$$

Equations (7.3) may be solved by iterative methods for $\hat{\gamma}$, the maximum likelihood estimate of γ.

Differentiating $\ln L$ with respect to γ a second time, we obtain:

$$\partial^2 \ln L/\partial \gamma \partial \gamma' = - \Sigma_{i=1}^{n} 1/[1 + \exp - (\gamma'Z_i)]^2 Z_i Z_i'.$$

If the matrix of independent variables $\begin{bmatrix} Z'_i \\ \vdots \\ Z'_n \end{bmatrix}$ is of full rank, then

$\Sigma_{i=1}^n \alpha_i Z_i Z'_i$, where $\alpha_i = [1 + \exp - (\gamma'Z_i)]^{-2} > 0$, $\forall$ i, will be a positive definite matrix, implying that the matrix of second derivatives of the logarithm of the likelihood function is negative definite.[4] This ensures that a unique maximum exists for the likelihood maximization problem. It follows that the maximum likelihood estimator of γ as defined in equation (7.3) is consistent, asymptotically normal, and asymptotically efficient.

Alternative specifications

In our empirical analysis the probability of adoption is specified to be

$$P(Y_i = 1 \mid Z_i) = [1 + \exp - (\gamma'Z_i)]^{-1}$$

where $\gamma'Z_i$, in its most general form, is set equal to

$$(7.4) \qquad \gamma'Z_i = \gamma_0 + \gamma_p \ln P_{0i} + \gamma_L \ln W_i + \gamma_C \ln PCN_i$$
$$+ \gamma_K \ln K_i + \gamma_T \ln T_i + \Sigma_{l=2}^4 R_{li}$$
$$+ \gamma_{A5} A5_i + \gamma_{A6} A6_i + \gamma_{EXT} EXT_i$$
$$+ \gamma_{A7} A7_i + \gamma_{HM} HM_i + \gamma_{CR} CR_i$$

where P_{0i} is the price of the output of the ith farm, W_i and PCN_i are, respectively, the normalized wage rate and the normalized price of chemical inputs; K_i and T_i are, respectively, the quantities of capital and land operated by the ith farm; and R_{li}, EXT_i, CR_i, and HM_i are respectively, the values of the dummy variables corresponding to each region, availability of agricultural extension, and availability of credit ($= 1$ if available, 0 otherwise), and sex of the head of household ($= 1$ if male, 0 otherwise). $A5_i$ is the maximum number of years of formal education of the head(s) of household, $A6_i$ is the average number of years of formal education for each adult member

---

4. Note that $\Sigma_{i=1}^n \alpha_i X'Z_iZ'_iX$ is a sum with positive coefficients of n nonnegative variables. Moreover, if $\Sigma_{i=1}^n \alpha_i X'Z_iZ'_iX = 0$ for any X, it implies that $X'Z_i = 0$ for all i, which implies that $X' \Sigma_{i=1}^n Z_iZ'_iX = 0$, contradicting the assumption that the matrix of independent variables is of full rank.

of the household, and $A7_i$ is the maximum age of the head(s) of household.

Equation (7.4) will be referred to as specification (1). It is the basic form of the estimating equations used in the empirical analysis. Two other specifications were also used. In specification (2), the formal education term, $\gamma_{A5}A5_i$, is replaced by $\gamma_{E5}E5_i$, where $E5_i$ is a dummy variable that takes the value 1 if the head of household is educated, and 0 if otherwise. In specification (3), the formal education term is replaced by

$$\gamma_{E2}E2_i + \gamma_{E3}E3_i + \gamma_{E4}E4_i$$

where $E2_i$ is a dummy variable taking the value 1 if the head of household has more than 0 but less than 4 years of formal education, $E3_i$ is a dummy variable taking the value 1 if the head of household has exactly 4 years of formal education, and $E4_i$ is a dummy variable taking the value 1 if the head of household has more than 4 years of formal education. The purpose of these alternative specifications is to explore the possibility of a nonlinear or threshold effect of education on the decision to adopt.

One possible specialization of the function $U_N(Z_i) - U_T(Z_i) = \gamma'Z_i$ is to assume that it is linear in the difference between the natural logarithm of the profits of the two alternative technologies.[5] Thus,

$$U_N(Z_i) - U_T(Z_i) = \ln \Pi_N^*(Z_i) - \ln \Pi_T^*(Z_i)$$

where $\Pi_N^*(Z_i)$ and $\Pi_T^*(Z_i)$ are, respectively, the nominal profit functions of the new technology and the traditional technology. Under the assumption that the output prices faced by the ith farm are the same under the new or the traditional technology, this is in turn equal to

$$= \ln \Pi_N(Z_i) - \ln \Pi_T(Z_i)$$

where $\Pi_N(Z_i)$ and $\Pi_T(Z_i)$ are, respectively, the normalized profit functions of the new technology and the traditional technology.

Under our assumptions of Cobb-Douglas production functions, each of the logarithmic normalized profit functions is a linear function in the natural logarithms of the normalized prices and the fixed inputs and linear in the characteristic variables, so that

5. This would be the case if it is assumed that the household utility function is a logarithmic function of profit and that the household maximizes expected utility.

$$U_N(Z_i) - U_T(Z_i) = \gamma' Z_i$$
$$= (\alpha_0^N - \alpha_0^T)$$
$$+ (\alpha*_L^N - \alpha*_L^T) \ln W_i + \alpha*_C^N \ln PCN_i$$
$$+ (\beta*_K^N - \beta*_K^T) \ln K_i + (\beta*_T^N - \beta*_T^T) \ln T_i$$
$$+ \Sigma_{l=2}^4 (\delta_l^N - \delta_l^T)R_{li} + (\delta_{EXT}^N - \delta_{EXT}^T)EXT_i$$
$$+ (\delta_{E5}^N - \delta_{E5}^T)E5_i$$

where the α_i^*'s, β_i^*'s and, δ_i's are the parameters of the normalized profit function, and the superscripts N and T denote, respectively, the technologies using chemical inputs and those not using chemical inputs. If this specialization were in fact true, then the coefficients of the logit regression on the prices of outputs and variable inputs and on the quantities of the fixed inputs should be the same as the differences in the corresponding coefficients between the chemical and nonchemical normalized profit functions. It is also possible to impose these constraints a priori. This has not been done here, since other considerations than just profit may have also been relevant to the decision of the farmer.

Caveats

Finally, a word needs to be said about the data. In principle, the price variables that are relevant for the decision to adopt technology should be the prices that the farmer expects to prevail over the production period. These expected prices may be different from the realized prices. Unfortunately, data are not available on expected prices. Therefore, we have used the actual realized prices instead. To the extent that the actual realized prices differ significantly from the expected prices, we have a problem of errors in the variables that may bias the estimates of the parameters.

The validity of the logit analysis depends on the assumption that the ε_i^*'s, the specific net benefits to the individual farm household, are independently and identically distributed as the logistic distribution. This assumption will be approximately valid if the true underlying probability density distribution is symmetric around its mean and has a relatively strong central tendency. For example, the normal distribution can be approximated to a high degree of accuracy by a logistic distribution. This binomial logit analysis has been generalized to the case of many alternatives.[6] Thus, this framework can be used to analyze the choice of crops and the choice of varieties, as well as the choice of inputs.

Adoption of Technology by Thai Farms

The empirical model developed above is applied to the sample of Thai farms. Out of 275 farms in the usable sample, 184 did not use chemical inputs, and 91 used chemical inputs. Using this sample we first ran logit regressions, using as independent variables the logarithms of the price of output, the normalized wage rate and the normalized price of chemical inputs, the logarithms of the quantities of capital and land, regional dummy variables, maximum education of head of household, average education of the adult members of the household, and availability of agricultural extension. The last three particular characteristic variables were selected because they were expected to have an effect on the probability of adoption. We also experimented with the alternative forms of the formal education variable. The results of the logit regressions of the three alternative specifications are summarized in Table 7–1.

Effects of prices and fixed inputs

Table 7–1 indicates that although the price of output does not have a statistically significant effect, the normalized wage rate has a positive and statistically significant effect. The higher the wage rate faced by a farm household, the more likely it is to adopt the technology using chemical inputs. There are two possible explanations for this phenomenon. The first explanation is based on the assumption that labor and chemical inputs are substitutes. The second explanation is based on the assumption that using chemical inputs requires higher quality labor, and hence the wage rate paid by the farm household tends to go up as it adopts the use of chemical inputs. We believe that the second explanation is the more plausible one, since almost all studies of agricultural production in Thailand suggest that labor and chemical inputs are more complements than substitutes. It is also consistent with the positive dependence of the wage

6. See, for example, McFadden (1974).

Table 7–1. *Logit Regressions for Thai Farms*
(sample = 275)

Independent variable	Specification			
	(0)	(1)	(2)	(3)
Constant	-5.352	-5.757	-5.567	-5.833
	(-2.301)	(-2.379)	(-2.297)	(-2.336)
Price of output (baht per kilogram) (ln)	2.226	2.014	1.816	2.280
	(1.655)	(1.440)	(1.302)	(1.582)
Price of labor (baht per day) (ln)	2.339	2.384	2.409	2.605
	(3.109)	(3.044)	(3.073)	(3.226)
Price of chemical inputs (baht per kilogram) (ln)	-1.054	-1.146	-1.152	-1.165
	(-2.524)	(-2.636)	(-2.661)	(-2.684)
Capital (baht) (ln)	-0.244	-0.312	-0.321	-0.335
	(-1.080)	(-1.320)	(-1.375)	(-1.384)
Land area (rai) (ln)	0.746	0.726	0.737	0.702
	(2.899)	(2.788)	(2.838)	(2.657)
Region 2	0.452	0.536	0.481	0.585
	(1.164)	(1.309)	(1.184)	(1.367)
Region 3	1.596	1.535	1.510	1.650
	(2.666)	(2.467)	(2.446)	(2.602)
Region 4	0.624	0.756	0.701	0.846
	(1.081)	(1.250)	(1.165)	(1.350)

A5 (education of head of household) (years)	—	0.089 (1.047)	—	—
A6 (average education) (years)	—	−0.012 (−0.099)	0.071 (0.617)	−0.034 (−0.267)
E2 (education, 0 < A5 < 4)	—	—	—	−0.186 (−0.321)
E3 (education, A5 = 4)	—	—	—	−0.161 (−0.419)
E4 (education, A5 > 4)	—	—	—/	2.339 (2.355)
E5 (education, A5 > 0)	—	—	−0.209 (−0.581)	—
EXT (1 if extension services available; 0 otherwise)	—	0.876 (2.831)	0.863 (2.797)	1.003 (3.095)
Log likelihood	−156.1	−151.2	−151.6	−147.6

Note: Numbers in parentheses are *t* ratios. The variables are defined in Table 4-4.
— Not applicable.

rate (price of labor) on the use of chemical inputs as reported in Chapter 6.

The normalized price of chemical inputs has a negative and statistically significant effect, as expected. The higher the price of chemical inputs faced by a farm household, the less likely it is to adopt the technology using chemical inputs.

The quantity of land has a consistently positive and statistically significant effect, although capital does not seem to have a significant effect, as in all the other chapters. Land captures two effects. First, with a larger quantity of land, the average cost per unit of land of adopting a new technology, which involves fixed costs, will be reduced, and the average net benefit per unit of land will be enhanced. Second, the quantity of land may be an indicator of the level of assets, and a higher level of assets implies a greater ability and willingness for the farm household to take risks. Land may also have been differentially productive for the chemical and nonchemical farms. The results in Chapter 6 indicate, however, that the elasticity of normalized profit with respect to land is approximately the same for chemical and nonchemical farms.

Effects of education and agricultural extension

Before examining the education and agricultural extension coefficients, we first test the hypothesis that the effects of these characteristic variables are zero. This is equivalent to testing the following hypotheses:

   a. For specification (1), H_0: $\delta_{A5} = 0$, $\delta_{A6} = 0$, $\delta_{EXT} = 0$.

   b. For specification (2), H_0: $\delta_{E5} = 0$, $\delta_{A6} = 0$, $\delta_{EXT} = 0$.

   c. For specification (3), H_0: $\delta_{E2} = \delta_{E3} = \delta_{E4} = 0$, $\delta_{A6} = 0$, $\delta_{EXT} = 0$.

Likelihood ratio tests are used for this purpose.

A likelihood ratio test can be explained as follows. Suppose that the admissible parameter space (the set of all values that can be taken by the parameters) is Ω and that under the null hypothesis H_0 of interest the parameter space is restricted to ω. ω must of course be a subset of Ω. The likelihood ratio λ is defined as

$$\lambda = L(\hat{\omega})/L(\hat{\Omega})$$

where $L(\hat{\omega})$ and $L(\hat{\Omega})$ are the maximized likelihoods when the parameter space is restricted to ω and Ω, respectively. Intuitively,

$L(\hat{\Omega}) \geqq L(\hat{\omega})$, because an unconstrained maximum must be greater than or equal to a constrained maximum, so that the likelihood ratio is always less than one. If H_0 were actually true, however, then the restriction of the parameter space to ω within Ω would not be a substantive restriction, and hence $L(\hat{\omega})$ would be very close in value to $L(\hat{\Omega})$, and the likelihood ratio would be close in value to unity. Thus, values of the likelihood ratio close to unity favor the null hypothesis, and values far from one suggest that the null hypothesis may be false.

It can be shown that under mild regularity conditions (which are satisfied in this case) the random variable $-2 \ln \lambda$, where λ is the likelihood ratio, is asymptotically distributed as χ^2 with degrees of freedom equal to the number of independent restrictions on the parameters implied by the null hypothesis H_0.

We compute $-2 \ln \lambda$ for the null hypotheses that all the education and extension effects are zero, as shown in Table 7–2. The critical values corresponding to alternative levels of significance are also shown, so that the reader can evaluate the robustness of our test procedure.

A level of significance 0.05 is assigned to the test of zero education and extension effects. This implies that the probability of falsely rejecting a hypothesis when it is in fact true using our procedure is 0.05. At this level of significance, we reject the hypothesis of zero effects for each of the three specifications embodying alternative representations of the formal education variable. We conclude that education and extension have significant effects on the probability of adoption.

Next, the coefficients of the education and extension variables are examined. The logit regression with the best fit is the one in which the education variable is disaggregated into *E2* (0 to 4 years), *E3*

Table 7-2. *Likelihood Ratio Tests for Zero Education and Extension Effects*

Null hypothesis	Degrees of freedom	$-2 \ln \lambda$	Critical values of χ^2 at given levels of significance		
			0.01	*0.05*	*0.10*
(1)	3	9.80	11.34	7.81	6.25
(2)	3	9.00	11.34	7.81	6.25
(3)	5	17.00	15.09	11.07	9.24

Table 7–3. *Logit Regressions for Thai Farms*
(sample = 275)

Independent variable	Specification		
	(1)	*(2)*	*(3)*
Constant	−6.022	−5.292	−5.949
	(−1.984)	(−1.778)	(−1.927)
Price of output	2.006	1.852	2.357
(baht per kilogram) (ln)	(1.369)	(1.285)	(1.571)
Price of labor	2.336	2.322	2.593
(baht per day) (ln)	(2.854)	(2.889)	(3.102)
Price of chemical inputs	−1.382	−1.304	−1.310
(baht per kilogram) (ln)	(−3.073)	(−2.930)	(−2.956)
Capital	−0.176	−0.225	−0.215
(baht) (ln)	(−0.718)	(−0.944)	(−0.869)
Land area	0.651	0.690	0.639
(rai) (ln)	(2.421)	(2.600)	(2.358)
Region 2	0.623	0.532	0.654
	(1.453)	(1.278)	(1.478)
Region 3	1.709	1.561	1.739
	(2.663)	(2.485)	(2.687)
Region 4	0.763	0.705	0.842
	(1.201)	(1.136)	(1.293)
A5 (education of head of household)	0.295	—	—
(years)	(2.838)		
A6 (average education) (years)	−0.066	0.061	−0.073
	(−0.505)	(0.521)	(−0.547)
E2 (education, 0 < *A5* < 4)	—	—	0.356
			(0.574)
E3 (education, *A5* = 4)	—	—	0.645
			(1.299)
E4 (education, *A5* > 4)	—	—	3.452
			(3.091)
E5 (education, *A5* > 0)	—	0.428	—
		(0.932)	
EXT (1 if extension services available;	0.927	0.846	1.012
0 otherwise)	(2.852)	(2.674)	(3.016)
A7 (age of head of household)	0.045	0.028	0.036
(years)	(2.836)	(1.793)	(2.206)
CR (1 if credit taken or available;	0.301	0.295	0.200
0 otherwise)	(0.766)	(0.762)	(0.499)
HM (1 if male; 0 if female)	−2.738	−2.294	−2.522
	(−1.882)	(−1.637)	(−1.739)
Log likelihood	−144.1	−147.9	−143.0

Note: Numbers in parentheses are *t* ratios. The variables are defined in Table 4–4.

   — Not applicable.

(exactly 4 years), and *E4* (more than 4 years). In this regression, *E4* is the only statistically significant education variable. This implies that more than 4 years of education is necessary before it affects the probability of adopting the new technology. Four or fewer years of education do not seem to have any statistically significant effect. When the education variable is represented by a single continuous variable, *A5*, it shows positive but statistically insignificant effects. When the education variable is measured by a single dummy variable, *E5*, it shows negative but statistically insignificant effects. These results suggest that there may be a threshold education level of 4 years, which must be exceeded before it affects the probability of adoption.

The average level of education per adult member of the household does not have a statistically significant coefficient in any one of the logit regressions reported in Table 7–1 at any reasonable level of significance. Availability of agricultural extension, however, is found to affect the probability of adopting the new technology in a positive and statistically significant manner. Its effect is between one-third to two-fifths of the effect of more than 4 years of formal education.

Effects of other characteristic variables

Our examination of the effects of the education and extension variables on the decision to adopt technology indicates that both the level of education of the head of household and the availability of agricultural extension have positive and statistically significant effects on the probability of adopting the technology using chemical inputs. The question that arises naturally is: do the other household characteristic variables, such as the age and sex of the head of household and the availability of credit, make a difference? To answer this question, logit regressions including these additional variables under each of the three alternative specifications of the formal education variable were estimated. These logit regressions are presented in Table 7–3. Likelihood ratio tests were also computed for the null hypothesis that the effects of all these other variables are zero for each of the three alternative specifications of the formal education variable. These statistics for the likelihood ratio tests are presented in Table 7–4 along with the critical values.

At a level of significance equal to 0.05, the hypothesis of zero other effects can be rejected for specifications (1) and (3) but not for specification (2). We consider this sufficient evidence that these

Table 7-4. *Likelihood Ratio Tests for Zero Other Effects*

Specification	Degrees of freedom	$-2 \ln \lambda$	Critical values of χ^2 at given levels of significance		
			0.01	*0.05*	*0.10*
(1)	3	14.20	11.34	7.81	6.25
(2)	3	7.40	11.34	7.81	6.25
(3)	3	9.20	11.34	7.81	6.25

other variables do have an effect on the probability of adoption. An examination of the specifications (1) and (3) indicates that the age of the head of household variable has a statistically significant and positive effect on the probability of adoption. It is possible that the age variable may be a proxy for experience. Still, it is somewhat remarkable that age, which is usually associated with conservatism, enhances the probability of adopting the new technology rather than diminishes it. One possible explanation may lie in the self-selection phenomenon: those young farmers who can respond quickly to changes in the environment have probably all left the agricultural sector to seek more remunerative employment. Another possible explanation may lie in the distribution of assets (excluding capital and land) across age groups: one may expect the distribution to be skewed in favor of farm households with older heads. If all heads of farm households had the same concave utility function, the older farm household heads would be more likely to take greater risks because they would have more assets. If data on assets were available, this hypothesis could be tested directly. The two remaining variables, sex of the head of household and the availability of credit, do not show statistically significant effects.

Robustness of the estimates

To assess the degree of robustness of our estimated effects of education, agricultural extension, and other household characteristics, logit regressions representing all possible distinct combinations of the independent variables corresponding to education, extension, and other household characteristics were run.[7] In all these

7. The reports of these regressions are in the technical annexes, which are not included in this volume because of their bulk. They are available from the authors on request.

regressions, the prices of the output and the variable inputs, the quantities of capital and land, and the regional dummy variables were always included.

The results of these logit regressions for each coefficient are summarized in Table 7–5. Columns 1 and 2 contain the minimum and the maximum estimates, respectively, that are found in the regressions. Column 3 contains the value of the estimate that has the highest absolute value of the *t* ratio in the regressions. Column 4 contains the estimates of the logit regression that has the highest value of the likelihood function across all the alternative specifications of the independent variables corresponding to education, extension, and household characteristics.

From the minimum and the maximum values of the estimates of each coefficient encountered one can gain an idea of the variability of the estimate for different but equally plausible specifications. If the range between the minimum and maximum estimates is large, it suggests that the estimated effect will be quite sensitive to the choice of the specification. From the estimate with the maximum absolute value of the *t* ratio, one can verify if an independent variable that may be found to be statistically significant in some specification may have been erroneously omitted, thus gaining additional protection against false conclusions. The maximum likelihood estimates provide in a sense the best-fitting regression. The likelihood criterion used here, however, does not take into account the differences in the number of independent variables for the different specifications.

Table 7–5 shows that the statistically significant estimates of the coefficients of the price of output, the wage rate, the price of chemical inputs, capital, and land are quite robust. The wage rate and the quantity of land have consistently positive and statistically significant effects on the probability of adoption. The price of chemical inputs has a consistently negative and statistically significant effect on the probability of adoption. The ranges of these estimates are relatively small.

It is also apparent from Table 7–5 that both formal education, as measured by $E4$ and to a lesser extent by $A5$, and agricultural extension have positive and statistically significant effects on the probability of adoption. Approximately 3 percent of sample farm households have $E4 = 1$. Among chemical farms it is 5.5 percent. Among nonchemical farms it is 1.6 percent. Average education of adult household members, however, has a consistently statistically

Table 7-5. Summary of Logit Regressions for Thai Farms
(sample = 275)

Independent variable	Minimum estimate	Maximum estimate	Estimate of highest t ratio	Maximum χ^2 (94.87)
Price of output (baht per kilogram) (ln)	1.744 (1.247)	2.622 (1.800)	2.545 (1.813)	2.407 (1.613)
Price of labor (baht per day) (ln)	2.214 (2.856)	2.625 (3.155)	2.616 (3.245)	2.604 (3.128)
Price of chemical inputs (baht per kilogram) (ln)	-1.417 (-3.185)	-1.051 (-2.517)	-1.417 (-3.185)	-1.289 (-2.929)
Capital (baht) (ln)	-0.341 (-1.423)	-0.103 (-0.433)	-0.341 (-1.423)	-0.212 (-0.861)
Land area (rai) (ln)	0.607 (2.230)	0.790 (2.993)	0.773 (2.998)	0.628 (2.330)
Region 1	-6.287 (-2.591)	-3.130 (-1.157)	-6.287 (-2.591)	-5.868 (-1.914)
Region 2	-5.854 (-2.541)	-2.644 (-1.016)	-5.854 (-2.541)	-5.200 (-1.763)
Region 3	-4.694 (-1.872)	-1.482 (-0.530)	-4.694 (-1.872)	-4.122 (-1.317)
Region 4	-5.727 (-2.561)	-2.571 (-1.023)	-5.727 (-2.561)	-5.056 (-1.779)

	Col 1	Col 2	Col 3	Col 4
A5 (education of head of household) (years)	0.070 (0.961)	0.294 (2.830)	0.272 (2.905)	—
A6 (average education) (years)	-0.079 (-0.592)	0.089 (0.994)	0.089 (0.994)	-0.076 (-0.574)
E2 (education, 0 < A5 < 4)	-0.188 (-0.327)	0.351 (0.567)	0.349 (0.578)	0.351 (0.567)
E3 (education, A5 = 4)	-0.201 (-0.570)	0.638 (1.315)	0.638 (1.315)	0.634 (1.281)
E4 (education, A5 > 4)	1.761 (2.025)	3.494 (3.133)	3.232 (3.179)	3.494 (3.133)
E5 (education, A5 > 0)	-0.209 (-0.581)	0.498 (1.147)	0.498 (1.147)	—
EXT (1 if extension services available; 0 otherwise)	0.832 (2.639)	1.018 (3.053)	1.003 (3.101)	1.018 (3.045)
A7 (age of head of household) (years)	0.017 (1.425)	0.048 (3.069)	0.048 (3.069)	0.038 (2.352)
CR (1 if credit taken or available; 0 otherwise)	0.208 (0.519)	0.578 (1.603)	0.578 (1.603)	—
HM (1 if male; 0 if female)	-2.882 (-2.089)	-2.029 (-1.465)	-2.874 (-2.103)	-2.569 (-1.784)

Note: Numbers in parentheses are t ratios. The variables are defined in Table 4-4.
— Not applicable.

Table 7–6. Logit Regressions for Thai Farms

(sample = 275)

Independent variable	Specification		
	(1)	(2)	$\ln \Pi_N^* - \ln \Pi_T^*$
Constant	−8.115	−7.443	0.237
	(−2.930)	(−2.833)	
Price of output	2.109	2.139	—
(baht per kilogram) (ln)	(1.441)	(1.496)	
Price of labor	2.692	2.680	−0.0331
(baht per day) (ln)	(3.274)	(3.282)	
Price of chemical inputs	−1.240	−1.209	−0.1028
(baht per kilogram) (ln)	(−2.876)	(−2.839)	
Capital	−0.298	−0.310	0.0050
(baht) (ln)	(−1.233)	(−1.293)	
Land area	0.647	0.678	−0.0245
(rai) (ln)	(2.444)	(2.595)	
Region 2	0.612	0.602	−0.0600
	(1.415)	(1.410)	
Region 3	1.693	1.674	−0.0095
	(2.650)	(2.648)	
Region 4	0.879	0.852	0.3778
	(1.392)	(1.367)	
E2 (education, 0 < A5 < 4)	0.183	—	—
	(0.301)		
E3 (education, A5 = 4)	0.391	—	—
	(0.865)		
E4 (education, A5 > 4)	2.992	2.614	—
	(3.004)	(2.983)	
E5 (education, A5 > 0)	—	—	0.1287
EXT (1 if extension services available;	1.030	1.027	−0.2336
0 otherwise)	(3.126)	(3.138)	
A7 (age of head of household)	0.033	0.025	—
(years)	(2.104)	(2.016)	
Log likelihood	−145.2	−145.6	—

Note: Numbers in parentheses are *t* ratios. The variables are defined in Table 4–4.

— Not applicable.

insignificant effect. Age of the head of household occasionally has a statistically significant positive effect. Availability of credit has a consistently positive but statistically insignificant effect. Sex of the head of the household occasionally has a marginally statistically significant effect. Since the proportion of female heads of household in the total sample was only 1 percent, the sex variable was dropped in further analysis.

On the whole, the results of these additional logit regressions confirm the robustness of our earlier results. For the purpose of further analysis we estimated a logit regression in which the education variable was represented by the dummy variables $E2$, $E3$, and $E4$. Variables for average education, availability of credit, and sex of the head of household were omitted. The dummy variables $E2$ and $E3$ were included even though they had been found to be statistically insignificant, because we wished to consider the complete set $(E2, E3, E4)$ as the education variable. For the purpose of comparison, the same logit regression was also estimated with $E2$ and $E3$ omitted. The results of these two regressions are reported in Table 7–6. The estimated coefficients of the two logit regressions do not differ significantly. This is also evidenced by the very small change in the logarithm of the likelihood.

Net benefit function

It is of some interest to see if the net benefit function, $U_N(Z_i) - U_T(Z_i)$, is in fact linear in the difference between the logarithms of the normalized profit functions of chemical and nonchemical farms. The net benefit function, however, is not a function of only the relative profitability of the new and traditional technologies. This is known from the fact that the age variable has a statistically significant positive effect on the probability of adoption. The profit function estimates reported in Tables 6–5 and 6–6 were used to compute the differences in the coefficients of each independent variable between the chemical and nonchemical farms; these numbers are presented in the third column of Table 7–6. If these differences are close to the corresponding estimates of the effect of the same independent variable on the probability of adoption, one may conclude that the probability of adoption is in fact a linear function in the difference in the logarithm of normalized profit. Under certain additional assumptions, this linearity in the difference of the logarithm of profit may be regarded as evidence in support of the proposition that the farmers chose the technology that maximized their expected utilities of profit. As the figures in column 3 indicate, however, the estimated net benefit function is substantially different from being a linear function of the logarithm of the relative profit of the two technologies.

Interpretation of Findings

The coefficients of the logit regressions cannot be readily interpreted. Table 7–7 shows the change in the probability of adoption of the technology using chemical inputs in response to a 1 percent change in the continuous independent variables in each region measured at the mean of the independent variables in that region. The table also includes the change in the probability of adoption in response to a one-year change in the age of the head of household from the mean age of that region. The change in the probability of adoption corresponding to a change in the value of each of the dummy variables from the base case in each region is also reported. For the base case, $E2 = E3 = E4 = 0$, and $EXT = 0$, and all other variables are set at the mean of that region. The values of the parameters used in these probability calculations were taken from Table 7–6, column 1. The means of the independent variables are presented in Table 7–8.

Table 7–7 shows that both education and extension strongly increase the probability of adopting the technology using chemical inputs. The probability of a farm household, the head of which had more than 4 years of education, adopting the technology is between 59 and 63 percentage points higher than that of a farm household, the head of which had no formal education. The probability of adoption is increased by between 14 and 20 percentage points by the availability of agricultural extension. It is also increased by between 0.3 and 0.5 of a percentage point by an increase of 1 year in the age of the head of household from the mean.

Changes in prices of output and variable inputs and the quantities of fixed inputs also have effects. A 10 percent increase in the price of output results in an increase of between 2 and 3 percentage points in the probability of adoption; a 10 percent increase in the wage rate results in an increase of between 2 and 4 percentage points in the probability of adoption; a 10 percent increase in the price of chemical inputs decreases the probability of adoption by between 1 and 2 percentage points; and a 10 percent increase in the quantity of land area results in an increase of approximately 1 percentage point in the probability of adoption. Since the estimated coefficient of capital is consistently statistically insignificant, no importance is attached to its effect on the probability of adoption. The estimated effect of the price of output should also be regarded as being more unreliable than the other estimated effects.

In our analysis of the decision of the farm household to adopt technology we have assumed that each farmer chooses the technology that gives him the highest net benefit. We have not subjected this assumption to a statistical test, nor are we able to test this assumption without additional knowledge on the possible distributions of the ε_i^*'s. In addition, since our concept of net benefit is allowed to contain elements of subjective benefits and costs, the assumption of maximization of net benefit does not necessarily imply the maximization of profit in the choice of technology. Indeed, we have not established that the individual farms adopted the technologies that would maximize their individual profits. Indications are that the decision of which technology to adopt depends on considerations other than profit maximization as well. In particular, the estimated net benefit function does not seem to be a simple function of relative profits of the two technologies. Thus it is conceivable that the technology chosen by an individual farmer may maximize net benefit (or expected net benefits) but may not be the technology to maximize profits (or expected profits), given the characteristics and the economic environment of the farmer.

It is indeed conceivable that the agricultural extension service may have caused some farms to adopt chemical inputs prematurely, with the consequence that these farms may fail to realize the full profit potential of the new technology. Thus, compared with farms that chose to adopt without encouragement from the agricultural extension service (which is interpreted to mean that they were also better equipped to implement the new technology) the farms that adopt because of the agricultural extension service will tend to show a lower level of profits, other things—normalized prices and quantities of fixed inputs—being equal. This provides an explanation of the apparent paradox that availability of agricultural extension actually lowers the profits for the farms using chemical inputs, as reported in Chapter 6, although such a negative effect is in general not statistically significant.

Table 7–7. Changes in the Probability of Adopting Technology Using Chemical Inputs, by Region
(percentage points)

Change in independent variable	Region 1 (base level = 10.02)	Region 2 (base level = 15.19)	Region 3 (base level = 17.29)	Region 4 (base level = 14.66)
Price of output (+ 1 percent)	0.190	0.272	0.302	0.264
Price of labor (+ 1 percent)	0.243	0.347	0.385	0.337
Price of chemical inputs (+ 1 percent)	-0.112	-0.160	-0.177	-0.155
Capital (+ 1 percent)	-0.027	-0.038	-0.043	-0.037
Land area (+ 1 percent)	0.058	0.083	0.092	0.081
E2 (0 < A5 < 4)	1.775	2.510	2.776	2.438
E3 (A5 = 4)	4.116	5.746	6.320	5.591
E4 (A5 > 4)	58.913	62.922	63.350	62.727
EXT (1 if extension services available; 0 otherwise)	13.756	18.218	19.640	17.822
A7 (age of head of household) (+ 1 year)	0.301	0.430	0.477	0.415

Note: The base level probabilities are evaluated at the means of the continuous variables: price of output, wage rate, price of chemical inputs, capital, land area, and age of head of household for each region and with dummy variables E2, E3, E4, and EXT set equal to zero.

Table 7-8. *Means of Independent Variables, by Region*

Independent variable	Region 1 n = 67	Region 2 n = 150	Region 3 n = 27	Region 4 n = 31
Price of output (baht per kilogram) (ln)	0.149	0.150	0.216	0.149
Price of labor (baht per day) (ln)	2.222	2.086	2.091	1.985
Price of chemical inputs (baht per kilogram) (ln)	1.641	1.423	2.045	1.358
Capital (baht) (ln)	4.140	4.322	4.622	4.268
Land area (rai) (ln)	2.028	2.043	1.708	1.700
E2 (education, 0 < A5 < 4)	0.104	0.073	0.222	0.065
E3 (education, A5 = 4)	0.672	0.653	0.593	0.581
E4 (education, A5 > 4)	0.045	0.033	0.000	0.000
EXT (1 if extension services available; 0 otherwise)	0.564	0.533	0.815	0.548
A7 (age of head of household) (years)	47.896	47.940	47.889	50.677

A second explanation of the observed negative relation between profits and the availability of agricultural extension service for chemical farms may lie in the fact that the agricultural extension service may recommend practices that maximize output rather than profit. Again, profits are expected to be lower for farms using chemical inputs with agricultural extension service than those without.

CHAPTER 8

The Rate of Return to Rural Education

THIS BRIEF CHAPTER PRESENTS the results of calculations of the internal rate of return to education based on the effects of education on the technological level of farmers. We stress the hypothetical character of this exercise: the results are sensitive to the assumptions about the time structure of the streams of benefits, and, of course, to the assumption that the benefits of education that we estimate with our production functions will continue to occur in the future. Of course, estimates of the rate of return to education in the wage sector are subject to these caveats and the additional, important one that wage differences may fail to reflect marginal productivity differences for the reasons discussed in Chapter 1.

Results are given from analysis of the internal rate of return to additional years of education completed in each of our samples. This is followed by a discussion of how these empirical findings may be helpful in World Bank project evaluation by using them to compute an internal rate of return to investment in educational radio in Thailand.

Rates of Return to Elementary Education in Korea, Malaysia, and Thailand

To calculate internal rates of return (that is, the value of the rate of discount that makes the present value of the time stream of differences between costs and benefits zero), we estimated the cost and benefit streams accruing to one additional year of completed

Table 8–1. *Expenditures per Pupil for Preprimary and Primary Education*
(1970 U.S. dollars per year)

Year	Korea	Thailand	Malaysia
1965	5.69	14.22	44.99
1970	35.75	19.95	52.18

Sources: Unesco (1975) and World Bank (1976).

schooling for the farmer. Table 8–1 presents the costs used in the analysis. Since these are costs per student per year and, at least in the case of Thailand, not all students who enroll during the year complete the grade, the actual cost-benefit calculations use the slightly higher figure of cost per year completed rather than cost per year attended. In computing the cost stream for a year of schooling, it is assumed that the individual incurs, at age 11, the cost in the 1970 row of Table 8–1, and that he incurs 0 cost each year from then until he is 60.

To compute the benefit stream we took the estimated percentage increase in output for one additional year of education from column 6 of Table 2–2. This was 2.27 percent for Korea, 5.11 for Malaysia, and 2.79 for Thailand. (The value for Thailand is the average for the chemical and nonchemical farms; the value for Korea was the average for mechanical and nonmechanical farms.) This percentage increase was multiplied by the level of output of the average farm in the sample and by the farmgate price of rice. Four different price estimates were used to obtain estimates of the sensitivity of the calculations to output price. We then assumed that benefits of the magnitude just computed would accrue to the farmer in each year from some initial age (17 and 25 years of age were used) until retirement at 60.

Table 8–2 shows the internal rate of return to rural primary education computed from the cost and benefit streams just described. The figures in the table should be viewed as approximations. They err on the high side in attributing the entire increase in output of a farm to the additional education of a single individual. They err on the low side in omitting allocative benefits, benefits from off-farm employment, and (for Thailand and Malaysia) benefits from second crops. Nonetheless, Table 8–2 does suggest high

Table 8–2. *Internal Rate of Return to Rural Education*
(percent per year)

Farmgate price of rice (U.S. dollars per metric ton)	Age at which benefits are assumed to commence					
	17			25		
	Korea	*Malaysia*	*Thailand*	*Korea*	*Malaysia*	*Thailand*
150	11.0	18.6	17.6	7.1	11.0	10.6
200	13.3	21.8	20.6	8.4	12.5	12.0
250	15.2	24.4	23.2	9.4	13.7	13.2
300	17.0	26.7	25.4	10.2	14.7	14.2

Table 8–3. *Sensitivity of the Rate of Return to Schooling to Error in Estimation of Its Effect on Productivity*

Deviation of actual from estimated effect of schooling on productivity[a]	Internal rate of return (percent per year)		
	Korea	Malaysia	Thailand
− 1.5	9.4	9.2	9.8
− 0.5	12.1	18.6	17.8
0	13.3	21.8	20.6
+ 0.5	14.3	24.4	23.0
+ 1.5	16.3	28.8	27.0

a. The unit of the deviation is in standard errors of the estimate of the percentage increase in output resulting from an additional year of schooling.

returns.[1] Estimated returns decline about 40 percent if benefits are assumed to commence at age 25 rather than 17; they increase by from 35 to 50 percent if the farmgate price of rice is assumed to be $300 per ton rather than $150 per ton.

To assess the sensitivity of the calculated rates of return to errors in the estimated effects of education on productivity, a sensitivity analysis was undertaken. The analysis assumed that the benefit stream began when the farmer reached 17 years of age and that the farmgate price of rice was $200 per ton. The benefit from a year of education was then allowed to vary from − 1.5 to + 1.5 standard errors of the estimates of the percentage increase in output for an additional year of education. These standard errors are reported in Appendix A, Table A–2. The probability is low that the "correct" value of the benefits would lie outside the range from − 1.5 to + 1.5 standard errors around the estimated value. Table 8–3 shows how returns vary in this range.

1. Several other studies (Blaug 1974, Chiswick 1978, Meesook 1980, Sabot 1977) report the benefits of education in Thailand. Blaug's analysis, for urban Bangkok, provides a complement to our findings concerning rural areas. He concludes that an additional year of education increases earnings by an average of 1.4 percent. Although this increase is not directly comparable to the 2.3 percent increase in farm output that we report as resulting from a year of education, it does suggest that there is no obvious efficiency argument for investing in urban rather than rural schools. Indeed, efficiency arguments would seem to reinforce equity ones (see Lim and others 1980, p. 27) to suggest reallocation of educational resources in favor of rural areas.

The Rate of Return to Educational Radio in Thailand

The Fifth World Bank Education project in Thailand includes substantial resources for expanding the use of educational radio in rural areas. It has been observed that effectively implemented educational radio tends to increase the progression rate of students from one grade to the next, principally by reducing repetition rates. This has the effect of increasing the number of years of schooling completed per year of schooling attended, and forms the basis for

Figure 8–1. *Variation of Internal Rate of Return with the Price of Rice*

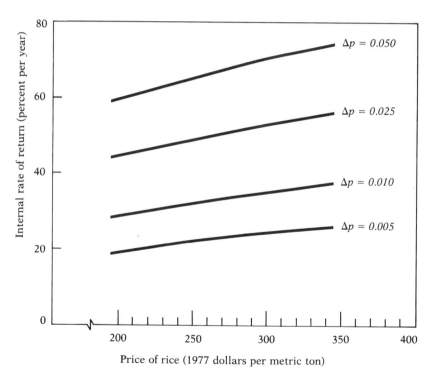

Note: MC = $2.50.

computing the internal rate of return to investment in educational radio.

The number of years completed per year attended in the traditional system is simply P_t, the progression rate. It is assumed that it is equal to P_r with radio and that P_r is greater than P_t. The additional number of years completed resulting from the introduction of radio is, then, $P_r - P_t = \Delta P$. Other studies (Jamison 1978) have found ΔP to be over 0.1, although 0.05 would probably be as much or more than could be routinely hoped for.

This then allows computation of a benefit stream for providing educational radio to one student for one year. This is simply equal to ΔP times the benefit figure for a year of schooling completed, as computed in the preceding section. The cost is simply the marginal cost per student per year of providing radio in the schools, which might run between US$1 and US$5 per year. For the calculations here, we assume a cost of US$2.50 per year, which is sufficient to get high quality.

Figure 8–1 shows how the internal rate of return varies as a function of the price of rice for several values of ΔP. Even with a very low ΔP and the minimum plausible price for rice, the internal rate of return to investment in educational radio is a respectable 20 percent.

PART THREE

Appendixes

Supplemental Information
on Studies of Farmer Education

THIS APPENDIX CONTAINS SUPPLEMENTAL INFORMATION on the studies reviewed in Chapter 2. It is organized into two tables. Table A–1 contains, for each sample of farms in each of the papers, information on the sample size, the nature of the education variable(s), and productivity variable(s) used, whether allocative or technical efficiency was examined, and other variables used in the analysis. Table A–2 summarizes quantitative information on the strength of the effects found for education in the various studies and contains information on the social context of the regions, such as per capita income, adult literacy rates, and degree modernity.

Note: This appendix, like Chapter 2, is drawn from Lockheed, Jamison, and Lau (1980).

Table A-1. Studies of Education and Small Farm Productivity

Country and city	Reference	Sample size, N	Modernizing environment	Education variable	Dependent variable	Kinds of analysis: efficiency/ specification[a]	Other variables
Brazil, Candelaria	Pachico and Ashby (1976)	117	No	$D > 5$ years of schooling completed by farm operator	Value of farm production	Technical/eqn. (2.3)	Land—Q; human labor; machine labor—V; animal labor—V; purchased inputs—V
Brazil, Garibaldi	Pachico and Ashby (1976)	101	Yes	$D > 5$ years of schooling completed by farm operator	Value of farm production	Technical/eqn. (2.3)	Land—Q; human labor; machine labor—V; animal labor—V; purchased inputs—V
Brazil, Guarani	Pachico and Ashby (1976)	63	No	$D > 5$ years of schooling completed by farm operator	Value of farm production	Technical/eqn. (2.3)	Land—Q; human labor; machine labor—V; animal labor—V; purchased inputs—V

Brazil, Taquari	Pachico and Ashby (1976)	101	Yes	$D > 5$ years of schooling completed by farm operator	Value of farm production	Technical/eqn. (2.3)	Land—Q; human labor; machine labor—V; animal labor—V; purchased inputs—V
Brazil Alto São Francisco	Patrick and Kehrberg (1973)	82	Transition	Years of schooling completed by farm operator	Value of farm production, less value of purchased nonlabor inputs	Technical and allocative/eqn. (2.2)	Farm resources—V
Brazil, Conceicao de Castelo	Patrick and Kehrberg (1973)	54	No	Years of schooling completed by farm operator	Value of farm production, less value of purchased nonlabor inputs	Technical and allocative/eqn. (2.2)	Farm resources—V
Brazil, Paracatu	Patrick and Kehrberg (1973)	86	No	Years of schooling completed by farm operator	Value of farm production, less value of purchased nonlabor inputs	Technical and allocative/eqn. (2.2)	Farm resources—V

(Table continues on the following page)

Table A–1 (*continued*)

Country and city	Reference	Sample size, N	Modern-izing environ-ment	Education variable	Dependent variable	Kinds of analysis: efficiency/ specification[a]	Other variables
Brazil, Resende	Patrick and Kehrberg (1973)	62	Yes	Years of schooling completed by farm operator	Value of farm production, less value of pur-chased non-labor in-puts	Technical and allocative/eqn. (2.2)	Farm re-sources—V
Brazil, Vicosa	Patrick and Kehrberg (1973)	337	Yes	Years of schooling completed by farm operator	Value of farm production, less value of pur-chased non-labor in-puts	Technical and allocative/eqn. (2.2)	Farm re-sources—V
Colombia, Chinchiná	Haller (1972)	77	Yes	Average of grades of schooling completed by working farm family mem-bers over 14 years; mean: 2.8 grades	Value of farm production	Technical/eqn. (2.1); internal rate of return	Land—V; family labor—Q; hired labor—Q; power capital—V; fixed capital—V

Colombia, Espinal	Haller (1972)	74	Yes	Average of grades of schooling completed by working farm family members over 14 years; mean: 2.4 grades	Value of farm production	Technical/eqn. (2.1)	Land—V; family labor—Q; hired labor—Q; power capital—V; fixed capital—V
Colombia, Málaga	Haller (1972)	74	No	Average of grades of schooling completed by working farm family members over 14 years; mean: 1.6 grades	Value of farm production	Technical/eqn. (2.1)	Land—V; family labor—Q; hired labor—Q; power capital—V; fixed capital—V
Colombia, Moniquirá	Haller (1972)	75	No	Average of grades of schooling completed by working farm family members over 14 years; mean: 1.6 grades	Value of farm production	Technical/eqn. (2.1)	Land—V; family labor—Q; hired labor—Q; power capital—V; fixed capital—V

(Table continues on the following page)

Table A–1 (*continued*)

Country and city	Reference	Sample size, N	Modern-izing environ-ment	Education variable	Dependent variable	Kinds of analysis: efficiency/ specification[a]	Other variables
Greece, Epirus	Yotopoulos (1967)	430	No	Average of years of schooling completed by farm house-hold mem-bers age 15 to 69 years; mean: 2.24 years	Value of agri-cultural production	Technical/eqn. (2.1)	Land—Q; human labor—Q; animal labor—V; machine labor—V; ser-vices—V
India, Punjab, Haryana, and Utter Pradesh	Chaudhri (1974)	1,038	n.a.	Average years of schooling completed by all agricultu-ral workers in household; years of schooling completed by household head	Value of agri-cultural production	Technical/eqn. (2.1)	Irrigated land—Q; cultivated land—Q; hu-man labor—V; chemical fer-tilizer—V; manure—V; bullocks—Q

India, Punjab	Sidhu (1976)	236 (traditional and Mexican wheat)	n.a.	Average years of schooling completed by farm household members over 13 years; mean estimated to be 2.6 from subsamples	Wheat production—Q; sale value of farm production	Technical/eqn. (2.1)	Land—Q; labor—Q; capital services—V; fertilizers—V; wheat type—D
India, Punjab	Sidhu (1976)	369 (Mexican wheat)	n.a.	Average years of schooling completed by farm household members over 13 years; mean estimated to be 2.6 from subsamples	Wheat production—Q; sale value of farm production	Technical/eqn. (2.1)	Land—Q; labor—Q; capital services—V; fertilizers—V; year
Israel	Sadan, Nachmias, and Bar-Lev (1976)	1,841	Mixed	Years of schooling completed by farm operator's wife	Gross value-added of farm production	Technical/eqn. (2.4)	Herd—Q; irrigation—D; family size

(Table continues on the following page)

237

Table A–1 (*continued*)

Country and city	Reference	Sample size, N	Modernizing environment	Education variable	Dependent variable	Kinds of analysis: efficiency/specification[a]	Other variables
Japan, Honshu, Shikoku, and Kyushu	Harker (1973)	971	Yes	Years of schooling completed by farmer	Gross farm sales	Technical/eqn. (2.4) (path-analysis)	Use of agricultural media and agents; ownership of power implements; father's education; farm location; age; land
Kenya, Vihiga	Moock (1973)	152	Yes	D > 4 years of schooling completed by farm manager	Bags of maize produced	Technical/eqn. (2.3)	Interplanted crop—D; hybrid seed—D; plant population—Q; insecticide—D; rate of phosphate—Q; previous season labor—Q; crop damage—Q; extension contact—D; loan recipient—D; migration/age —Q; female manager—D

238

Kenya	Hopcraft (1974)	674	Mixed	Dummy variables for schooling of household head	Bags of maize produced (other regressions examined livestock, tea, and aggregate output)	Technical/eqn. (2.3)	Cultivated land—Q; labor—Q; purchased inputs—V; extension visits—Q
Korea	Hong (1975)	895	n.a.	Years of schooling completed by farm operator; mean: 4.2 years	Value of rice production	Technical	Land—Q; labor—Q; capital—V; extension—V; age of farm operator; age 2; interactions
Korea	Jamison and Lau (this volume)	1,363 (mechanical farms)	n.a.	Average number of years of education	Value of agricultural production	Technical/eqn. (2.2)	Land—Q; human labor—Q; animal labor—Q; machine labor; capital—V; fertilizers and pesticides; regions—D; sex of head of household—D; age of head of household—Q

(Table continues on the following page)

Table A–1 (*continued*)

Country and city	Reference	Sample size, N	Modern-izing environ-ment	Education variable	Dependent variable	Kinds of analysis: efficiency/specification[a]	Other variables
Korea	Jamison and Lau (this volume)	541 (nonme-chan-ical farms)	n.a.	Average num-ber of years of education for household members aged 17 to 60; mean: 4.95 years	Value of agri-cultural production	Technical/eqn. (2.2)	Land—Q; human labor—Q; animal labor—Q; capital—V; fertilizers and pesticides; re-gions—D; sex of head of household—D; age of head of household—Q
Malaysia, Kedah and Perlis	Jamison and Lau (this volume)	403	Yes	$D = 0, D = 1$ to 3, $D = 4$ years of schooling completed by head of household	Rice produc-tion—Q	Technical/eqn. (2.3)	Cultivated land—Q; capital input—V; variable in-put—V; labor—Q; years of double-cropping—D

						Technical/eqn.	
Nepal, Bara	Pudasaini (1976)	102	Mixed	Years of schooling completed by farm operator	Gross farm revenue	Technical/eqn. (2.2)	Land; labor; cash expenses; bullocks—V; machines and tools—V; land fragments; animal labor; tractor labor; pumpset use; tractor and pumpset used—D
Nepal, Nuwakot	Calkins (1976)	540	No	$D \geq 6$ years total schooling obtained by family members	Value of farm production	Technical	Land—V; family labor—Q; hired labor—Q; bartered labor—Q; farmyard manure—Q; chemical fertilizer—Q; capital—V; altitude—Q; nutritional status of laborers—Q; interaction terms

(*Table continues on the following page*)

Table A–1 (continued)

Country and city	Reference	Sample size, N	Modernizing environment	Education variable	Dependent variable	Kinds of analysis: efficiency/specification[a]	Other variables
Nepal, Rupandehi	Sharma (1974)	87 (wheat farms)	Yes	D = literate	Wheat production—Q	Technical/eqn. (2.3)	Cultivated land—Q; labor—Q; seed—Q; organic manure—Q
Nepal, Rupandehi	Sharma (1974)	138 (rice farms)	Yes	D = literate	Rice production—Q	Technical/eqn. (2.3)	Cultivated land—Q; labor—Q; seed—Q; organic manure—Q
Philippines, Laguna (1963)	Halim (1976)	274	n.a.	Average years of schooling completed by all agricultural workers in household (weighted)	Average annual rice production; net farm earnings	Technical/eqn. (2.2)	Cultivated land—Q; labor—Q; operating expenditures—V; extension contacts—Q; barrio development index—D; type of extension—D

Location	Study	Sample	Schooling	Schooling measure	Dependent variable	Function/eqn.	Independent variables
Philippines, Laguna (1968)	Halim (1976)	273	n.a.	Average years of schooling completed by all agricultural workers in household (weighted)	Average annual rice production; net farm earnings	Technical/eqn. (2.2)	Cultivated land—Q; labor—Q; operating expenditures—V; extension contacts—Q; barrio development index—D; type of extension—D
Philippines, Laguna (1973)	Halim (1976)	220	n.a.	Average years of schooling completed by all agricultural workers in household (weighted)	Average annual rice production; net farm earnings	Technical/eqn. (2.2)	Cultivated land—Q; labor—Q; operating expenditures—V; extension contacts—Q; barrio development index—D; type of extension—D
Taiwan	Wu (1971)	333 (rice farms)	Yes	Years of schooling completed by farm operator; 25 percent are primary graduates	Gross farm income	Technical/eqn. (2.2)	Owned land—V; family labor—Q; livestock expenses; poultry and livestock—V; farm tools and machinery—V

(Table continues on the following page)

243

Table A–1 (continued)

Country and city	Reference	Sample size, N	Modernizing environment	Education variable	Dependent variable	Kinds of analysis: efficiency/specification[a]	Other variables
Taiwan	Wu (1971)	316 (banana and pineapple farms)	No	Years of schooling completed by farm operator; 25 percent are primary graduates	Gross farm income	Technical/eqn. (2.2)	Owned land—V; family labor—Q; livestock expenses; poultry and livestock—V; farm tools and machinery—V
Taiwan	Wu (1977)	310	Yes	Years of schooling completed by farm operator; mean: 6.7 years	Gross crop income	Technical and allocative/various equations	Land—Q; labor—V; capital—V; fertilizer—V; other expenses—V
Thailand, Chiang Mai	Jamison and Lau (this volume)	91 (chemical farms)	Yes	Years of schooling completed by head of household	Rice production—Q	Technical and allocative/eqn. (2.2)	Land—Q; labor—Q; capital—V; region—D; extension—D

| Thailand, Chiang Mai | Jamison and Lau (this volume) | 184 (non-chemical farms) | Yes | Years of schooling completed by head of household | Rice production—Q | Technical and allocative/eqn. (2) | Land—Q; labor—Q; capital—V; region—D; extension—D |

Note: D = dummy variable, Q = measure of quantity, V = measure of value.
n.a. Not available.

a. The specifications are labeled equation (1) to equation (5) and these refer to the equations in the first part of the paper that show the alternatives used in specifications.

Table A–2. *Effects of Education and Environmental Variables*

					Formal education	
Author	Region	Sample	N	Func-tional form[a]	Percentage gain in output for each year of education	Standard error of estimate of percentage gain[b]
Halim	Philippines	1963	274	2	2.2	1.3
		1968	273	2	1.92	1.5
		1973	220	2	2.74	1.2
Haller	Chinchiná		77	1	−0.29	2.2
	Espinal		74	1	6.10	3.5
	Málaga		74	1	3.09	3.3
	Moniquirá		75	1	−3.12	3.0
Jamison and Lau	Korea	mechanical nonmechan-ical	1,363 541	2 2	2.22 2.33	0.4 0.8
Jamison and Lau	Malaysia		403	3	5.11	2.2
Jamison and Lau	Thailand	chemical nonchemical	91 184	2 2	3.15 2.43	1.5 1.1
Moock	Kenya		152	3	1.73	1.1
Pachico and Ashby	Candalaria		117	3	2.69	3.3
	Garibaldi		101	3	4.60	2.7
	Guarani		63	3	1.49	2.9
	Taquari		101	3	5.53	3.8
Patrick and Kehrberg	Alto São Francisco		82	2	−1.29	2.0
	Conceicao de Castelo		54	2	−0.90	1.2
	Paracatu		86	2	−1.79	1.2
	Resende		62	2	1.01	0.9
	Viscosa		337	2	2.33	0.8
Pudasaini	Nepal		102	2	1.3	0.8
Sharma	Nepal	wheat rice	87 138	3 3	5.09 2.85	3.1 1.7
Sidhu	India	wheat Mexican wheat	236 369	1 1	1.49 1.41	0.8 0.6

	Nonformal education		Environmental variables				
Variable	Regression coefficient on output	t ratio	Modernizing environment[c]	Extension present or not[d]	GNP per capita[e]	Crop	Adult literacy rate (percent)[f]
Nonlog; number of	0.006	3.435	0	1	285.16	Rice	72.0
ber of	0.004	2.4	0	1	343.83	Rice	
weighted	−0.000	−0.772	0	1	314.38	Rice	
contacts							
			1	0		Coffee	74.0
			1	0		Mixed	
			−1	0	452.66	Tobacco	
			−1	0		Mixed	
			1	0	525.23	Mixed	91.0
			1	0		Mixed	
Adult education participation	0.237	1.732	1	1	764.20	Rice	89.0
Nonlog; whether extension was available in village	−0.092	−1.098	1	1	317.42	Rice	82.0
	0.085	2.225	1	1		Rice	
Factored variables	0.003	0.77	1	1	216.00	Maize	30.0
Number of contacts	−0.010	−2.5	−1	1		Mixed	68.0
			1	1		Mixed	
			−1	1	1,225.87	Mixed	
			1	1		Mixed	
Nonlog; number of visits	0.004	0.977	0	1		Mixed	68.0
	0.009	2.65	−1	1		Coffee	
	0.001	0.203	−1	1	955.04	Mixed	
	0.001	0.124	1	1		Dairy	
	0.003	1.026	1	1		Mixed	
			0	−1	97.21	Rice	14.0
			1	−1	108.62	Wheat	14.0
			0	−1		Rice	
			0	0	125.02	Wheat	36.0
			0	0		Wheat	36.0

(Table continues on the following page)

Table A–2 (*continued*)

					Formal education	
Author	Region	Sample	N	Func-tional form[a]	Percentage gain in output for each year of education	Standard error of estimate of percentage gain[b]
Wu (1971)	Taiwan	rice	333	2	0.70	1.3
Wu (1971)		banana and pineapple	316	2	3.87	1.4
Wu (1977)			310	2	0.9	1.0
Yotopoulos	Greece		430	1	6.47	3.2

a. The numbers correspond to the following Cobb-Douglas production function specifications:

(1) $\ln Y = \alpha_0 + \alpha_1 \ln L + \alpha_2 \ln T + \beta \ln E + \gamma EXT$

(2) $\ln Y = \alpha_0 + \alpha_1 \ln L + \alpha_2 \ln T + \beta E + \gamma EXT$

(3) $\ln Y = \alpha_0 + \alpha_1 \ln L + \alpha_2 \ln T + \beta D + \gamma EXT$

where E is the educational level of the head of household and D is an indicator variable equal to 1 for some specific range of E, and 0 otherwise.

b. In order to calculate the standard error (s.e.) in the estimate of the percentage gain in output for 1 year of education, one needs the value of the coefficient on education in the original regression (β), the estimated standard error in the estimate of β (σ_β), and the functional form of the original regression. For all studies reported in this table the functional form was that of equation (1), (2), or (3) above, and the corresponding formulas for the standard error are:

| | *Nonformal education* | | | *Environmental variables* | | | |
Variable	*Regression coefficient on output*	*t ratio*	*Modernizing environment*[c]	*Extension present or not*[d]	*GNP per capita*[e]	*Crop*	*Adult literacy rate (percent)*[f]
			1	0	583.69	Rice	73.0
			1	0		Mixed	
			1	0	997.35	Mixed	73.0
			−1	0	1,356.68	Mixed	82.0

(1) s.e. $= [e^{2\beta \ln [(E + 0.5)/(E - 0.5)]} \, e^{\{\ln [(E + 0.5)/(E - 0.5)]\}^2 \sigma_\beta^2} \, (e^{\{\ln [(E + 0.5)/(E - 0.5)]\}^2 \sigma_\beta^2} - 1)]^{1/2}$,

where E is the mean number of years of education in the sample;

(2) s.e. $= [e^{2\beta} \, e^{\sigma_\beta^2} \, (e^{\sigma_\beta^2} - 1)]^{1/2}$; and

(3) s.e. $= [1/N^2 \, (e^{2\beta} \, e^{\sigma_\beta^2} \, (e^{\sigma_\beta^2} - 1))]^{1/2}$,

where N is the number of years of education completed signified by the indicator variable D.

c. − 1, a nonmodernizing environment; 1, a modernizing environment; and 0, no information or a transitional environment.

d. − 1, no extension service available; 1, availability of extension service in region; and 0, no information on availability of extension.

e. *Source*: World Bank, *World Tables* (1980).

f. *Source*: World Bank, *World Tables* (1976); India GNP figures are for 1973.

APPENDIX B

Aggregation Bias

SUPPOSE THE INDIVIDUAL FUNCTIONS are identical and Cobb-Douglas in form, so that

$$Y_i = Y_0 K_i^{\alpha_1} L_i^{\alpha_2} \qquad (i = 1, \ldots, N)$$

where $K_i > 0$; $L_i > 0$; $i = 1, \ldots, N$; and Y_0, α_1, α_2 are positive constants. In addition, it is assumed that the K_i's are not proportional to the L_i's. The true aggregate output is then given by

(B.1) $$Y = Y_0 \sum_{i=1}^{N} K_i^{\alpha_1} L_i^{\alpha_2}.$$

If instead of equation (B.1), aggregate output is taken to be

(B.2) $$Y = Y_0 \left(\sum_{i=1}^{N} K_i\right)^{\alpha_1} \left(\sum_{i=1}^{N} L_i\right)^{\alpha_2}$$

there will be, in general, a bias. We shall show that the bias is always upward if $\alpha_1 + \alpha_2 \geq 1$, that is, equation (B.2) always overstates the true aggregate output if there are constant or increasing returns to scale. We shall also show that the bias is indeterminate if $\alpha_1 + \alpha_2 < 1$.

First consider the case $\alpha_1 + \alpha_2 > 1$. Jensen's theorem states that if $\alpha_1 > 0, \alpha_2 > 0$, and $\alpha_1 + \alpha_2 > 1$, and $K_i > 0, L_i > 0, i = 1, \ldots, N$, then

$$\sum_{i=1}^{N} K_i^{\alpha_1} L_i^{\alpha_2} < \left(\sum_{i=1}^{N} K_i\right)^{\alpha_1} \left(\sum_{i=1}^{N} L_i\right)^{\alpha_2}$$

for all K_i's and L_i's.[1] The theorem extends readily to the case of more than two inputs. Thus, the bias due to the use of equation (B.2) is always upward if $\alpha_1 + \alpha_2 > 1$.

Next, consider the case $\alpha_1 + \alpha_2 = 1$. Hölder's inequality states that if $\alpha_1 > 0$, $\alpha_2 > 0$, and $\alpha_1 + \alpha_2 = 1$, then

1. See Hardy, Littlewood, and Polya (1952), p. 29.

$$\Sigma_{i=1}^{N} K_i^{\alpha 1} L_i^{\alpha 2} < (\Sigma_{i=1}^{N} K_i)^{\alpha 1} (\Sigma_{i=1}^{N} L_i)^{\alpha 2}$$

unless either (a) the K_i's and L_i's are proportional or (b) either the K_i's or the L_i's are all zeroes.[2] The inequality extends readily to the case of more than two inputs. Thus, a straightforward application of the inequality shows that the bias due to the use of equation (B.2) is always upward if $\alpha_1 + \alpha_2 = 1$.

Finally, consider the case $\alpha_1 + \alpha_2 < 1$. Two examples show that the bias can be both upward and downward. First, let $K_i = \bar{K}$, and $L_i = \bar{L}$, $i = 1, \ldots, N$. Then

$$\Sigma_{i=1}^{N} K_i^{\alpha 1} L_i^{\alpha 2} = N\bar{K}^{\alpha 1}\bar{L}^{\alpha 2}$$
$$> N^{(\alpha 1 + \alpha 2)} \bar{K}^{\alpha 1}\bar{L}^{\alpha 2}$$
$$= (N\bar{K})^{\alpha 1} (N\bar{L})^{\alpha 2}$$
$$= (\Sigma_{i=1}^{N} K_i)^{\alpha 1} (\Sigma_{i=1}^{N} L_i)^{\alpha 2}.$$

Second, let $K_i = \bar{K}$, $K_2 = \ldots = K_N = 0$;

$$L_1 = 0, L_2 = \bar{L}, L_3 = \ldots = L_N = 0.$$

Then

$$\Sigma_{i=1}^{N} K_i^{\alpha 1} L_i^{\alpha 2} = 0$$
$$< \bar{K}^{\alpha 1}\bar{L}^{\alpha 2}$$
$$= (\Sigma_{i=1}^{N} K_i)^{\alpha 1} (\Sigma_{i=1}^{N} L_i)^{\alpha 2}.$$

By continuity, the inequality is unaffected if all the zero quantities are replaced by very small but positive quantities. Thus, we have shown that the bias is indeterminate if $\alpha_1 + \alpha_2 < 1$.

If instead of equation (B.1), average output is taken to be

$$Y/N = \Sigma_{i=1}^{N} Y_i/N$$
$$= Y_0 (1/N \, \Sigma_{i=1}^{N} K_i)^{\alpha 1} (1/N \, \Sigma_{i=1}^{N} L_i)^{\alpha 2}$$

so that the aggregate output is given by

(B.3) $$Y = N^{[1 - (\alpha 1 + \alpha 2)]} Y_0 (\Sigma_{i=1}^{N} K_i)^{\alpha 1} (\Sigma_{i=1}^{N} L_i)^{\alpha 2}$$

there will also be, in general, a bias. We shall show that the bias is always upward if $\alpha_1 + \alpha_2 \leqq 1$, that is, equation (B.3) always overstates the true aggregate output if there are constant or decreasing

2. See Hardy, Littlewood, and Polya (1952), pp. 21–24.

returns to scale. We shall also show that the bias is indeterminate if $\alpha_1 + \alpha_2 > 1$.

First, consider the case $\alpha_1 + \alpha_2 < 1$. Under the conditions stated, the Cobb-Douglas production function is strictly concave, so that

$$1/N \sum_{i=1}^{N} K_i^{\alpha_1} L_i^{\alpha_2} < (1/N \sum_{i=1}^{N} K_i)^{\alpha_1} (1/N \sum_{i=1}^{N} L_i)^{\alpha_2}$$

or

$$\sum_{i=1}^{N} K_i^{\alpha_1} L_i^{\alpha_2} < N^{[1 - (\alpha_1 + \alpha_2)]} (\sum_{i=1}^{N} K_i)^{\alpha_1} (\sum_{i=1}^{N} L_i)^{\alpha_2}.$$

Thus, the bias due to the use of equation (B.3) is always upward if $\alpha_1 + \alpha_2 < 1$.

For the case $\alpha_1 + \alpha_2 = 1$, equations (B.2) and (B.3) coincide, so that the bias is always upward.

Finally, consider the case $\alpha_1 + \alpha_2 > 1$. Two examples again show that the bias can be both upward and downward. First, let $K_1 = \bar{K}$, $L_1 = \bar{L}$, $K_2 = \ldots = K_N = 0$, $L_2 = \ldots = L_N = 0$. Then

$$\sum_{i=1}^{N} K_i^{\alpha_1} L_i^{\alpha_2} = \bar{K}^{\alpha_1} \bar{L}^{\alpha_2}$$

$$> N^{[1 - (\alpha_1 + \alpha_2)]} \bar{K}^{\alpha_1} \bar{L}^{\alpha_2}, \text{ since}$$

$$N^{[1 - (\alpha_1 + \alpha_2)]} < 1$$

$$= N^{[1 - (\alpha_1 + \alpha_2)]} (\sum_{i=1}^{N} K_i)^{\alpha_1} (\sum_{i=1}^{N} L_i)^{\alpha_2}.$$

Second, let $K_1 = \bar{K}$, $K_2 = \ldots = K_N = 0$;

$$L_1 = 0, L_2 = \bar{L}, L_3 = \ldots = L_N = 0.$$

Then

$$\sum_{i=1}^{K} K_i^{\alpha_1} L_i^{\alpha_2} = 0$$

$$< N^{[1 - (\alpha_1 + \alpha_2)]} \bar{K}^{\alpha_1} \bar{L}^{\alpha_2}$$

$$= N^{[1 - (\alpha_1 + \alpha_2)]} (\sum_{i=1}^{N} K_i)^{\alpha_1} (\sum_{i=1}^{N} L_i)^{\alpha_2}.$$

By continuity, the inequalities in both examples are unaffected if all the zero quantities are replaced by very small but positive quantities. Thus, we have shown that the bias is indeterminate if $\alpha_1 + \alpha_2 > 1$.

Now suppose the individual production functions are not Cobb-Douglas but instead are of the constant-elasticity-of-substitution (CES) form, so that

$$Y_i = Y_0[(1 - \delta) K_i^{\rho} + \delta L_i^{\rho}]^{1/\rho} \qquad (i = 1, \ldots, N)$$

where $Y_0 > 0$, $1 \geq \delta \geq 0$, $\rho \leq 1$.[3] What, then, are the biases in the values of the aggregate output obtained from using the equivalents of equations (B.2) and (B.3) for the CES case?

The equivalent of equation (B.2) takes the form

(B.4) $\qquad Y = Y_0[(1 - \delta)(\Sigma_{i=1}^{N} K_i)^{\rho} + \delta(\Sigma_{i=1}^{N} L_i)^{\rho}]^{1/\rho}$.

The equivalent of equation (B.3) takes the form

$$Y = NY_0[(1 - \delta)(1/N \, \Sigma_{i=1}^{N} K_i)^{\rho} + \delta(1/N \, \Sigma_{i=1}^{N} L_i)^{\rho}]^{1/\rho}$$

(B.5)

$$= Y_0[(1 - \delta)(\Sigma_{i=1}^{N} K_i)^{\rho} + \delta(\Sigma_{i=1}^{N} L_i)^{\rho}]^{1/\rho}$$

which is identical to equation (B.4). Thus, whatever biases may exist, they are the same whether the aggregate or the average representation is used. This is a direct consequence of the property of constant returns to scale of the CES production function.

To determine the direction of the bias, Minkowski's inequality[4] is used, which states that

$$\Sigma_{i=1}^{N} [(1 - \delta) K_i^{\rho} + \delta L_i^{\rho}]^{1/\rho} > [(1 - \delta)(\Sigma_{i=1}^{N} K_i)^{\rho} + \delta(\Sigma_{i=1}^{N} L_i)^{\rho}]^{1/\rho}$$

$$\text{if } \rho > 1$$

and

$$\Sigma_{i=1}^{N} [(1 - \delta) K_i^{\rho} + \delta L_i^{\rho}]^{1/\rho} < [(1 - \delta)(\Sigma_{i=1}^{N} K_i)^{\rho} + \delta(\Sigma_{i=1}^{N} L_i)^{\rho}]^{1/\rho}$$

$$\text{if } \rho < 1, \rho \neq 0$$

for all finite ρ, where $K_i > 0$, $L_i > 0$, $i = 1, \ldots, N$, and the K_i's and the L_i's are not proportional. The inequality extends readily to the case of more than two inputs. Moreover, if $\rho = 1$, it can be verified directly that

$$\Sigma_{i=1}^{N} [(1 - \delta) K_i + \delta L_i] = [(1 - \delta)(\Sigma_{i=1}^{N} K_i) + \delta(\Sigma_{i=1}^{N} L_i)].$$

Thus, we conclude that the bias is always upward if $\rho < 1$, $\rho \neq 0$. The bias is zero if $\rho = 1$.

Finally, suppose the individual production functions are identical, monotonically increasing, concave, and take the values zero at the origin but are otherwise unrestricted in form. What can be said

---

3. For $\rho > 1$, the production function is not concave.
4. See Hardy, Littlewood, and Polya (1952), pp. 30–31.

about the biases? The aggregate and average representations are given, respectively, by

(B.6) $$Y = F(\Sigma_{i=1}^{N} K_i, \Sigma_{i=1}^{N} L_i)$$

and

(B.7) $$Y = NF(1/N \ \Sigma_{i=1}^{N} K_i, 1/N \ \Sigma_{i=1}^{N} L_i).$$

Two cases can be distinguished: constant returns to scale and decreasing returns to scale. Under constant returns to scale, equations (B.6) and (B.7) coincide. By concavity,

$$1/N \ \Sigma_{i=1}^{N} F(K_i, L_i) \leqq F(1/N \ \Sigma_{i=1}^{N} K_i, 1/N \ \Sigma_{i=1}^{N} L_i)$$

or

$$\Sigma_{i=1}^{N} F(K_i, L_i) \leqq F(\Sigma_{i=1}^{N} K_i, \Sigma_{i=1}^{N} L_i)$$

by homogeneity of degree one. Under decreasing returns to scale, equation (B.7) continues to have an upward bias, since by concavity,

$$\Sigma_{i=1}^{N} F(K_i, L_i) \leqq NF(1/N \ \Sigma_{i=1}^{N} K_i, 1/N \ \Sigma_{i=1}^{N} L_i).$$

Equation (B.6) has an indeterminate bias, as shown in two examples. First, let $K_i = \bar{K}$ and $L_i = \bar{L}$, $i = 1, \ldots, N$. Then

$$\Sigma_{i=1}^{N} F(\bar{K}, \bar{L}) = NF(\bar{K}, \bar{L})$$

$$> F(N\bar{K}, N\bar{L}), \text{ by decreasing returns to scale}$$

$$= F(\Sigma_{i=1}^{N} K_i, \Sigma_{i=1}^{N} L_i).$$

Second, let $K_1 = \bar{K}, K_2 = \ldots = K_N = 0;$

$$L_1 = 0, L_2 = \bar{L}, L_3 = \ldots = L_N = 0.$$

Then

$$\Sigma_{i=1}^{N} F(K_i, L_i) = F(\bar{K}, 0) + F(0, \bar{L}).$$

Take the extreme example of

$$F(K_i, L_i) = [\min (K_i, L_i)]^{1/\rho}, \rho > 1$$

which can be verified to be a concave function with decreasing returns to scale. Then clearly,

$$F(\bar{K}, 0) + F(0, \bar{L}) < F(\bar{K}, \bar{L})$$

$$= F(\Sigma_{i=1}^{N} K_i, \Sigma_{i=1}^{N} L_i).$$

APPENDIX C

Alternative Measures of Goodness of Fit

CONSIDER A STANDARD LINEAR REGRESSION MODEL:

$$y = X\beta + \varepsilon$$

where y is a vector of observations on the dependent variable, X is a fixed matrix of observations on the independent variables with full rank, and ε is a vector of stochastic disturbances with expectation equal to zero and variance-covariance matrix equal to $\sigma^2 I$. Under these assumptions, the ordinary least-squares estimator $(X'X)^{-1}X'y$ is the unique, minimum variance, linear, and unbiased estimator of β.

In general, however, it is not known whether the set of independent variables contained in the matrix X is the correct one. Very often, there will be more than one set of independent variables that seems equally plausible. One way to compare these different regressions is to use a summary statistic that provides a scalar measure of the degree to which the variations in the independent variables explain the variations in the dependent variable. In general the higher the value of the summary statistic, the better, in some sense, is the regression. Many such summary statistics are available.

Three such summary statistics are examined: the coefficient of multiple determination, R^2; the coefficient of multiple determination adjusted for the degrees of freedom, $\bar{R}^2$; and the prediction criterion, R^{*2}.

The summary statistic R^2 is probably the best-known measure of the goodness of fit of a regression. It is defined as the proportion of the total sum of squares of the dependent variable around its mean that is explained by the regression. It is measured by the formula

$$R^2 = 1 - e'e/(y - \bar{y})'(y - \bar{y})$$

where e is the vector of residuals from the regression, y is the vector of observations on the dependent variable, and $\bar{y}$ is a vector of units times the average value of the dependent variable.[1] The difficulty with using R^2 as a summary statistic for comparing regressions is that it can be increased by simply adding more independent variables.

The summary statistic $\bar{R}^2$ is proposed by Theil (1961) as a criterion for choosing between two competing regression models. Let the two models be given by

Model I: $y = X_1\beta_1 + \varepsilon_1$

where X_1 has full rank equal to K_1

$E(\varepsilon_1) = 0; V(\varepsilon_1) = \sigma_1^2 I$

and   Model II: $y = X_2\beta_2 + \varepsilon_2$

where X_2 has full rank equal to K_2

$E(\varepsilon_2) = 0; V(\varepsilon_2) = \sigma_2^2 I$.

Suppose the first model is the true model. Then the sum of squared residuals from an ordinary least squares regression of the first model divided by the degrees of freedom is an unbiased estimator of σ_1^2, the true variance of the errors in the equation. The sum of squared residuals from an ordinary least-squares regression of the second model, divided by the degrees of freedom, however, will be in general a biased estimator of σ_1^2 and, in particular, will be biased upward. This can be shown as follows. The sum of squared residuals from the second regression is given by

$$e_2'e_2 = [X_1\beta_1 + \varepsilon_1 - X_2(X_2'X_2)^{-1}X_2'(X_1\beta_1 + \varepsilon_1)]'$$
$$[X_1\beta_1 + \varepsilon_1 - X_2(X_2'X_2)^{-1}X_2'(X_1\beta_1 + \varepsilon_1)]$$
$$E(e_2'e_2) = \beta_1'X_1'[I - X_2(X_2'X_2)^{-1}X_2']X_1\beta_1$$
$$+ E\{\varepsilon_1'[1 - X_2(X_2'X_2)^{-1}X_2']\varepsilon_1\}$$
$$= \beta_1'X_1'[1 - X_2(X_2'X_2)^{-1}X_2']X_1'\beta_1 + \sigma_1^2(N - K_2).$$

---

1. R^2 may become negative if the regression does not include a vector of units as an independent variable.

Since $[I - X_2(X_2'X_2)^{-1}X'_2]$ is an idempotent matrix, it is positive semi-definite, and thus the first term is necessarily nonnegative. Thus,

$$E[e_2'e_2/(N - K_2)] \geq \sigma_1^2 = E[e_1'e_1/(N - K_1)].$$

In other words, the expected value of the sum of squared residuals of the true model divided by the number of degrees of freedom is always smaller than the expected value of the sum of squared residuals of the false model divided by the number of degrees of freedom. Since these expected values are unknown, however, Theil suggests using the unbiased estimates $\hat{\sigma}_1^2$ and $\hat{\sigma}_2^2$ to choose the true model. This amounts to choosing the model with the lowest $e_i'e_i/(N - K_i)$. But $e'e$ is related to the traditional R^2 by

$$R^2 = 1 - e'e/(y - \bar{y})'(y - \bar{y}).$$

Thus, choosing the lowest $e_i'e_i/(N - K_i)$ amounts to choosing the lowest $(1 - R^2)/(N - K_i)$ or, equivalently, the lowest $(1 - R^2)N/(N - K_i)$, since N is fixed. $\bar{R}^2$ is defined as

$$(1 - \bar{R}^2) = [N/(N - K)](1 - R^2)$$

so that choosing the lowest $(1 - R^2)N/(N - K)$ is equivalent to choosing the highest $\bar{R}^2$. $\bar{R}^2$ is referred to as the coefficient of multiple determination adjusted for degrees of freedom. Although increasing the number of independent variables necessarily decreases $(1 - R^2)$, it also simultaneously increases $N/(N - K)$, so that $\bar{R}^2$ can decrease if the additional independent variable does not increase the goodness of fit substantially. Thus, it offers some protection against choosing a regression model that includes an indiscriminately large number of independent variables.

The summary statistic R^{*2}, proposed by Amemiya (1980), is based on minimizing the unconditional mean square error of prediction. Consider again the choice between two models. Suppose again that the first model is the true model, and that the purpose of the estimation is to obtain a good prediction of y_0 given a vector X_{10} or X_{20}. The mean square error of prediction, conditional on X_{10}, using the ordinary least-squares estimator for the first model is

$$E[X_{10}'(X_1'X_1)^{-1}X_1'(X_1\beta_1 + \varepsilon_1) - X_{10}'\beta_1 - \varepsilon_0]^2$$
$$= \sigma_1^2[1 + X_{10}'(X_1'X_1)^{-1}X_{10}].$$

If, in addition, X_{10} is treated as a random vector satisfying $E(X_{10}X_{10}') = (1/N)(X_1'X_1)$, the unconditional mean square error of prediction for the first model is

$$E(\sigma_1^2(1 + X'_{10}(X'_1 X_1)^{-1} X_{10})) = \sigma_1^2 + K_1/N.$$

The mean square error of prediction, conditional on X_{20}, using the ordinary least squares estimator for the second model, is

$$E[X'_{20}(X'_2 X_2)^{-1} X'_2(X_1 \beta_1 + \varepsilon_1) - X'_{10}\beta_1 - \varepsilon_0]^2$$
$$= \sigma_1^2[1 + X'_{20}(X'_1 X_2)^{-1} X_{20}] + [X'_{20}(X'_2 X_2)^{-1} X'_2 X_1 \beta_1 - X'_{10}\beta_1]^2.$$

The unconditional mean square error of prediction for the second model is

$$\sigma_1^2(1 + K_2/N) + \beta'_1 X'_1 X_2 X'_2 X_1 \beta_1/N + \beta'_1 X'_1 X_1 \beta_1/N$$
$$- 2\beta_1 X'_1 X_2 (X'_2 X_2)^{-1} X'_2 X_1 \beta_1/N.$$

The sum of the last three terms is always nonnegative. Thus, the unconditional mean square error of the false model is always greater than that of the true model. Again, the unconditional mean square error is in general unknown. Amemiya suggests using unbiased estimates $\hat{\sigma}_1^2$ and $\hat{\sigma}_2^2$ to choose the true model. Minimizing the estimate of the unconditional mean square error is thus equivalent to minimizing

$$e'_i e_i (1 + K_i/N)/(N - K_i)$$

which, since N is fixed, is in turn equivalent to minimizing

$$e'_i e_i (N + K_i)/(N - K_i).$$

R^{*2} is defined as

$$1 - R^{*2} = (1 - R^2)(N + K)/(N - K)$$
$$= [e'e/(y - \bar{y})'(y - \bar{y})]/[(N + K)/(N - K)]$$

so that choosing the lowest estimate of the unconditional mean square error of prediction is equivalent to choosing the highest R^{*2}. R^{*2} can be seen to be even more conservative in guarding against the increase in the number of included independent variables than is $\bar{R}^2$.

APPENDIX D

The Normalized
Restricted Profit Function

IN THIS APPENDIX WE INTRODUCE the concept of a normalized restricted profit function and formulate a model within which questions of allocative efficiency can be studied. We largely follow the
approach developed by Lau and Yotopoulos (1971).
Let

$$Y = F(X_1, \ldots, X_m; Z_1, \ldots, Z_n)$$

be the production function of a farm, where Y is the quantity of
output, and the X_i's and the Z_j's are the quantities of variable and
the fixed inputs, respectively. Examples of variable inputs are labor
and fertilizers. Examples of fixed inputs are capital and land. Of
course, in the very long run, all inputs are potentially variable. This
analysis is concerned with only the short-to-intermediate run, in
which (for reasons of either institutional rigidities or market im-
perfections) the supply of certain inputs to any individual farm may
be considered as essentially fixed. Then short-run profit, defined as
revenue less variable costs, is given by

$$P^* = p_o F(X, Z) - \Sigma_{i=1}^m q_i^* X_i$$
$$= p_o[F(X, Z) - \Sigma_{i=1}^m q_i X_i]$$
$$= p_o[F(X, Z) - q'X]^1$$

where p_o = nominal price of output; q_i^* = nominal price of the ith

---

1. $X'Y \equiv \Sigma_i X_i Y_i$.

variable input; $q_i = q_i^*/p_o$, normalized price of the ith variable input; and X, Z, and q are the vectors of X_i's, Z_j's, and q_i's, respectively.

It is assumed that the objective of productive activity is to maximize short-run profit and that the farm is a price-taker in the output and variable input markets. Thus, the farm maximizes profit with respect to X, taking p, q^*, and Z as given. This short-run profit is referred to as restricted profit, because it is the profit that can be attained when the quantities of certain inputs, the fixed inputs in this case, are restricted. The restricted profit function, Π, is a function of p_o, q^*, and Z, which gives the maximized value of restricted profit for each set of values p_o, q^*, and Z:

$$\Pi^*(p_o, \mathrm{q}^*; Z) = \underset{X}{\mathrm{Max}} \{p_o[F(X, Z) - q'X]\} = p_o[F(X^*, Z) - q'X^*]$$

where the X_i^*'s are the optimized quantities of the variable inputs.

Before proceeding further, one may observe that maximization of restricted profit, P^*, is equivalent to the maximization of normalized restricted profit, P, defined by

$$P = P^*/p_0 = F(X, Z) - q'X$$

so that the X_i^*'s are identical for the two maximization problems. The normalized restricted profit function is a function of q and Z that gives the maximized value of normalized profit for each set of values q and Z:

$$\Pi(q, Z) = F(X^*, Z) - q'X^* .$$

The normalized restricted profit function, $\Pi(q, Z)$, is more convenient to work with for the purpose at hand, but the one-to-one correspondence between $\Pi^*(p_o, q^*, Z)$ and $\Pi(q, Z)$ should be obvious.

Assumptions on the Production Function

The production function is assumed to have certain properties. Let $\bar{R}_+^n$ and $\bar{R}_+^m$ denote the closed nonnegative orthants of R^n and R^m, and let R_+^m be the interior of the nonnegative orthant of R^m. The assumptions on the production function are as follows:

(F.1) Domain: F is a finite, nonnegative, real-valued function defined on $\bar{R}_+^m \times \bar{R}_+^n$. For each $Z\varepsilon R_+^m$, $F(0, Z) = 0$.

(F.2) Continuity: F is a continuous on $\bar{R}_+^m \times \bar{R}_+^n$.

(F.3) Smoothness: For each $Z \varepsilon \bar{R}^n_+$, F is continuously differentiable on R^m_+, and the Euclidean norm of the gradient of F with respect to X is unbounded for any sequence of X in R^m_+ converging to a boundary point of $\bar{R}^m_+$. For each $X \varepsilon \bar{R}^m_+$, F is continuously differentiable on R^n_+.[2]

(F.4) Monotonicity: F is nondecreasing in X and Z on $\bar{R}^m_+ \times \bar{R}^n_+$ and strictly increasing in X and Z on $R^m_+ \times R^n_+$.

(F.5) Concavity: For each $Z \varepsilon \bar{R}^n_+$, F is concave on $\bar{R}^m_+$ and locally strongly concave on R^m_+.[3]

(F.6) Twice differentiability: For each $Z \varepsilon \bar{R}^n_+$, F is twice continuously differentiable on R^m_+.

The concavity and twice differentiability assumptions together imply that for each $Z \varepsilon \bar{R}^n_+$ the Hessian matrix of F with respect to X is negative definite on R^m_+.

(F.7) Boundedness: For each $Z \varepsilon \bar{R}^n_+$, $\lim_{\lambda \to \infty} F(\lambda X, Z)/\lambda = 0$, $\forall X \varepsilon \bar{R}^m_+$.

The boundedness assumption ensures that a bounded and attainable solution exists for the normalized profit maximization problem for all $q \varepsilon R^m_+$.

Assumptions (F.1) through (F.6) are sufficient to ensure that, if a solution X^* to the normalized profit maximization problem exists for a given q and Z, the solution will be unique and lies in R^m_+. The additional assumption (F.7) is needed to ensure that such a solution exists for arbitrary $q \varepsilon R^m_+$ and $Z \varepsilon \bar{R}^n_+$.[4]

From any production function that satisfies assumptions (F.1) through (F.7), a unique normalized restricted profit function can always be derived, under the assumption of restricted profit max-

---

2. The Euclidean norm of a vector X is defined to be $(X'X)^{1/2}$. The gradient of a real-valued function $F(X)$ with respect to X is the vector of its first-order partial derivatives with respect to X.

3. A function is *strongly concave on* a convex set C if there exists $\delta > 0$ such that

$$F[(1-\lambda)X_1 + \lambda X_2] \geqq (1-\lambda)F(X_1) + \lambda F(X_2) + \lambda(1-\lambda)\delta(X_1-X_2)'(X_1-X_2).$$
$$(0 \leqq \lambda \leqq 1, \forall X_1, X_2 \varepsilon C).$$

See Roberts and Varberg (1973), p. 268. An example of a strongly concave function is $F(X) = -X^2$. A function is *locally strongly concave* if there exists such a δ for every proper convex subset of C. An example of a locally strongly concave (but not strongly concave) function on $\bar{R}_+$ is $F(X) = 1 - e^{-X}$.

4. See Lau (1978) for a proof of these propositions.

imization. This may be accomplished by solving from the equations corresponding to the first-order conditions for profit maximization,

$$\partial F/\partial X (X, Z) = q$$

for the optimum input demand functions, $X_i^* (q, Z), i = 1, \ldots, m$, and substituting these into the expression for normalized restricted profit:

$$\Pi = F(X^*, Z) - q'X^*$$

(D.1)

$$= F[X^* (q, Z), Z] - q'X^* (q, Z)$$

$$= G(q, Z).$$

Every such normalized restricted profit function must possess certain properties that are consequences of the assumptions on the production function and of profit maximization.

Properties of the Normalized Profit Function

The properties of a normalized restricted profit function that corresponds to a production function that satisfies assumptions (F.1) through (F.7) have been established by Lau (1978). They may be listed as follows:

(G.1) Domain: G is a finite, positive, real-valued function defined on $R_+^m \times \bar{R}_+^n$.

(G.2) Continuity: G is continuous on $R_+^m \times \bar{R}_+^n$.

(G.3) Smoothness: For each $Z \varepsilon \bar{R}_+^n$, G is continuously differentiable on R_+^m, and the Euclidean norm of the gradient of G with respect to q is unbounded for any sequence of q in R_+^m converging to a boundary point of $\bar{R}_+^m$. For each $q \varepsilon R_+^m$, G is continuously differentiable on R_+^n.

(G.4) Monotonicity: $G(q, Z)$ is nonincreasing in q and nondecreasing in Z on $R_+^m \times \bar{R}_+^n$.

(G.5) Convexity: For each $Z \varepsilon \bar{R}_+^n$, $G(q, Z)$ is locally strongly convex on R_+^m.[5]

---

5. A function F is locally strongly convex if $-F$ is locally strongly concave.

(G.6) Twice differentiability: For each $Z\epsilon\bar{R}^n_+$, $G(q, Z)$ is twice continuously differentiable on R^m_+.

The convexity and twice differentiability assumptions together imply that for each $Z\epsilon\bar{R}^n_+$ the Hessian matrix of G with respect to q is positive definite on R^m_+.

(G.7) Boundedness: For each $Z\epsilon\bar{R}^n_+$, $\lim_{\lambda\to\infty} G(\lambda q, Z)/\lambda = 0$, $\forall$ $q\epsilon R^m_+$.

Given a normalized restricted profit function $G(q, Z)$ its conjugate may be defined as:

$$F^*(X, Z) = \inf_q \{G(q, Z) + q'X\}.$$

Under assumptions (G.1) through (G.7), $G(q, Z)$ is a closed proper convex function on R^m_+ for each $Z\epsilon\bar{R}^n_+$, hence its conjugate function is unique and equal to $F(X, Z)$ itself. Thus, there is a one-to-one correspondence between a production function that satisfies assumptions (F.1) through (F.7) and a normalized restricted profit function which satisfies assumptions (G.1) through (G.7). Given either one, the other is uniquely determined through the conjugacy operation:

$$G(q, Z) = \sup_X \{F(X, Z) - q'X\}$$
$$F(X, Z) = \inf_q \{G(q, Z) + q'X\}.$$

Under the assumption of restricted profit maximization, the normalized restricted profit function $G(q, Z)$ then contains all the technological information on $F(X, Z)$. Hence in the study of technology under profit maximization it is sufficient to focus on $G(q, Z)$ alone.[6]

Hotelling-Shephard Lemma

Because of the duality of the production function and the normalized restricted profit function under the assumption of restricted profit maximization, it is equivalent in the study of technology to start with either the production function or the normalized restricted profit function.

---

6. The duality between production functions and normalized restricted profit functions is further discussed in Lau (1978).

What makes the use of the normalized restricted profit function, $G(q, Z)$, particularly attractive, however, is the fact that its first-order partial derivatives with respect to q are the negatives of profit-maximizing input demand functions, and its first-order partial derivatives with respect to Z are the marginal products of the fixed inputs. This set of relations is known as the Hotelling (1932)-Shephard (1953) lemma.

Under the assumptions on the production and normalized restricted profit functions, it is easy to prove the Hotelling-Shephard lemma. By partially differentiating equation (D.1) with respect to q, using the chain rule,

$$\partial \Pi^* / \partial q = \Sigma_{i=1}^{m} (\partial F / \partial X_i)(\partial X_i^* / \partial q) - \Sigma_{i=1}^{m} q_i \, \partial X_i^* / \partial q - X^*(q, Z).$$

But, by the first-order conditions of profit maximization,

$$\partial F / \partial X = q.$$

Hence,

(D.2) $\partial \Pi^* / \partial q = \partial G(q, Z) / \partial q = - X^*(q, Z).$

Similarly, by partially differentiating equation (D.1) with respect to Z, using the chain rule, we obtain

$$\partial \Pi^* / \partial Z = \Sigma_{i=1}^{m} (\partial F / \partial X_i)(\partial X_i^* / \partial Z) - \Sigma_{i=1}^{m} q_i \, \partial X_i^* / \partial Z + \partial F / \partial Z$$

which, again by the first-order conditions of profit maximization, becomes

(D.3) $\partial \Pi^* / \partial Z = \partial G(q, Z) / \partial Z = \partial F / \partial Z.$

It follows from equation (D.2) and the definition of restricted profit that the output supply function is given by

(D.4) $Y^* = \Pi^* + q' X^*(q, Z)$

$$= G(q, Z) - q' \, \partial G / \partial q \, (q, Z).$$

Thus, given a normalized restricted profit function, $G(q, Z)$, that satisfies assumptions (G.1) through (G.7), the input demand functions can be obtained explicitly by simple partial differentiation. From duality, there must be a unique underlying production function satisfying assumptions (F.1) through (F.7), which gives rise to the normalized restricted profit function and hence to the derived input demand functions, under the assumption of restricted profit maximization.

Effect of Returns to Scale

A production function, $F(X, Z)$, is homogeneous of degree $k, k > 0$, if

$$F(\lambda X, \lambda Z) = \lambda^k F(X, Z), \; \forall \, \lambda > 0, \; \forall \, X, Z.$$

If $k > 1$, $F(X, Z)$ is said to exhibit increasing returns to scale.

If $k = 1$, $F(X, Z)$ is said to exhibit constant returns to scale.

If $k < 1$, $F(X, Z)$ is said to exhibit decreasing returns to scale.

The assumption of concavity of $F(X, Z)$ in X for any Z is perfectly consistent with increasing returns of $F(X, Z)$ in X and Z.

What does homogeneity of the production function imply about the normalized restricted profit function? Euler's theorem for homogeneous functions requires that

(D.5) $\qquad (\partial F/\partial X)'X + (\partial F/\partial Z)'Z = kF(X, Z).$

By substituting equations (D.2) through (D.4) into equation (D.5) and making use of the first-order conditions for profit maximization,

(D.6) $\qquad - q' \, \partial G/\partial q \, (q, Z) + \partial G/\partial Z \, (q, Z)'Z$
$$= k[G(q, Z) - q' \, \partial G/\partial q \, (q, Z)].$$

Equation (D.6) simplifies into

(D.7) $\quad (k - 1)q' \, \partial G/\partial q \, (q, Z) + \partial G/\partial Z(q, Z)'Z = kG(q, Z).$

Equation (D.7) is the generalized Euler's equation for almost homogeneous functions.[7] Under constant returns, $k = 1$, in which case equation (D.7) becomes

(D.8) $\qquad \partial G/\partial Z \, (q, Z)'Z = G(q, Z).$

Equation (D.8) says that $G(q, Z)$ is homogeneous of degree one in Z for any q. Starting from equation (D.8), the reverse substitutions can be made:

---

7. For a discussion of almost homogeneous normalized restricted profit functions, see Lau (1978).

$$G(q, Z) = F(X, Z) - q'X$$

$$\partial G/\partial Z \ (q, Z) = \partial F/\partial Z \ (X, Z)$$

to obtain

$$[\partial F'/\partial Z]'Z = F(X, Z) - [\partial F/\partial X]'X$$

or

$$[\partial F/\partial X \ (X, Z)]'X + [\partial F/\partial Z \ (X, Z)]'Z = F(X, Z).$$

Thus, we have proved

THEOREM. *A production function $F(X, Z)$ is homogeneous of degree one in X and Z if and only if the normalized restricted profit function $G(q, Z)$ is homogeneous of degree one in Z.*

Effect of Neutral Differences in the Level of Technology

Two production functions,

$$Y_1 = F_1(X_1, Z_1)$$

$$Y_2 = F_2(X_2, Z_2)$$

are said to exhibit neutral difference in the level of technology if

$$F_1(X_1, Z_1) = A_1F(X_1, Z_1)$$

$$F_2(X_2, Z_2) = A_2F(X_2, Z_2).$$

In other words, the two production functions differ only by a scalar, multiplicative factor, which is independent of the quantities of the variable and fixed inputs. A_1 and A_2 will be referred to as the technological level parameters. Since the scalar factor can always be absorbed into the function $F(X_1, Z_1)$ one may take $A_1 = 1, A_2 = A$ without loss of generality. A then measures the difference in the technological level between the two production functions, to use the terminology of Chapter 3.

How do the normalized restricted profit functions differ between two production functions that differ only by a multiplicative technological level parameter? Let $Y_1 = F(X_1, Z_1)$, $Y_2 = AF(X_2, Z_2)$ and

$$\Pi_1(q, Z_1) = \underset{X_1}{\text{Max}} \ \{F(X_1, Z_1) - q'X_1\} = G(q, Z_1).$$

Then

$$\Pi_2(q, Z_2) = \underset{X_2}{\text{Max}} \{AF(X_2, Z_2) - q'X_2\}$$
$$= A \underset{X_2}{\text{Max}} \{F(X_2, Z_2) - q'/A\, X_2\}$$
$$= AG(q/A, Z_2).$$

The $G(\cdot, \cdot)$ is the same function for Π_1^* and Π_2^*. Thus, there are two differences between the two normalized restricted profit functions. First, there is a difference in the scalar factor. Second, the normalized prices, q, are scaled by the reciprocal of the technological level parameter.

If $A \geqq 1$, then, by the monotonicity property of $G(q, Z)$ in q,

$$G(q/A, Z) \geqq G(q, Z), \forall\, q, Z$$

and hence

$$AG(q/A, Z) \geqq G(q, Z), \forall\, q, Z.$$

We therefore conclude that, for given q and Z, the farm with the production function with the higher technological level parameter will always have higher nomalized profits if both farms face the same normalized prices and have the same quantities of fixed inputs. This is true regardless of the form of the production function as long as the difference is technology between the farms is neutral.

Effect of Allocative Inefficiency

We next consider two farms with identical production functions, but with different degrees of success in equating the marginal products of the variable inputs to the normalized prices. If both farms are successful in maximizing normalized restricted profit, then the normalized restricted profit function can be realized and will be identical for both farms. It is possible, however, that the farms may be consistently and systematically allocatively inefficient.

Let us represent the situation as follows: for each farm, the marginal conditions are given by

$$\partial F(X_1, Z_1)/\partial X_1 = K_1 q_1 \,;\; \partial F(X_2, Z_2)/\partial X_2 = K_2 q_2$$

(D.9)

$$k_1 = \text{Diag}\, [K_1] \geqq 0 \,;\; k_2 = \text{Diag}\, [K_2] \geqq 0$$

where each K_i is a diagonal matrix, and the subscript refers to the farm. If both farms are equally allocatively "efficient" in optimizing with respect to the variable inputs, then $k_1 = k_2$. A farm is allocatively efficient only if it maximizes profit, that is, if and only if $k_i = [1]$, a unit vector. Equation (D.9) may be interpreted as a set of decision rules for the individual farms. k_1 and k_2 may assume any nonnegative values, and in particular, the special values of $[0]$, a zero vector, and $[1]$. They will be referred to in the allocative efficiency parameters.

The fact that decision rules for the farm consist of equating the marginal product to a constant times the normalized price of each variable input may be rationalized as follows: (a) Consistent over- and undervaluation of the opportunity costs of the resources by the farms; (b) Satisficing behavior; (c) Divergence of expected and actual normalized prices; (d) The elements of k_i may be interpreted as the first-order coefficients of a Taylor's series expansion of arbitrary decision rules of the type:

$$\partial F_i / \partial X_{ij} = f_{ij}(q_{ij})$$

where $f_{ij}(0) = 0$. A wide class of decision rules may be encompassed under (d).

From equation (D.9), the farms may be regarded to behave as if they maximize normalized restricted profits subject to given normalized price vectors $K_1 q_1$ and $K_2 q_2$, respectively. Let $G(q, Z)$ be the normalized restricted profit function corresponding to $F(X, Z)$. The behavior of the two farms may then be derived from the "behavioral" normalized restricted profit functions:

$$\Pi_1^b = G(k_{11}q_{11}, \ldots, k_{1m}q_{1m}; Z_{11}, \ldots, Z_{1n})$$

$$\Pi_2^b = G(k_{21}q_{21}, \ldots, k_{2m}q_{2m}; Z_{21}, \ldots, Z_{2n}).$$

Treating $K_1 q_1$ and $K_2 q_2$ as the given price vectors, the input demand functions are given by the Hotelling-Shephard lemma as

$$X_{ij}^* = -\partial G(K_i q_i; Z_i) / \partial k_{ij} q_{ij} \qquad (i = 1, 2; j = 1, \ldots, m).$$

The supply functions are given by

$$Y_i^* = G(K_i q_i; Z_i) - \Sigma_{j=1}^m k_{ij} q_{ij} \, \partial G(K_i q_i; Z_i) / \partial k_{ij} q_{ij} \qquad (i = 1, 2).$$

The actual normalized restricted profit function is not, however, in general equal to the "behavioral" normalized restricted profit function, because transactions are effected in actual normalized prices,

q_i, rather than the hypothetical normalized prices $K_i q_i$. The actual normalized profit functions are given by

$$\Pi_i^a = Y_i^* - \Sigma_{j=1}^m q_{ij} X_{ij}^* .$$

First, if $k_i = [1]$, that is, if the farm actually maximizes profit, the "behavioral" and the actual normalized restricted profit functions coincide. Second, actual normalized restricted profit functions and the output supply and input demand functions are identical for both farms if and only if $k_1 = k_2$. This last result provides the basis for testing the null hypothesis of no difference in allocative efficiency. When an appropriate algebraic functional form is specified for $G(q, Z)$, the null hypothesis that $k_1 = k_2$ may be tested by comparing the coefficient estimates obtained from the actual normalized restricted profit functions or the output supply functions and input demand functions of the two farms.

Measurement of Relative Economic Efficiency

In general, of course, two farms may differ in both their technological level parameters and allocative efficiency parameters. Then

$$Y_1 = A_1 F(X_1, Z_1); \; Y_2 = A_2 F(X_2, Z_2)$$

(D.10) $\partial F(X, Z_1)/\partial X_1 = K_1 q_1/A_1 ; \; \partial F(X_2, Z_2)/\partial X_2 = K_2 q_2/A_2$

$$k_1 = \text{Diag} [K_1] \geqq 0 ; \; k_2 = \text{Diag} [K_2] \geqq 0 .$$

Let $G(q, Z)$ be the normalized profit function corresponding to $F(X, Z)$; then the "behavioral" normalized profit functions are given by

$$\Pi_1^b = G(k_{11}q_{11}/A_1, \ldots, k_{1m}q_{1m}/A_1; Z_{11}, \ldots, Z_{1n})$$

$$\Pi_2^b = G(k_{21}q_{21}/A_2, \ldots, k_{2m}q_{2m}/A_2; Z_{21}, \ldots, Z_{2n}) .$$

Again, treating $K_1 q_1/A_1$ and $K_2 q_2/A_2$ as the given price vectors, the input demand functions are given, by the Hotelling-Shephard lemma, as

$$X_{ij}^* = - \partial G[(K_i q_i/A_i); Z_i]/\partial k_{ij}q_{ij}/A_i \quad (i = 1, 2; j = 1, \ldots, m).$$

The supply functions are given by

$$Y_i^* = A_i F(X_i, Z_i)$$

$$= A_i[G((K_i q_i/A_i); Z_i)$$

$$- \Sigma_{j=1}^m k_{ij} q_{ij}/A_i \, \partial \, G[(K_i q_i/A_i); Z_i]/\partial \, k_{ij} q_{ij}/A_i] \quad (i = 1, 2).$$

And the actual normalized restricted profit functions are given by

$$\Pi_i^{*a} = Y_i^* - \Sigma_{j=1}^m q_{ij} X_{ij}^*$$

$$= A_i G[(K_i q_i/A_i); Z_i]$$

$$+ \Sigma_{j=1}^m (1 - k_{ij}) q_{ij} \, \partial \, G[(K_i q_i/A_i); Z_i]/\partial k_{ij} q_{ij}/A_i \quad (i = 1, 2).$$

These expressions may be simplified by applying the chain rule of differentiation, so that

$$X_{ij}^* = - A_i/k_{ij} \, \partial G[(K_i q_i/A_i); Z_i]/\partial q_{ij} \quad (i = 1, 2; j = 1, \ldots, m)$$

$$Y_i^* = A_i \{ G[(K_i q_i/A_i); Z_i]$$

$$- \Sigma_{j=1}^m q_{ij} \, \partial G[(K_i q_i/A_i); Z_i]/\partial q_{ij} \} \quad (i = 1, 2)$$

$$\Pi_i^{*a} = A_i \{ G[(K_i q_i/A_i); Z_i]$$

$$- \Sigma_{j=1}^m [1 - (1/k_{ij})] q_{ij} \, \partial G[(K_i q_i/A_i); Z_i]/\partial q_{ij} \} \quad (i = 1, 2).$$

One may differentiate Π_i^a with respect to A_i:

$$\partial \Pi_i^a/\partial A_i = G[(K_i q_i/A_i); Z_i]$$

$$- A_i \Sigma_{j=1}^m \{ \partial G[(K_i q_i/A_i); Z_i]/\partial k_{ij} q_{ij}/A_i \} k_{ij} q_{ij}/A_i^2$$

$$- \Sigma_{j=1}^m (1 - k_{ij}) q_{ij} \Sigma_{l=1}^m$$

$$\{ \partial^2 G[(K_i q_i/A_i); Z_i]/\partial(k_{ij} q_{ij}/A_i) \, \partial(k_{il} q_{il}/A_i) \} k_{il} q_{il}/A_i^2$$

$$= G[(K_i q_i/A_i); Z_i]$$

$$- A_i \Sigma_{j=1}^m \{ \partial G[(K_i q_i/A_i); Z_i]/\partial k_{ij} q_{ij}/A_i \} k_{ij} q_{ij}/A_i^2$$

$$- \Sigma_{j=1}^m \Sigma_{l=1}^m q_{ij} \{ \partial^2 G[(K_i q_i/A_i); Z_i]/$$

$$\partial(k_{ij} q_{ij}/A_i) \, \partial(k_{il} q_{il}/A_i) \} k_{il} q_{il}/A_i^2$$

$$+ \Sigma_{j=1}^m \Sigma_{l=1}^m k_{ij} q_{ij} \{ \partial^2 G[(K_i q_i/A_i); Z_i]/$$

$$\partial(k_{ij} q_{ij}/A_i) \, \partial(k_{il} q_{il}/A_i) \} k_{il} q_{il}/A_i^2$$

whereas the first, second, and fourth terms are in general positive because of assumptions (G.1) through (G.7) on the normalized restricted profit function (the fourth term is a positive definite quadratic form because of the local strong convexity of $G(q, Z)$), the third term is indeterminate in sign. Thus, in general, $\partial \Pi_i^a / \partial A_i$ cannot be signed unambiguously.

Observe that if and only if $A_1 = A_2$ and $k_1 = k_2$, the actual normalized restricted profit functions and the output supply and input demand functions are identical. If and only if $k_i = [1]$, there is perfect allocative efficiency. Two farms can be equal in allocative efficiency $(k_1 = k_2)$, however, without being equal in the level of technology $(A_1 = A_2)$ and vice versa.

In general, the actual normalized restricted profit functions may be identical without either the technological level parameters or the allocative efficiency parameters being equal. The difference between the two actual normalized restricted profit functions may be used as a measure of relative economic efficiency between two farms. A farm is relatively more efficient than another farm (for normalized prices within a prespecified domain) if its actual normalized restricted profit function is higher for all such prices. Relative economic efficiency may change as the price domain of interest changes. Hence it is always important to define the exact domain over which relative economic efficiency holds.

Specialization to the Case of Cobb-Douglas Production Function

We now specialize the analysis to the case of Cobb-Douglas production function. Let

$$Y = A \, \Pi_{i=1}^m \, X_i^{\alpha_i} \, \Pi_{j=1}^n \, Z_j^{\beta_j}$$

where $\alpha_i > 0, \beta_j > 0, \forall \, i, j$, and by the local strong concavity assumption $\Pi_{i=1}^m \, \alpha_i < 1$. The first-order necessary conditions for profit maximization are

$$\partial Y / \partial X_i = \alpha_i A \, \Pi_{k=1}^m \, X_k^{\alpha_k} \, \Pi_{j=1}^n \, Z_j^{\beta_j} / X_i = q_i \qquad (i = 1, \ldots, m)$$

where the farm subscripts on the normalized prices have been suppressed. Taking natural logarithms,

$$\Sigma_{k=1}^m \, \alpha_k \ln X_k - \ln X_i = \ln (q_i / \alpha_i) - \ln (A \, \Pi_{j=1}^n \, Z_j^{\beta_j}) \quad (i = 1, \ldots, m).$$

This system of equations in $\ln X_k$'s may be written in matrix form as

$$
\begin{bmatrix}
\alpha_1 - 1 & \alpha_2 & \dots & \alpha_m \\
\alpha_1 & \alpha_2 - 1 & \dots & \alpha_m \\
\vdots & \vdots & & \vdots \\
\alpha_1 & \alpha_2 & & \alpha_m - 1
\end{bmatrix}
\begin{bmatrix}
\ln X_1 \\
\ln X_2 \\
\vdots \\
\ln X_m
\end{bmatrix}
$$

$$
=
\begin{bmatrix}
\ln (q_1/\alpha_1) - \ln [A \, \Sigma_{j=1}^n Z_j^{\beta_j}] \\
\ln (q_2/\alpha_2) - \ln [A \, \Sigma_{j=1}^n Z_j^{\beta_j}] \\
\vdots \\
\ln (q_m/\alpha_m) - \ln [A \, \Sigma_{j=1}^n Z_j^{\beta_j}]
\end{bmatrix}.
$$

We shall solve this system of equations by finding an inverse to the matrix on the left-hand side, say A. The elements of A^{-1} are given by

$$
A^{-1} = - (1 - \Sigma_{i=1}^m \alpha_i)^{-1}
\begin{bmatrix}
(1 - \Sigma_{\substack{j=1 \\ j \neq 1}}^m \alpha_i) & \dots & \alpha_2 & \dots & \alpha_m \\
\vdots & & \vdots & & \vdots \\
\alpha_1 & & (1 - \Sigma_{\substack{j=1 \\ j \neq 2}}^m \alpha_i) & & \vdots \\
\vdots & & \vdots & & \vdots \\
\alpha_1 & \dots & \alpha_2 & \dots & (1 - \Sigma_{\substack{j=1 \\ j \neq m}}^m \alpha_i)
\end{bmatrix}
$$

a result that may be verified by direct computation.

By making use of A^{-1} the input demand functions can be solved as

$$
\ln X_i^* = - (\alpha_i/(1 - \Sigma_{j=1}^m \alpha_j) + 1) \ln (q_i/\alpha_i)
$$
$$
- \Sigma_{\substack{j=1 \\ j \neq i}}^m \alpha_j/(1 - \Sigma_{j=1}^m \alpha_j) \ln (q_j/\alpha_j)
$$
$$
+ 1/(1 - \Sigma_{j=1}^m \alpha_j) \ln [A \, \Pi_{j=1}^n Z_j^{\beta_j}]
$$
$$
(i = 1, \dots, m)
$$

or

$$
X_i^* = (q_i/\alpha_i)^{-[\alpha_i/(1-\mu)+1]} \Pi_{\substack{j=1 \\ j \neq i}}^m (q_j/\alpha_j)^{\alpha_j/(1-\mu)}
$$
$$
A^{(1-\mu)^{-1}} \Pi_{j=1}^n Z_j^{\beta_j/(1-\mu)} \qquad (i = 1, \dots, m)
$$

where $\mu \equiv \Sigma_{i=1}^m \alpha_i$. By substituting these values of X_i^* into the production function, we obtain the output supply function:

$$Y^* = A \, \Pi_{i=1}^m \, X_i^{*\alpha_i} \, \Pi_{j=1}^n \, Z_j^{\beta_j}$$
$$= A^{(1-\mu)^{-1}} \, \Pi_{i=1}^m \, (q_i/\alpha_i)^{-\alpha_i/(1-\mu)} \, \Pi_{j=1}^n \, Z_j^{\beta_j}.$$

The normalized restricted profit function $G(q, Z)$ is therefore given by

$$G(q, Z) = Y^* - \Sigma_{i=1}^m \, q_i X_i^*$$
$$= A^{(1-\mu)^{-1}} \, (1 - \mu) \, \Pi_{i=1}^m \, (q_i/\alpha_i)^{-\alpha_i/(1-\mu)}$$
$$\Pi_{j=1}^n \, Z_j^{\beta_j/(1-\mu)}.$$

One can verify directly that

$$\partial G/\partial q = -X^*$$
$$G(-\partial G/\partial q)'q = Y^*.$$

Given $G(q, Z)$, the formulas derived in the previous section can be applied to obtain the actual normalized profit functions and the demand functions for a farm with technological level parameter A_i and allocative efficiency parameter k_i as

$$\Pi_i^a = A_i^{(1-\mu)^{-1}} \, (1 - \Sigma_{j=1}^m \, \alpha_j/k_{ij}) \, [\Pi_{j=1}^m \, k_{ij}^{-\alpha_j \, (1-\mu)^{-1}}] \, [\Pi_{j=1}^m \, \alpha_j^{\alpha_j \, (1-\mu)^{-1}}]$$
$$[\Pi_{j=1}^m \, q_j^{-\alpha_j \, (1-\mu)^{-1}}] \, [\Pi_{j=1}^n \, Z_j^{\beta_j \, (1-\mu)^{-1}}] \qquad\qquad i = 1, 2$$

$$X_{ij} = A_i^{(1-\mu)^{-1}} \, (\alpha_j/k_{ij}q_j) \, [\Pi_{j=1}^m \, k_{ij}^{-\alpha_j \, (1-\mu)^{-1}}] \, [\Pi_{j=1}^m \, \alpha_j^{\alpha_j \, (1-\mu)^{-1}}]$$
$$[\Pi_{j=1}^m \, q_j^{-\alpha_j(1-\mu)^{-1}}] \, [\Pi_{j=1}^n \, Z_j^{\beta_j \, (1-\mu)^{-1}}], \quad (i = 1, 2; j = 1, \ldots, m).$$

From these two equations, one may derive

$$q_j X_{ij}/\Pi_i^a = (\alpha_j/k_{ij})/(1 - \Sigma_{j=1}^m \, \alpha_j/k_{ij}) \qquad (i = 1, 2; j = 1, \ldots, m)$$

so that the ratio of expenditure on the jth input to the actual restricted profit is a constant. Moreover, this constant depends only on the allocative efficiency parameters, k_i, and the elasticities of production of the variable inputs. It is independent of the technological level parameter and the elasticities of production of the fixed inputs. If and only if $k_{ij} = 1, j = 1, \ldots, m$, then the constants become

$$q_j X_{ij}/\Pi_i^a = (\alpha_j/k_{ij})/(1 - \Sigma_{l=1}^m \, \alpha_l/k_{il}) = \alpha_j/(1 - \Sigma_{l=1}^m \, \alpha_l)$$

$$(j = 1, \ldots, m).$$

Sufficiency is obvious. Necessity can be shown as follows. Cross-multiplying both sides by the denominators,

$$(1 - \Sigma_{l=1}^m \alpha_l)/k_{ij} = (1 - \Sigma_{j=1}^m \alpha_l/k_{il}) \qquad (j = 1, \ldots, m).$$

This defines a system of simultaneous equations in the unknowns $1/k_{ij}$, $j = 1, \ldots, m$, which may be written in the matrix form:

$$\begin{bmatrix} (1 - \Sigma_{\substack{j=1 \\ j\neq 1}}^m \alpha_j) & \ldots & \alpha_2 \ldots & \alpha_3 & \ldots & \alpha_m \\ \alpha_1 & & (1 - \Sigma_{\substack{j=1 \\ j\neq 2}}^m \alpha_j) & \alpha_3 & \ldots & \alpha_m \\ \vdots & & & & & \vdots \\ \alpha_1 \ldots\ldots\ldots & & \alpha_2 \ldots\ldots\ldots & & (1 - \Sigma_{\substack{j=1 \\ j\neq m}}^m \alpha_j) \end{bmatrix} \begin{bmatrix} 1/k_{i1} \\ 1/k_{i2} \\ \vdots \\ 1/k_{im} \end{bmatrix} = \begin{bmatrix} 1 \\ 1 \\ 1 \\ 1 \\ \vdots \\ 1 \\ 1 \end{bmatrix}.$$

The matrix on the left-hand side, say A^*, is $- (1 - \Sigma_{i=1}^m \alpha_i)A^{-1}$, which has been derived earlier. $A^{*-1} = - (1 - \Sigma_{j=1}^m \alpha_i)^{-1}A$, which is equal to

$$A^{*-1} = - (1 - \Sigma_{i=1}^m \alpha_i)^{-1} \begin{bmatrix} \alpha_1 - 1 & \alpha_2 \ldots & \ldots \alpha_m \\ \alpha_1 & \alpha_2 - 1 & \ldots \alpha_m \\ \vdots & \vdots & \vdots \\ \alpha_1 & \alpha_2 \ldots & \alpha_m - 1 \end{bmatrix}.$$

It then follows by multiplying the right-hand side of the system of equations by A^{*-1} that

$$1/k_{ij} = 1 \qquad (j = 1, \ldots, m)$$

which in turn proves that

$$k_{ij} = 1. \qquad (j = 1, \ldots, m)$$

Taking natural logarithms of the actual normalized restricted profit function,

$$\ln \Pi_i^a = \ln A_i^* + \Sigma_{j=1}^m \alpha_j^* \ln q_j + \Sigma_{j=1}^n \beta_j^* \ln Z_j$$

where

$$\ln A_i^* = (1 - \mu)^{-1} \ln A_i + \ln (1 - \Sigma_{j=1}^m \alpha_j/k_{ij})$$
$$- \Sigma_{j=1}^m \alpha_j (1 - \mu)^{-1} \ln k_{ij} + \Sigma_{j=1}^m \alpha_j (1 - \mu)^{-1} \ln \alpha_j$$
$$\alpha_j^* \equiv - \alpha_j (1 - \mu)^{-1} \qquad (i = 1, \ldots, m)$$
$$\beta_j^* \equiv \beta_j (1 - \mu)^{-1} \qquad (j = 1, \ldots, m)$$

so that the actual normalized restricted profit function of two different farms differ by only a scalar multiplicative factor A_j^*. The ith farm is said to be relatively more economically efficient than the jth farm if the ith actual normalized restricted profit function is greater than the ith actual normalized restricted profit function. In the Cobb-Douglas case, this implies $A_i^* > A_j^*$, which is also sufficient for the ith farm to be globally (for all normalized prices and fixed inputs) relatively more efficient than the jth farm. We note further that for the Cobb-Douglas case, $\partial \Pi_i^{*a} / \partial A_i > 0$, $\forall$ i, so that an increase in the technological level of the ith farm always increases the actual normalized restricted profit function of the ith farm. Consequently the farm with a higher technological level parameter also has a higher normalized restricted profit function.

The ratio of expenditure on the ith input to profit for the ith farm may be written as

$$- q_j X_{ij} / \Pi_i^a \equiv \alpha_{ij}^{**} \quad (i = 1, 2; j = 1, \ldots, m)$$

where

$$\alpha_{ij}^{**} \equiv - \alpha_j / k_{ij} / (1 - \Sigma_{l=1}^m \alpha_l / k_{il}) \quad (i = 1, 2; j = 1, \ldots, m).$$

Four observations may be made. First, two farms are equally allocatively (in)efficient ($k_1 = k_2$) if and only if $\alpha_{ij}^{**} = \alpha_{2j}^{**}, j = 1, \ldots, m$; second, a farm is allocatively efficient ($k_i = 1$) if and only if $\alpha_{ij} = \alpha_j^*, j = 1, \ldots, m$; third, two farms are equally economically efficient if and only if $\ln A_1^* = \ln A_2^*$; finally, two farms are equal in technological level and allocative efficiency if and only if $\ln A_1^* = \ln A_2^*$ and $\alpha_{ij}^{**} = \alpha_{2j}^{**}, j = 1, \ldots, m$. These four observations form the basis of the empirical tests of relative economic efficiency between two groups of farms.

Finally, if $\ln A_1^*$ is greater than $\ln A_2^*$, then the marginal product of the actual normalized restricted profit function with respect to the kth fixed input will be greater in the first farm than in the second farm if the normalized prices and the fixed inputs are the same on both farms. To the extent that the latter variables are different, the marginal products, or quasi-rents, will be different. By the Hotelling-Shephard lemma, the marginal profit of the profit function with respect to the kth fixed input is precisely the marginal product of the production function with respect to the kth fixed input. Therefore the marginal products of the fixed inputs may be compared by comparing the partial derivatives of the actual normalized restricted profit functions with respect to the fixed inputs. Such a comparison may have important implications on the relative desirability of alternative distributions of the fixed inputs among the farms.

Bibliography

The word *"processed"* indicates works that are reproduced by mimeograph, xerography, or similar means; such works may not be cataloged or commonly available through libraries, or may be subject to restricted circulation.

Amemiya, Takeshi. 1980. "Selection of Regressors." *International Economic Review*, vol. 21, pp. 331–54.

Arrow, Kenneth J., Hollis B. Chenery, Bagicha Minhas, and Robert M. Solow. 1961. "Capital-Labor Substitution and Economic Efficiency." *Review of Economics and Statistics*, vol. 43, pp. 225–50.

Arrow, Kenneth J., and Frank Hahn. 1971. *General Competitive Analysis.* San Francisco, Calif.: Holden-Day.

Barnum, Howard N., and Lyn Squire. 1978. "Technology and Relative Economic Efficiency." *Oxford Economic Papers*, vol. 30, pp. 181–98.

————. 1979. *A Model of an Agricultural Household: Theory and Evidence.* Baltimore, Md.: Johns Hopkins University Press.

Beal, D. W. 1963. "The Capacity to Succeed in Farming." *Farm Economist*, vol. 10, pp. 114–24.

Belshaw, Cyril S. 1965. *Traditional Exchange and Modern Markets.* Englewood Cliffs, N.J.: Prentice-Hall.

Benor, Daniel, and James Q. Harrison. 1977. *Agricultural Extension: The Training and Visit System.* Washington, D.C.: World Bank.

Berkson, Joseph. 1951. "Why I Prefer Logits to Probits." *Biometrics*, vol. 7, pp. 327–39.

————. 1955. "Maximum Likelihood and Minimum Chi-square Estimates of the Logistic Function." *Journal of the American Statistical Association*, vol. 50, pp. 130–62.

Berry, S. Albert. 1980. "Education, Income, Productivity, and Urban Poverty." In *Education and Income.* Edited by Timothy King. World Bank Staff Working Paper no. 402. Washington, D.C.: World Bank.

Bhalla, Surjit S. 1979. "Farm Size, Productivity, and Technical Change in Indian Agriculture." Appendix A of R. A. Berry and W. R. Cline, *Agrarian Structure and Productivity in Developing Countries*. Baltimore, Md.: Johns Hopkins University Press, pp. 141–93.

Bhati, U. N. 1973. "Farmers' Technical Knowledge and Income—A Case Study of Padi Farmers of West Malaysia." *Malayan Economic Review*, vol. 18, pp. 36–47.

Binswanger, Hans P. 1980. "Attitudes towards Risk: Experimental Measurement in Rural India." *American Journal of Agricultural Economics*, vol. 62, pp. 395–407.

Blaug, Mark. 1974. "An Economic Analysis of Personal Earnings in Thailand." *Economic Development and Cultural Change*, vol. 23, pp. 1–31.

Bowles, Samuel, and Herbert Gintis. 1976. *Schooling in Capitalist America*. New York: Basic Books, Inc.

Bowman, Mary Jean. 1976(a). "Rural People and Rural Economic Development." Seminar Paper, no. 21. Paris: Unesco International Institute for Educational Planning. Processed.

————. 1976(b). "Through Education to Earnings?" *Proceedings of the National Academy of Education*, vol. 3, pp. 221–92.

————. 1980. "Education and Economic Growth: An Over-view." In *Education and Income*. Edited by Timothy King. World Bank Staff Working Paper, no. 402. Washington, D.C.: World Bank.

Bridge, J. L. 1971. *Applied Econometrics*. Amsterdam: North-Holland.

Buck, John Lossing. 1937. *Land Utilization in China*. Nanking: University of Nanking. (Reproduced in 1956 by The Council on Economic and Cultural Affairs, Inc., New York.)

Calkins, Peter. 1976. "Shiva's Trident: The Effect of Improving Horticulture on Income, Employment, and Nutrition." Ph.D. dissertation. Ithaca: Cornell University. Processed.

Chaudhri, D. P. 1968. "Education and Agricultural Productivity in India." Ph.D. dissertation. New Delhi: Department of Economics, University of Delhi. Processed.

————. 1974. "Effect of Farmer's Education on Agricultural Productivity and Employment—A Case Study of Punjab and Haryana States of India." Armidale, Australia: Faculty of Economic Studies, University of New England. Processed.

————. 1979. *Education, Innovations, and Agricultural Development*. London: Croom Helm.

Chiswick, Carmel U. 1978. "The Determinants of Earnings in Thailand." Washington, D.C.: World Bank. Processed.

Chow, Gregory C. 1960. "Tests for Equality of Coefficients in Two Linear Regressions." *Econometrica*, vol. 28, pp. 591–605.

Cochrane, Susan H. 1979. *Fertility and Education: What Do We Really Know?* Baltimore, Md.: Johns Hopkins University Press.

Cochrane, Susan H., Joanne Leslie, and Donald O'Hara. 1982. "Parental Education and Child Health: Intracountry Evidence." *Journal of Health Policy and Education*, forthcoming.

Cole, Michael, Donald W. Sharp, and Charles Lave. n.d. "The Cognitive Consequences of Education: Some Empirical Evidence and Theoretical Misgivings." *Urban Review*, in press.

Debreu, Gerard. 1959. *Theory of Value.* New York: Wiley.

Evenson, Robert E. 1974. "Research, Extension, and Schooling in Agricultural Development." In *Education and Rural Development.* Edited by J. Sheffield and P. Foster. London: Evans Brothers, Ltd, pp. 163–84.

Evenson, Robert E., and Yoav Kislev. 1975. *Agricultural Research and Productivity.* New Haven, Conn.: Yale University Press.

Evenson, Robert E., Paul E. Waggoner, and Vernon W. Ruttan. 1979. "Economic Benefits from Research: An Example from Agriculture." *Science*, vol. 205, pp. 1101–07.

Fane, George. 1975. "Education and the Managerial Efficiency of Farmers." *Review of Economics and Statistics*, vol. 57, pp. 452–61.

FAO. 1976. *1975*, FAO *Production Yearbook*, vol. 28–1. Rome: FAO.

FAO/World Bank. 1975. "The Muda Study: A First Report." Rome: Food and Agriculture Organization. Processed.

Fields, Gary S. 1980. "Education and Income Distribution in Less Developed Countries." In *Education and Income.* Edited by Timothy King. World Bank Staff Working Paper, no. 402. Washington, D.C.: World Bank.

Figlewski, Stephen. 1978. "Market 'Efficiency' in a Market with Heterogenous Information." *Journal of Political Economy*, vol. 86, 581–97.

Folks, Gertrude. 1920. "Farm Labor vs. School Attendance." *American Child*, vol. 2, pp. 73–89.

Førsund, Finn R., C. A. Knox Lovell, and Peter Schmidt. 1980. "A Survey of Frontier Production Functions and of Their Relationship to Efficiency Measurement." *Journal of Econometrics*, vol. 13, pp. 5–25.

Freire, Maria. 1980. "Education and Agricultural Efficiency." In *Malnourished Children of the Rural Poor.* Edited by Judith B. Balderston, Alan B. Wilson, Maria E. Freire, and Mari S. Simonen. Boston: Auburn House Publishing Company, pp. 107–45.

Friedman, Milton, and Simon Kuznets. 1945. *Income from Independent Professional Practice.* New York: National Bureau of Economic Research.

Gerhart, John. 1975. *The Diffusion of Hybrid Maize in Western Kenya* (abridged). Mexico City: Centro Internacional de Mejoramiento de Maiz y Trigo (CIMMYT).

Gisser, Micha. 1965. "Schooling and the Farm Problem." *Econometrica*, vol. 33, pp. 582–92.

Glass, Gene. 1976. "Primary, Secondary, and Metaanalysis of Research." *Educational Researcher*, vol. 5, pp. 3–8.

Griliches, Zvi. 1963(a). "Estimates of Aggregate Agricultural Production Functions from Cross-sectional Data." *Journal of Farm Economics*, vol. 45, pp. 419–28.

_____. 1963(b). "The Sources of Measured Productivity Growth: United States Agriculture, 1940–60." *Journal of Political Economy*, vol. 71, pp. 331–46.

_____. 1964. "Research Expenditures, Education, and the Aggregate Agricultural Production Function." *American Economic Review*, vol. 54, pp. 961–74.

_____. 1970. "Notes on the Role of Education in Production Functions and Growth Accounting." In *Education, Income, and Human Capital*. Edited by W. L. Hansen. New York: Columbia University Press, pp. 71–127.

Halim, Abdul. 1976. *Schooling and Extension and Income Producing Philippine Household*. Bangladesh: Department of Agricultural Extension and Teachers Training, Bangladesh Agricultural University.

Halim, Abdul, and Mohammed M. Husain. 1979. *Time Allocation and Its Effect on Rice Production and Farm Income in Three Villages of Mymensingh District*. Publication no. 12. Mymensingh, Bangladesh: Graduate Training Institute, Bangladesh Agricultural University.

Haller, Thomas E. 1972. "Education and Rural Development in Colombia." Ph.D. dissertation. Lafayette, Ind.: Purdue University. Processed.

Hardy, G. H., J. E. Littlewood and G. Polya. 1952. *Inequalities*, 2d ed., Cambridge: Cambridge University Press.

Harker, Bruce R. 1973. "The Contribution of Schooling to Agricultural Modernization: An Empirical Analysis." In *Education and Rural Development*. Edited by P. Foster and J. R. Sheffield. London: Evans Brothers, Ltd, pp. 350–71.

_____. n.d. "Rural Literacy's Influence on Indian Agriculture." Department of Education, Oakland University. Processed.

Harma, Risto. 1978. "Farmer Entrepreneur and His Prerequisite Prior Education in Agricultural Development." Washington, D.C.: World Bank. Processed.

Hayami, Yujiro. 1969. "Sources of Agricultural Productivity Gap among Selected Countries." *American Journal of Agricultural Economics*, vol. 51, pp. 564–75.

Hayami, Yujiro, and Vernon W. Ruttan. 1970. "Agricultural Productivity Differences among Countries." *American Economic Review*, vol. 60, pp. 895–911.

Henderson, John W. et al. 1971. *Area Handbook for Thailand*, 3rd edition. Washington, D.C.: Government Printing Office.

Herdt, Robert W. 1971. "Resource Productivity in Indian Agriculture." *American Journal of Agricultural Economics*, vol. 53, pp. 517–21.

Hicks, Norman. 1980. *Economic Growth and Human Resources*. World Bank Staff Working Paper no. 408. Washington, D.C.: World Bank.

Hoch, Irving. 1958. "Simultaneous Equation Bias in the Context of the Cobb-Douglas Production Function." *Econometrica*, vol. 26, pp. 556–78.

Hong, K. Y. 1975. "An Estimated Economic Contribution of Schooling and Extension in Korean Agriculture." Ph.D. dissertation. Los Banos: University of the Philippines. Processed.

Hopcraft, Peter N. 1974. "Human Resources and Technical Skills in Agricultural Development: An Economic Evaluation of Educative Investments in Kenya's Small Farm Sector." Ph.D. dissertation. Stanford, Calif.: Stanford University. Processed.

Hopper, W. David. 1979. "Distortions of Agricultural Development Resulting from Government Prohibitions." In *Distortions of Agricultural Incentives*. Edited by T. W. Schultz. Bloomington: Indiana University Press, pp. 69–78.

Horowitz, Stanley A., and Allan Sherman. "A Direct Measure of the Relationship between Human Capital and Productivity." *Journal of Human Resources*, vol. 15, pp. 67–76.

Hotelling, Harold. 1932. "Edgeworth's Taxation Paradox and the Nature of Demand and Supply Functions." *Journal of Political Economy*, vol. 40, pp. 577–616.

Huffman, Wallace E. 1974. "Decisionmaking: The Role of Education." *American Journal of Agricultural Economics*, vol. 56, pp. 85–97.

―――. 1977. "Allocative Efficiency: The Role of Human Capital." *Quarterly Journal of Economics*, vol. 91, pp. 59–79.

―――. 1980. "Farm and Off-farm Work Decisions: The Role of Human Capital." *Review of Economics and Statistics*, vol. 42, pp. 14–23.

Ishii, Yoneo (ed). 1978. *Thailand: A Rice Growing Society*. Honolulu: University Press of Hawaii.

Jamison, Dean T. 1970. "Studies in Individual Choice Behavior." Ph.D. thesis. Cambridge, Mass.: Department of Economics, Harvard University. Processed.

―――. 1978. "Radio Education and Student Repetition in Nicaragua." In *The Radio Mathematics Project: Nicaragua 1976–77*. Edited by Patrick Suppes, Barbara Searle, and Jamesine Friend. Stanford: Stanford University, Institute for Mathematical Studies in the Social Sciences.

Jamison, Dean T. and Peter R. Moock. 1981. "Farmer Education and Farm Efficiency in Nepal: The Role of Schooling, Extension Services, and

Cognitive Skills." Population and Human Resources Division Discussion Paper no. 81–60. Washington, D.C.: World Bank. Processed.

Jamison, Dean T., Patrick Suppes, and Stuart J. Wells. 1974. "The Effectiveness of Alternative Instructional Media: A Survey." *Review of Educational Research*, vol. 44, pp. 1–67.

Jorgenson, Dale W., and Lawrence J. Lau. 1974. "Duality of Technology and Economic Behavior." *The Review of Economic Studies*, vol. 41, pp. 181–200.

Just, R. E. 1978. "The Welfare Economics of Agricultural Risk." Study by the Division of Agricultural Sciences, University of California, Davis. Processed.

Kennedy, Charles, and A. P. Thirwall. 1972. "Surveys in Applied Economics: Technical Progress." *Economic Journal*, vol. 82, pp. 11–72.

Khaldi, Nabil. 1975. "Education and Allocative Efficiency in U.S. Agriculture." *American Journal of Agricultural Economics*, vol. 57, pp. 650–57.

Kim, Hing (ed.). 1979. *Korean Statistical Yearbook*, 26th edition. Republic of Korea: National Bureau of Statistics, Economic Planning Board.

King, Kenneth. 1978. *Education and Self-employment*. Working Paper no. 544/10A. Paris: Unesco International Institute for Educational Planning.

Krantz, David, R. Duncan Luce, Patrick Suppes, and Amos Tversky. 1971. *Foundations of Measurement*, volume 1. New York and London: Academic Press.

Lau, Lawrence J. 1976. "A Characterization of the Normalized Restricted Profit Function." *Journal of Economic Theory*, vol. 12, pp. 131–63.

––––––. 1978. "Applications of Profit Functions." In *Production Economics: A Dual Approach to Theory and Applications*. Edited by Melvyn A. Fuss and Daniel L. McFadden. Amsterdam: North-Holland, pp. 133–216.

Lau, Lawrence J., and Pan A. Yotopoulos. 1971. "A Test for Relative Efficiency and Application to Indian Agriculture." *American Economic Review*, vol. 61, pp. 94–109.

––––––. 1972. "Profit, Supply, and Factor Demand Functions." *American Journal of Agricultural Economics*, vol. 54, pp. 11–18.

––––––. 1979. "Summary and Conclusions." In *Resource Use in Agriculture: Applications of the Profit Function to Selected Countries*. Edited by Pan A. Yotopoulos and Lawrence J. Lau. Special issue of *Food Research Institute Studies*, vol. 17, pp. 107–14.

Levin, Henry M. 1976. "Concepts of Economic Efficiency and Educational Production." In *Education as an Industry*. Edited by Joseph T. Froomkin, Dean T. Jamison, and Roy Radner. Cambridge, Mass.: Ballinger Publishing Co. for the National Bureau of Economic Research, pp. 149–96.

Lim, Edwin R., et al. 1980. "Thailand: Toward a Development Strategy of Full Participation." Washington, D.C.: World Bank. Processed.

Lockheed, Marlaine E., Dean T. Jamison, and Lawrence J. Lau. 1980. "Farmer Education and Farm Efficiency: A Survey." *Economic Development and Cultural Change*, vol. 29, pp. 37–76.

McFadden, Daniel L. 1974. "Conditional Logit Analysis of Qualitative Choice Behavior." In *Frontiers in Econometrics*. Edited by P. Zarembka. New York: Academic Press, pp. 105–42.

———. 1978. "Cost, Revenue, and Profit Functions." In *Production Economics: A Dual Approach to Theory and Applications*. Edited by Melvyn A. Fuss and Daniel L. McFadden. Amsterdam: North-Holland, pp. 1–110.

Meesook, Oey A. 1980. "The Formation of Income in the Household Sector in Thailand." In *Asian Socioeconomic Development: A National Accounts Approach*. Edited by Kazushi Ohkowa and Bernard Key. Tokyo: University of Tokyo Press, pp. 267–99.

Mellor, John, W. 1976. *The New Economics of Growth*. Ithaca, N.Y.: Cornell University Press.

Moock, Peter R. 1973. "Managerial Ability in Small Farm Production: An Analysis of Maize Yields in the Vihiga Division of Kenya." Ph.D. dissertation. New York: Columbia University. Processed.

———. 1981. "Education and Technical Efficiency in Small Farm Production." *Economic Development and Cultural Change*, vol. 29, pp. 723–39.

Morss, Elliott, John Hatch, Donald Mickelwait, and Charles Sweet. 1976. *Strategies for Small Farmer Development*. Boulder, Colorado: Westview Press.

Müller, Jurgen. 1974. "On Sources of Measured Technical Efficiency: The Impact of Information." *American Journal of Agricultural Economics*, vol. 56, pp. 730–38.

Mundlak, Yair, and Hoch, Irving. 1965. "Consequences of Alternative Specifications in Estimation of Cobb-Douglas Production Functions." *Econometrica*, vol. 33, pp. 814–28.

Nadiri, M. Ishaq. 1970. "Some Approaches to the Theory and Measurement of Total Factor Productivity: A Survey." *Journal of Economic Literature*, vol. 8, pp. 1137–77.

Nerlove, Marc. 1960. "Returns to Scale in Electricity Supply." In *Measurement in Economics: Studies in Mathematical Economics and Econometrics in Memory of Yehuda Grunfield*. Edited by C. F. Christ, et al. Stanford, Calif.: Stanford University Press, pp. 167–98.

Orivel, François. 1981. "The Effectiveness of Agricultural Extension Programs: A Review of Research." Population and Human Resources Division Discussion Paper no. 20. Washington, D.C.: World Bank. Processed.

Pachico, Douglas H. 1979. "Estimating the Allocative Productivity of Human Capital: Some Results from Nepal." Ithaca, N.Y.: Cornell University. Processed (preliminary version).

Pachico, Douglas H., and Jacqui A. Ashby. 1976. "Investments in Human Capital and Farm Productivity: Some Evidence from Brazil." Study prepared for Cornell University. Processed.

Page, John M. 1978. "Technical Efficiency and Economic Performance: Some Evidence from Ghana." Study prepared for Woodrow Wilson School, Princeton University. Processed.

———. 1979. "Firm Size, the Choice of Technique and Technical Efficiency: Evidence from India's Soap Manufacturing Industry." Washington, D.C.: World Bank. Processed.

Patrick, George F., and Earl W. Kehrberg. 1973. "Costs and Returns of Education in Five Agricultural Areas of Eastern Brazil." *American Journal of Agricultural Economics*, vol. 55, pp. 145–54.

Psacharopolous, George. 1973. *Returns to Education*. Amsterdam: Elsevier Scientific Publishing Company.

———. 1980. "Returns to Education: An Updated International Comparison." In *Education and Income*. Edited by Timothy King. World Bank Staff Working Paper no. 402. Washington, D.C.: World Bank.

Pudasaini, Som P. 1976. "Resource Productivity, Income, and Employment in Traditional and Mechanized Farming of Bara District, Nepal." M.A. dissertation. Los Banos: University of the Philippines. Processed.

Ram, Rati. 1976. "Education as a Quasi-factor of Production: The Case of India's Agriculture." Ph.D. dissertation. Chicago: School of Education, University of Chicago. Processed.

Republic of Korea. 1975a. *Report on the Result of the Farm Household Economy Survey, 1975*. Seoul: Ministry of Agriculture and Fisheries.

———. 1975b. *1975 Yearbook of Agriculture and Forestry Statistics*. Seoul: Ministry of Agriculture and Fisheries.

Roberts, Arthur W., and Dale E. Varberg. 1973. *Convex Functions*. New York: Academic Press.

Rogers, Everett M. 1969. *Modernization among Peasants: The Impact of Communication*. New York: Holt, Rinehart, and Winston, Inc.

Rogerson, W. P. 1978. "Aggregated Expected Consumer Surplus as a Welfare Index with an Application to Price Stabilization." Social Science Working Paper no. 205. Pasadena: California Institute of Technology. Processed.

Rosen, Sherwin. 1977. "Human Capital: A Survey of Empirical Research." In *Research in Labor Economics*, vol. 1. Edited by R. G. Ehrenberg. Greenwich, Connecticut, JAI Press, pp. 3–39.

Rosenzweig, Mark R. April 1978. "Schooling, Allocative Ability and the Green Revolution." Paper presented at the Meetings of the Eastern Economic Association, Washington, D.C. Processed.

Roumasset, James, A. 1976. *Rice and Risk: Decisionmaking among Low-income Farmers*. Amsterdam and London: North Holland.

Roy, Prodipto, Frederick Waisanen, and Everett Rogers. 1969. *The Impact of Communication on Rural Development: An Investigation in Costa Rica and India*. Paris: Unesco.

Sabot, Richard H. 1977. "Education and the Labor Market in Thailand." Washington, D.C.: World Bank. Processed.

Sachs, Reinhold E. G. 1979. "Educational Needs of Farmers—A Cross-national Study." *Sociologia Ruralis*, vol. 19, pp. 29–42.

Sadan, Ezra, C. Nachmias, and Gideon Bar-Lev. 1976. "Education and Economic Performance of Occidental and Oriental Family Farm Operators." *World Development*, vol. 4, pp. 445–55.

Saxonhouse, Gary R. 1977. "Productivity Change and Labor Absorption in Japanese Cotton Spinning, 1891–1935." *Quarterly Journal of Economics*, vol. 91, pp. 195–219.

Schultz, Theodore W. 1964. *Transforming Traditional Agriculture*. New Haven, Conn.: Yale University Press.

_____. 1965. "Education and Research in Rural Development." In *Rural Development in Tropical Latin America*. Edited by K. L. Turk and L. V. Crowder. Ithaca: New York State College of Agriculture, Cornell University, pp. 391–402.

_____. 1975. "The Value of the Ability to Deal with Disequilibria." *Journal of Economic Literature*, vol. 13, pp. 872–76.

_____. "On Economics and Politics of Agriculture." In *Distortions of Agricultural Incentives*. Edited by Theodore W. Schultz. Bloomington: Indiana University Press, pp. 3–23.

_____. 1979. "The Economics of Being Poor." Nobel lecture in economics. Stockholm: Nobel Foundation. Processed.

Sen, Amartya K. 1971. "Crisis in Indian Education." In *Aspects of Indian Economic Development*. Edited by Pramit Chaudhuri. London: George Allen & Unwin Ltd., pp. 144–59.

Shapiro, Kenneth H. 1974. "Efficiency and Modernization in African Agriculture: A Case Study in Geita District, Tanzania." Ph.D. dissertation. Stanford, Calif.: Food Research Institute, Stanford University. Processed.

Shapiro, Kenneth H., and Jurgen Müller. 1977. "Sources of Technical Efficiency: The Roles of Modernization and Information." *Economic Development and Cultural Change*, vol. 25, pp. 293–310.

Sharma, Shalik R. 1974. "Technical Efficiency in Traditional Agriculture: An Econometric Analysis of the Rupandehi District of Nepal." M.A. dissertation. Canberra: Australian National University. Processed.

Shephard, Ronald. 1953. *Cost and Production Functions*. Princeton: Princeton University Press.

Shotelersuk, V. 1977. "Economic Efficiency: A Test for Paddy Farms in Chiang Mai Valley, Northern Thailand." Ph.D. dissertation. Honolulu: University of Hawaii. Processed.

Sidhu, Surjit S. 1978. "The Productive Value of Education in Agricultural Development." Processed. (Forthcoming in *Economic Development and Cultural Change*.)

Sidhu, Surjit S., and Carlos A. Baanante. 1979(a). "Farm-level Fertilizer Demand for Mexican Wheat Varieties in the Indian Punjab." *American Journal of Agricultural Economics*, vol. 61, pp. 455–62.

———. 1979(b). "The Environmental Factors and Farm-level Input Demand and Wheat Supply in the Indian Punjab: An Application of the Translog Profit Function." Processed.

Simmons, John. 1976. "The Determinants of Earnings: Towards an Improved Model." In *Change in Tunisia*. Edited by R. A. Stone and J. Simmons. Albany: State University of New York Press, pp. 249–62.

Singh, Baldev. 1974. "Impact of Education on Farm Production." *Economic and Political Weekly* (September), pp. A-92–96.

Singh, Inderjit J. 1979. "Small Farmers and the Landless in South Asia." World Bank Staff Working Paper no. 320. Washington, D.C.: World Bank.

Theil, Henri. 1961. *Economic Forecasts and Policy*, 2d ed. Amsterdam and London: North-Holland.

Thodey, Alan R. 1977. "Farm-level Crop Marketing in Chiang Mai." Chiang Mai, Thailand: University of Chiang Mai. Processed.

Timmer, C. Peter. 1970. "On Measuring Technical Efficiency." *Food Research Institute Studies in Agricultural Economics, Trade, and Development*, vol. 9, pp. 99–171.

Tongsiri, Benjawan, Pichit Lerttamrab, and Alan R. Thodey. 1975. "Agroeconomic Characteristics of the Chiang Mai Valley, 1972–1973." Agricultural Economics Report no. 5. Chiang Mai, Thailand: Chiang Mai University.

Unesco, 1975. *Statistical Yearbook*. Geneva: UNESCO.

Valdes E., Alberto. 1971. "Wages and Schooling of Agricultural Workers in Chile." *Economic Development and Cultural Change*, vol. 19, pp. 313–29.

Villaume, John M. 1977. "Literacy and the Adoption of Agricultural Innovations." Ph.D. dissertation. Cambridge, Mass: Harvard University. Processed.

Vreeland, Neva, et al. 1977. *Area Handbook for Malaysia*, 3rd edition. Washington, D.C.: U.S. Government Printing Office.

Welch, Finis. 1970. "Education in Production." *Journal of Political Economy*, vol. 78, pp. 32–59.

_____. 1979. "The Role of Investments in Human Capital in Agriculture." In *Distortions of Agricultural Incentives*. Edited by Theodore W. Schultz. Bloomington: Indiana University Press, pp. 259–81.

Wharton, Clifton R., Jr. 1965. "Education and Agricultural Growth: The Role of Education in Early-stage Agriculture." In *Education and Economic Development*. Edited by C. Arnold Anderson and Mary J. Bowman. Chicago: Aldine, pp. 202–28.

Wheeler, David. 1980. "Human Resource Development and Economic Growth in LDCs: A Simultaneous Model." World Bank Staff Working Paper no. 407. Washington, D.C.: World Bank.

World Bank. 1976, 1980. *World Tables*. Baltimore: Johns Hopkins University Press.

_____. 1980. *Education Sector Policy Paper*, 3d ed. Washington, D.C.: World Bank.

_____. 1980. *World Development Report 1980*. Washington, D.C.: World Bank.

Wu, Craig C. 1971. "The Contribution of Education to Farm Production in a Transitional Farm Economy." Ph.D. dissertation. Nashville, Tenn.: Vanderbilt University. Processed.

_____. 1977. "Education in Farm Production: The Case of Taiwan." *American Journal of Agricultural Economics*, vol. 59, pp. 699–709.

Yotopoulos, Pan A. 1967. "The Greek Farmer and the Use of His Resources." *Balkan Studies*, vol. 8, pp. 365–86.

Yotopoulos, Pan A., and Lawrence J. Lau. 1973. "A Test for Relative Efficiency: Some Further Results." *American Economic Review*, vol. 63, pp. 214–23.

Zellner, Arnold, Jan Kmenta, and Jacques Dreze. 1966. "Specification and Estimation of Cobb-Douglas Production Function Models." *Econometrica*, vol. 34, pp. 784–95.

Index

The full range of World Bank publications is described in the *Catalog of World Bank Publications*; the continuing research program is outlined in *World Bank Research Program: Abstracts of Current Studies*. Both booklets are updated annually; the most recent edition of each is available without charge from the Publications Distribution Unit, World Bank (Dept. B), 1818 H Street, N.W., Washington, D.C. 20433, U.S.A.

DEAN T. JAMISON, currently senior project officer for the Population, Health, and Nutrition Department of the World Bank, was a senior economist in the Bank's Development Economics Department when this book was written. LAWRENCE J. LAU is a professor of economics at Stanford University and a consultant to the World Bank.